FINDING WAYP◈INTS

FINDING
WAYPINTS

A Warrior's Journey Towards Peace *and* Purpose

TERESE SCHLACHTER
AND COLONEL GREGORY GADSON (RET.)

schaffner
press

This is the First Hardcover edition, published by Schaffner Press, Inc.
POB 41567, Tucson, AZ 85717.

Cover and interior book design by David Ter-Avanesyan/Ter33Design

Library of Congress Control Number: 2023938076

ISBN: 978-1-63964-024-9
EPUB: 978-1-63964-034-8
EPDF: 978-1-63964-055-3

Printed in the United States of America

TABLE OF CONTENTS

"I'll lay me down and bleed awhile,
And then I'll rise and fight again."
—Scottish ballad by Sir Andrew Barton

PROLOGUE

We're sitting up on the second floor of the Walter Reed Army Medical Center—the Lieutenant Colonel and I, side by side on a white-sheeted therapy bed. It's October of 2007. We're talking about biking, or the weather, or something, and he makes some sort of football reference. I have no idea what he's talking about.

"When did you graduate from West Point?" I ask, changing the subject slightly.

" '89- and went straight into the Army."

In 1989 I was working as a television news producer in my hometown of Toledo, Ohio, and worried mostly about dating, paying my rent, and my feathered hair. The term "soldier" was not even in my vocabulary.

. . .

I became a television news producer after failing at being on TV. Years of watching Jane Pauley on "The Today Show" had created in me the notion that I could be a news anchor. At 17, I was an intern at WTVG in Toledo and was reporting on camera before I even graduated from college, then after, until company layoffs landed me in the unemployment line. There were *lines* then. I remember because I would regularly stand in one and cry. I recall sniveling with abandon on my final day of eligibility, only to find upon my return home that the news director of WSPD radio had left a message on my answering machine. (There were answering machines then, too). As a reporter, I covered the Toledo City Council for the all-talk radio station, regularly breaking stories there. I dated a firefighter. I had a decent apartment on Key Street near where the Toledo Mudhens played. Eventually I was invited to produce the 11 p.m. newscast at WTOL-TV. I gave up the on-air dream (I was terrible!). I got a raise. Things were going smoothly. But if I was going to get to a big city, I knew I'd better get a move on.

From Toledo, I became a news gypsy, moving to Louisville, Detroit, Miami, Baltimore and then Washington, D.C., where I freelanced, working mostly for NBC News, even helping to launch their new cable channel, MSNBC, in 1996. I worked for the network and cable channel for about a dozen years, spending a lot of time on Capitol Hill and some at the White House, but I'd barely sideswiped the Pentagon. I babysat a lot of live shots, transcribed press conferences and scrambled together stories for various correspondents. But I did little writing there and I missed it. I knew when I took the job at the Pentagon Channel I'd get out in the field more and I'd probably write a lot.

If you've ever attended a house party, gone looking for the restroom and accidentally opened a closet door instead—well, working at the Pentagon Channel felt a little like that. I'd invaded a private space containing ordinary, recognizable things but nothing which met my immediate need: substantive work. I'd arrived at what is now known as "Defense Media Activity" after spending a decade covering mainstream national news— presidents, Congress, and more natural disasters. Some might think a decade working at a major network would qualify a person to write curated stories for the Pentagon. But my new bosses made it clear that I was to sit down, and, in as much as it was possible, look pretty, or at least less annoyed. I had to stare into the closet for a bit. A few weeks in, after a small kerfuffle, the gate was raised. I was released into a press conference at Walter Reed Army Medical Center. "How much trouble could she possibly get into?" the news desk probably figured. Turns out, plenty.

When I first walked into Walter Reed Army Medical Center, I was mostly unaware of the number of wounded soldiers coming back from Iraq and Afghanistan. At first, I was sad. Then I was mesmerized. Hundreds of wounded soldiers, sailors, airmen and marines were all going about their business as though missing an arm or an eye or a foot was normal. And it had become that to them—their new normal. All these busted up men and women were working out or resting and shooting the breeze and "ma'am-ing" me, like I deserved some sort of respect just for standing around. And they were part of a team: team recovery. Each had been assigned to the Wounded Warrior Unit. This was their new AOR, Area of Responsibility. It was their *job* to get well. It was also their job on that September day to demonstrate and explain all the new rehabilitation equipment that had been installed in the MATC. For his part, Lieutenant Colonel Greg Gadson had been attached to a pulley system that guided him along a circular track where he was learning to use his prosthetic legs. I was standing alongside the track when he took a spill right in front of me. Greg Gadson literally tumbled into my universe. I had no idea how this one moment would change my life.

Back in the newsroom that day, I talked about what I'd seen, who I'd met. Managers squirmed and braced as if these stories should not be told—as if the nation's wounded should be kept under wraps, so as not to undermine the Pentagon's depiction of the wars. I don't know why but they gave way easily and the very next week I was back at WRAMC. So began my years-long coverage of, and occasional controversy over, the externally and internally wounded.

And that is how I came to be sitting next to Greg that afternoon, as he grew somber, staring down at his legs. The look was not sad, or even introspective. It was incredulous. He was wearing the bionic version of his prosthetics, the upper parts of which were shaped like small motorcycle gas tanks. Maybe they were supposed to mimic really muscular thighs.

He'd had the things for weeks. But he was looking at them like he'd never seen them before. Then Lieutenant Colonel Gregory D. Gadson turned to me and quietly said, "T, can you imagine getting up every morning and putting these things on?"

"Nope, I can't," I answered.

"I mean, sometimes I just think, what *happened*?"

CHAPTER ONE

"Your commander is invincible."
—First Sergeant Fredrick Johnson

Days like these formed the glue.

The security cordon established a perimeter inside the shadowy, heavily curtained meeting quarters of the Iraqi National Dialogue Council. Empty plastic water bottles and cups crusted with dried chai tea sat where they were discarded by council members. Some were wearing traditional robes and head scarves, others rumpled fatigues. Lieutenant Colonel Gregory D. Gadson handed off his camera to a member of his detail, who snapped a few photos, with most of the men smiling. Gadson was not rumpled. Nor did he smile.

Outside, the getaway guy and the gunner were flawlessly executing their jobs: they were waiting.

Private First Class Matthew Reeder shifted in the driver's seat of the Humvee (HMMWV or High Mobility Multipurpose Wheeled Vehicle) tentatively touching the wheel. "Least it's not like last week. Felt like 130 degrees in here."

"That AC got it all the way down to 125, I bet," answered Specialist Travis Ueke, shifting his gaze from the locked door of the building to the covered windows.

"It's something like 60 back home."

It didn't matter where home was. It was a universal term, one that

1

meant a better place, better times, better food.

"Bet they're getting some chow in there," Reeder said.

"LTC Gadson always gets chow. People love to feed him, man," said Ueke, maintaining his watch from the turret. "But I don't think he eats. I mean, just enough to be polite." He ran his fingers over the butt of his M240 Bravo 7.62 mm machine gun, muzzle pointed skyward, his voice echoing off the four metal protective shields forming a box around his midsection.

"Be polite. Be professional. But be prepared to kill everyone you meet," Reeder chuckled, quoting Gadson.

"Hot as Jesus."

"Bizarro-hot as Jesus."

Ueke lifted his head into the hot, ugly wind hoping for some relief. No bizarro luck. Everything manmade was a dirty gray. If it was made by God or something else, it was brown. He resumed his security stare.

"Patriot Six, headed out," a voice from the lieutenant colonel's detail came over the radio.

"Guess we're outta here," said Reeder.

The cordon exited the building as methodically as it had gone in, securing doors, windows and high spots, making sure there was no danger to the lieutenant colonel. Captain Brad Bandy came out first and got in the vehicle behind the passenger seat. Mike Oro, Lieutenant Colonel Gadson's interpreter, climbed in behind Reeder. The lieutenant colonel, sliding on his Army-issued sunglasses, the slightest glisten of perspiration on his forehead, strode purposefully toward the Humvee. A man of average height, Gadson seemed taller, his steps elongating with the afternoon shadows. He slid in one easy motion into shotgun position. Gadson always rode shotgun. The rest of the detail assembled in three more trucks, about 20 soldiers in all. The first part of the day's mission was complete.

The second part was becoming rote.

In the spring of 2007, improvised explosive devices, or IEDs, were increasingly the enemy's weapon of choice. The word "improvised" was misleading because it implied a weakness, a suggestion that it might not work, or would not work very well. Indeed, the IED was the Iraqi terrorist's most successful weapon. It could be hidden behind a pole, disguised as a rock, even tucked inside an animal carcass. It could blow up a 16-ton truck. It could throw shrapnel hundreds of yards, piercing flesh with plastics and coppers and irons. It could hurl bodies and tear off limbs. It most often would lie roadside awaiting an errant tire or foot. It could be detonated remotely. It was made with paper clips, rubber bands, cardboard and homemade explosives. It was sometimes toxic, often lethal, and almost always debilitating. The number of U.S. troops wounded in action was nearing 25,000. Almost 3,000 had been killed. That May alone, 127 U.S. troops had been killed in action.

Two of those men were members of the 4th Special Troops Battalion. They had died five days earlier, on May 2, when their Humvee struck an IED. A memorial service was being held for 23-year-old First Lieutenant Ryan Jones and 20-year-old Specialist Astor Sunsin-Pineda at Forward Operating Base Falcon. The deaths of the two young soldiers seemed no different than others. The Department of Defense posted its typical stark announcement on the Internet. Two dead, vehicle hit, names, ranks and posts were blandly described. No talk of service, heroism, dreams, goals or last words. They were exploded into thin air on a dusty, dirty Iraqi road. They were part of that landscape now, off-loaded onto a DOD website.

Lieutenant Colonel Gadson had never met Jones and Sunsin-Pineda, not that he remembered, anyway. He had some 400 soldiers under his own command, the 32nd Field Artillery, which was serving at the moment as infantry. They were the fighters, the guys who pulled the triggers. Jones and Sunsin-Pineda were part of Special Troops, which was traditionally a support unit, providing communications, intelligence and engineering personnel. The units' paths rarely crossed in theater. But they were a "sister" battalion. And they had lost two men. Gadson had stepped out of the Sunni meeting a little early so he and his troops could drive over to the memorial service before dark.

The M1151 up-armored Humvee pulled away from the building, Reeder making sure he gave the truck ahead of him about 40 meters of space. If one of them was hit, best not to take out the others. That was standard procedure, despite the fact the truck was equipped with an SSVJ cell jammer, which could interfere with the enemy's ability to detonate explosives using a phone. It also had a device known as a "Duke" which was supposed to do the same with radio waves. The rest of the four-truck convoy fell in line. The lieutenant colonel's was third. Bandy and Oro stared through the two-inch thick glass separating them from what they sometimes called the "Wild West." Reeder swerved the truck slightly from side to side, the theory being that they would be less likely to take a hit directly to the more exposed underbelly, in the middle. Ueke steadied his clanky perch, thankful for the paved road's smoothness. The road leading to FOB Falcon was fairly well traveled. An Iraqi checkpoint stood about a mile away. They arrived for the funeral service before dark.

. . .

The sobering ceremony made for a quiet ride back to Forward Operating Base Liberty, where they were stationed. Bandy, a company commander for Forward Support for the 2nd Brigade, 32nd Field Artillery, G Company, knew one of the soldiers who had been killed. The captain was not normally a part of the lieutenant colonel's security team. He had come along to pay his respects. The overseas ceremonies were a military tradition—he thought they were a good one. Sacrifice should be remembered. Honored. Jones and Sunsin-Pineda were not the first KIA. Would not be the last, which brought up the matter of who would be next. He still had almost a year to put in here—to survive. Seemed like there was an incident damned near every day. Hurt or killed. Just clicking them off almost, save for the ceremonies. Tomorrow they would move on. It was getting late, just before 8:30. Darkness rested on the desert. Behind a security fence, square block buildings rose randomly from the dirt. There would be paperwork waiting for him when he got back to FOB Liberty—about 10 miles away. His stomach rumbled. The dining facility would be closed.

Gadson mulled that afternoon's exchange with the Sunnis. It seemed more style than substance. He had been introduced to some local community organizers and Iraqi military leaders. Abu Muhammad and Colonel Gassan would be learning security tactics and ways of maintaining their own peace, so U.S. forces could eventually go home. For now it was all about introductions, good will, the "hearts and minds" stuff. They had not talked particulars regarding what sorts of security his troops could provide, or how much the Iraqis could muster. Muhammad and Gassan's people had put out a spread, though, served, of course, with chai. What they lacked in military force and strength they occasionally made up for in plain old belly-filling. He was glad they had taken pictures—proof of their cooperation and commitment to improving relations with each other and residents. Tomorrow he would make a report. Incremental progress. Impotent pixie dust in the wake of two more deaths. The costs weighed on him like four days of desert sweat.

Gadson felt around for his camera, touching the rough notches around the lens, making sure he had gotten it back. Rubbing his palms over his kneecaps, he stretched back into the well-worn seat, breathing in the cool, comfortable night air. It was a peaceful, almost Bible black night.

Ninety percent of IED victims describe an attack the same way. "I didn't see anything at first. I heard it. Just for a few seconds, everything slows down."

Thundering decibels belched from beneath the front right tire of the Humvee, lifting the side of the 10-ton truck, hammering the clear night air.

White, searing light glowed and flickered like an old-time movie, revealing shrapnel and smoke, driving them horizontally through the cab. Metal, plastic, shards of glass, dirt and other debris seemed to be attached to the sonic force, piercing the night, shredding rubber, bending steel. Three 130 mm artillery shells penetrated the cocoon so carefully woven by the security cordon. Chaos spilled out.

Gadson sensed himself going airborne, then hurtling across the asphalt. He knew they had hit an IED. There was no physical pain. All he could feel in that blink of time was rage. "*Mother . . . fuck. God, don't let me die in this country.*"

All Bandy could see, after the flash, was smoke filling the back seat. The vehicle had been lifted off the ground and came back down flat on the road, then careened, skidding forward. What was left of 10 tons of metal stumbled on its shattered frame, rear wheels still propelling them forward. It seemed to take forever to stop. *Nonsensical. They hadn't been going that fast. Maybe he was dreaming. Maybe he was dead already.* After what seemed like minutes, the lurching stopped. He caught his breath and in an oddly instinctive moment snapped his flashlight off the barrel of his gun and shined it on his own legs. Still there. Feet too.

"Ueke!" Bandy called.

"I'm okay!"

"Reeder!"

"Good. Okay."

"I'm hit!" yelled Oro.

The Humvee was so filled with smoke Bandy couldn't see across it to where Mike Oro was sitting. Bandy pushed open his door, barely noticing the inch-wide holes that pocked it, and ran around the back to the other side of the truck. Clear of some of the smoke, he could see Mike, still in his seat. His pant leg was ripped and he was hurting, but it was impossible to see how bad things were. There was no blood yet. Bandy and Reeder dragged the translator out of his seat and to the ground. Trying to muddle past his own confusion, Bandy knelt down beside Oro.

Private First Class Eric Brown, Gadson's personal security medic, had been riding in the fourth vehicle. He watched along with the others in his truck as the third vehicle lit up, then disappeared into a dark cloud. "We've lost our visual on the truck ahead!" he called. It took a moment for the smoke to clear enough to see the Humvee, rudderless, cross the highway then finally coast to a stop. They pulled up to the right of the battered truck on the hit side. Brown jumped out and stuck his head inside the blasted carcass of the vehicle. The lieutenant colonel's side door was open, but he was not there. Must have gotten out.

"Hey, can I use your spotlight?" Brown asked Ueke, who handed over his field light. Brown shined it around. Odd, he did not see the lieutenant colonel.

"Medic!" someone called from the other side of the truck. Brown handed the light back to the gunner and ran around the back end of the wrecked vehicle. Bandy stepped aside to allow Brown a better view of the injured man.

"My foot!" yelled Oro.

Brown assessed the 58-year-old interpreter. Best he could tell he had sustained a nasty shrapnel wound to his foot—enough to send the Iraqi-born U.S. citizen back to his home in Michigan—but luckily not life-threatening. Damn, it was dark. He pulled a tourniquet out of his bag and twisted it around the wounded leg. Amazing little devices.

"Have you seen Colonel Gadson?" Fredrick Johnson, the raspy voiced, fast-talking first sergeant, who had been riding in the truck with Brown, asked as he stood over Bandy and Brown like The Hulk. At 6-feet, 240 pounds, Johnson, who was the acting sergeant major on the detail, loomed above the fray.

"No, man, I thought he got out and went ahead," Brown said.

Johnson disappeared into the night.

It was not until that moment that it hit Bandy. The grunt. The white light flashed again in his mind. "Ummph." *The Colonel.* He had been hit. Bandy was sure of it. He struggled to put it into words, but it seemed to dawn on everyone at once. The search was on for the lieutenant colonel but the sudden understanding that Gadson was down meant Bandy was next in line. Now the highest-ranking soldier on the scene, he was in charge. Aside from tending to the wounded, the biggest concern was a secondary attack. He looked around the blast site—there was no security perimeter. Truck number one had made a U-turn south, back to the bomb site, in search of the lieutenant colonel.

"Truck two! Secure the road north!" Bandy yelled. The driver quickly positioned the truck sideways across the road, keeping the gunner in place. "Soldier!" Bandy called to a rifleman on foot. "Take the west side. Ueke! Take your position—look east!" The gunner climbed back into the damaged truck and swung the gun to the right, watching for any sort of motion. The IED had been on that side of the road. If the triggerman or any of his friends were still hanging around, it was likely they would be over there.

In the distance, a low hum quickly turned into a roar, as reinforcements arrived. Delta Company 1st Battalion, 28th Infantry—the Black Lions—along with four more trucks and 20 men, were a welcome sight. They would help secure the site and move casualties. Some of Bandy's burden was lifted but still it was his scene to manage. He looked back at Oro. Could be some broken bones in his foot or ankle but Brown thought he would be okay. There were bigger problems.

On the other side of the misshapen vehicle, Johnson stuck his head through the blown-open door. Where the fuck was Gadson? Black smoke stung his eyes. He bent further into the truck, turning his head closer to the floor. Oh, no. Oh, Jesus, there were the remnants of the lieutenant colonel's tracking equipment, blown to bits on the floor of the truck. Gear, weapons and ammunition were scattered everywhere. Maybe Gadson had escaped and ran ahead to check on his troops. Please God. Please let that be it. But there was not much left of the forward quarter of that truck. And Gadson always rode shotgun.

Johnson's breath grew short. He could not hear—either a result of the deafening blast or the yelling of 40 adrenaline-charged men. If Gadson's was one of the voices, he couldn't hear it. He scanned the fence line. Dust and rocks. And more fucking dust. Through the clearing haze he thought he saw a dark form lying along the side of the road, about 150 feet behind the mangled truck. Was it another explosive device? There was no movement. He looked out into the desert, squinting at the few barely habitable homes nearby, watching for the men who likely rigged the bomb, who may have planted more. Johnson moved closer to the figure, keeping the landscape in his peripheral vision while also glancing down, searching for trip wires. Those motherfuckers. If it was another bomb, he was about to find out in the most deadly of ways. Gradually, as he inched closer, the form took shape—a head, an arm, a face. With a cry, he recognized his commanding officer's distinctive profile—the cheekbones that nearly cut into the corners of his eyes. It was Gadson.

"Sir!" screamed Johnson, fearless now, running toward him.

Silence.

"Colonel Gadson!"

Nothing. No sound. No movement. The acting sergeant major drew in his breath. He knew about death. He had seen it creep up before. He was not watching it again. This was not happening. Commanding officers did not get hurt. They did not die. Not in the company of their own security detail. Not with the younger soldiers watching. This was not going to happen.

"Sir! Can you hear me? Colonel Gadson. Jesus. Mother of God."

Johnson stared for a few seconds at the lieutenant colonel's chest. It could have been the Interceptor Body Armor that was masking its rise and fall. But he did not seem to be breathing. He pulled up the lieutenant colonel's eyelids. All he could see were whites.

"*Sir!!* You're not fucking going to die!" He began to notice the wetness on the dark pavement. It was blood.

Johnson leaned directly over his friend and opened his mouth. Cupping his hand around the lieutenant colonel's jaw, he inhaled as much air as his lungs could contain, then forced it out of his own abdomen into the lieutenant colonel's. Johnson gasped. Then he did it again. And again. He was dizzy. There was so much blood.

"*Medic!*" he wheezed between bursts of air. "*Medic!* Man down! Man *down!* It's the *Colonel!*" The slightest fraction of a sob caught his throat. Another breath. Stay calm.

Johnson checked the lieutenant colonel's pupils again. This time his eyes rolled forward and seemed to see him. Johnson held the gaze for a split second, then turned his ear sideways to listen to his chest. Yes. There it was. He was breathing. It was shallow. But Gadson was still alive. The lieutenant colonel stirred a little, then spat something up.

If there was one thing Johnson knew it was the sound of his own voice. Stevie Nicks meets Barry White calling the Kentucky Derby. Distinctive. That is what he had always been told. He used it to call the lieutenant colonel's name over and over. He was probably in shock. He fixated on the commander's face, looking for any additional sign of life, keeping his middle finger on his neck, searching for a pulse.

"Colonel Gadson. Colonel. *Colonel!*" His voice scratched the air. He felt a strange tightening on his other wrist. The lieutenant colonel's long fingers, calloused and dirty, reached around his forearm.

"Don't leave me out here, man," Gadson whispered.

"No sir!" Johnson answered. Gadson had recognized him, or more likely, the sound of him.

"I can't get up," he told Johnson. "My legs hurt."

"Yes, sir." Hurt seemed an understatement. But panic pushed away every other thought or possible response, as Gadson dipped back to blackness.

"Reeder! Keep an eye on Mike," Brown called as he double-timed the 150 feet back to where Johnson had found the lieutenant colonel.

"He's breathing," Johnson said. "Barely."

"*Sir!* You're hurt, *Sir!*" Brown yelled.

Blood ran from the lieutenant colonel's body to the other side of the road, pooling in a small hole. There was no way for the medic to tell how much he had lost but it was definitely enough to kill a guy. Brown pulled two more tourniquets out of his bag and put them on each of the lieutenant colonel's thighs. That stemmed the flow but the damage to his calves was inconceivable. Brown thought the body armor might be restricting his breathing. With a pair of trauma shears and a knife, he hacked at the chest straps and rough canvas, trying to pry it from his chest. Time was short. The medevac helicopter was on its way to FOB Falcon. If they could only get the lieutenant colonel there he might be stabilized, then on his way to a real field hospital.

The commander needed to be moved onto a vehicle. Gadson, who had played football at the United States Military Academy, weighed in at 210. Somehow, Brown, Johnson, Bandy and a few others had to lift him into one of the Humvees. The rest of the patrol had all they could do to maintain security and arrange for reinforcements. They needed more trucks and some fresh gear. Their position was still vulnerable. And they needed to stay square. Brown heard their strained voices as the rest of the detail neatly formed a disciplined chain. Just get it done.

Johnson, running now on pure adrenaline, put his right arm under Gadson's shoulders and his left one under his legs. His right arm strained under the man's weight, but his left swept clumsily through the air. Johnson gasped as he realized there was little flesh left to grab, nothing to balance the weight of his chest. Gadson's legs seemed to have been shredded.

Johnson lost his footing, slipping in the streams of blood. He was going to have to lift him by grabbing under his arms. The driver of the truck backed up closer to them. Staff Sergeant Patrick Whaley sat at the tailgate, facing them, ready to pull up. The truck configuration inside made loading 6 feet and 210 pounds of dead weight even more difficult. A 4-inch high rear dashboard where they stored ammunition took up a lot of room. Any gear that was not attached was thrown to the pavement.

"Are you still with me, sir?" yelled Johnson. "We need to get you onto the truck, sir. Stay with me. Stay with me." That's when Johnson took his first blow. Gadson's fist smashed into his jaw with shocking power.

"Let me *go!*" yelled Gadson. "My legs are hurting!" He struggled to get free of Johnson's grip.

"Sir, your legs are *messed up.*"

Thwack.

The lieutenant colonel clocked him again, this time higher, closer to his cheek.

"Shit, that hurt!" yelled Johnson. "You can pound on me all you like, sir, I'm not letting go!" Gadson was clearly in excruciating pain, screaming now, delirious, fighting his every move.

It was with a certain amount of mad love, dedication and frustrated energy that Johnson and the others managed to get the lieutenant colonel into a bear hug, lifting his full body weight up, holding him under the arms. Whaley grabbed from behind at his commander, yanking at the back of his shirt. Johnson slipped again in the blood and the two of them fell back on the ground. Gadson continued to struggle and scream. The tourniquets had curbed some of the bleeding, but they all knew the situation was grave. If they did not get their commanding officer to a medical clinic soon, he would certainly die. Even if they did, he might not make it.

It took four more tries and at least one more punch, thrown with amazing force from a man so close to death, before Gadson was finally secured, lying on his side, in the truck. Brown saw that his legs were not going to clear the tailgate and grabbed the lieutenant colonel's calves to bend them at the knees. Bags of ground, raw chicken. That is how they felt. Bandy went for his ankles. They folded backwards.

What looked like gallons of blood were on the ground; it was hard to imagine there was enough left to feed the lieutenant colonel's heart. But somehow, it was still beating. Johnson wondered for how long.

He watched the truck pull away gently at first, the driver conscious of his oddly perched and folded cargo, then thunder its way back toward Falcon. One of the other trucks escorted. It was getting closer to 9:00 p.m. now. They needed to get Gadson to a hospital inside of the "golden hour"—the one that, statistically, determines whether someone lives or dies. They would make it back to Falcon well before that lethal deadline, but he would then have to survive a medevac flight.

Inside the vehicle, Gadson came to enough to hear the familiar hum of the engine. He knew he was being transported but it seemed to him that they had been driving for hours—making circles—with no destination. His own security detail was just driving *around*! They needed a command, some direction. Brown was talking to him. Gadson could see the medic's face, but he sounded so far away. Maybe he was trying to tell him why they could not get to their destination. Somewhere. The kid was new to his detail but there was something in particular about him, something familiar.

"Colonel. Colonel Gadson, sir you're not going to die here. We promise. Just hold on please, sir," Brown said.

Gadson looked down to see his own foot, lying in his crotch. He pulled his head back up, fighting the image. The look on Brown's face was not helping. He needed his higher power. *That's* what he remembered about PFC Eric Brown. The prayer. Each day at FOB Liberty began with a prayer.

The day it was Brown's turn to lead a blessing, he had loved the prayer so much he had asked the private for a copy.

"Brown," Gadson said quietly.

"Colonel? We're almost there, sir, just hold on."

"Brown. The prayer. Say the prayer."

"The Soldier's Prayer, sir?"

"Say it."

It took the medic a moment to remember how it started. It was on a piece of paper stuck in the back of his Bible. Not standard patrol gear.

"Almighty and all present power
Short is the prayer I make to Thee.
I do not ask in this battle hour
For any shield to cover me.
I seek no hope to smite my foe,
I seek no petty victory here.
The enemy I hate I know,
To Thee dear Lord is also dear.
The vast unalterable way
From which the stars do not depart
Shall not be turned aside to stay
The bullets flying to my heart.
But this I pray: be at my side
When death is drawing through the sky . . ."

Brown paused.

"Almighty God who also died

Teach me the way that I should die.[1]

"But you're not going to die, sir. See? We're here."

The gurney was ready. Help was fresh. The lieutenant colonel somehow, soothed.

It was strange, the lieutenant colonel thought, to feel no pain.

---

1. The prayer is actually called "The Airman's Prayer" and was written by Royal Australian Air Force Sergeant Hugh Brodie during World War II. He and the other four members of his bomber crew would later never return from a mission over Essen, Germany, June 2-3, 1942.

CHAPTER TWO

*"I was holding his head, whispering in his ear, 'You're going
to be okay.' I did NOT think he was going to be okay.
It was my scariest day in the Army."*
—Colonel Ricky Gibbs, Commander, Forward Operating Base Falcon

It was after 8 p.m. when Brigade Commander Ricky Gibbs had seen his six battalion commanders out the door of his office. The memorial service for Jones and Sunsin-Pineda provided a rare opportunity for the officers, who each managed a designated land parcel in and around Baghdad, to gather, so he had asked them all to come in, mostly to compare notes on what had become known as the "surge," President George Bush's strategy to secure Baghdad by clearing neighborhoods, supporting Iraqi military and winning the trust of the civilian population. Gibbs relished seeing the half dozen men all together. Their combination of knowledge, talent and the simple camaraderie made the overwhelming task at hand seem doable.

Of the battalion commands, LTC Gadson's and LTC Patrick Frank's contiguous areas of operation were the most interesting. They shared a boundary: Route Irish. Gadson's area, to the north, was populated with wealthy Sunnis who after the fall of Saddam Hussein saw the benefits of working with the Americans. Neighborhoods there were known as the "Beverly Hills" of Iraq. Its residents were once the power brokers in Baghdad—Hussein's constituency. Now the power was up for grabs, and U.S. troops could help deter the poverty-stricken minority Shia from entering their neighborhoods, threatening their property, their way of life. The Americans called it peacekeeping. The Sunnis called it preservation. South of Route Irish, LTC Frank and his troops struggled with a frustrated, violent population. Some less fortunate Sunnis were being forced from their homes by Muqtada al-Sadr's Mahdi Army, which then rented the houses to Shia families who were looking for better living conditions. There was great concern the movement would work its way north. The power struggles, like in many poor, urban American neighborhoods, were volatile. The Shia regularly made targets of each other and of U.S. soldiers. Through a 15-month deployment Frank's battalion would lose 19 soldiers. Gadson and Frank had paired off in the meeting.

"How are your charges in Mansour?" Frank had asked Gadson. "Still cooperating?"

"Mostly. Mostly, they're just watchin' out for yours," Gadson answered, smirking slightly. Peacekeeping was always temporary there. He was not so sure about this manpower surge he found himself a part of. He did believe in the hearts and minds stuff, though. He spent enough time around Iraqi families to know they wanted peace more than anyone.

"How's Kim doing? What's she up to?" Frank asked. The Frank and Gadson families were neighbors back at Fort Riley, in Kansas.

"She's good. She's still teaching in Junction City. She's got her hands full with the kids doing all their, I guess, teenage stuff. Pre-teen. Gabby plays soccer—her grades are good. Jaelen is on the track team. His academics are more, well, more of a wild card."

It would be the midmorning at home in Fort Riley. He imagined Kim at work, having earlier that morning wrangled the kids, getting them to school. Mondays were always a little slower for everyone. There would probably be soccer or track practice that night. He felt a small pang of homesickness. Watching his kids play sports was one of the best parts of parenting. It reminded him of his own childhood neighborhood football team. He wondered if either of his kids would wind up following his legacy at West Point—whether Jaelen might even play football. It was a dream he shared with his best friend, and former teammate, LTC Chuck Schretzman, who had a son close to Gabby's age. Schretzman was currently enjoying a comparatively cushy duty in Canada.

"How's Jenn?" he asked Frank.

"She's fine—holding down the fort, keeping up with things at the base. We got a new puppy."

"Oh, I'm sure our kids are all over that!" Greg said, happy for Gabby's and Jaelen's new diversion. "You know, you hear all those stories about how kids get into trouble while a parent is deployed. We're just lucky I guess or we're doing something right. Ours are fine, really. They help Kim out. No complaints."

Gadson and Frank had chatted for a half an hour maybe. Then Gadson and his detail had pulled out in their convoy, in the dark, headed back to Camp Liberty. Normally, Frank would have returned to his quarters at the nearby joint security station, which was sort of like an urban outpost. He was one of the officers tasked with living among the people of Iraq. A number of security stations were established in various neighborhoods. It was about showing U.S. presence and solidarity with Iraqi forces and police, and hopefully stemming the violence. General David Petraeus, commander of multinational forces in Iraq, had created the stations following President Bush's request for 20,000 more troops in Iraq and Al Anbar. The general wanted less shooting, more bonding. But tonight, instead of returning to the outpost, Frank had some odds and ends to tie up at FOB Falcon. So, he planned to work and bunk down there for the night.

Colonel Gibbs sat down at his desk, his laptop flickering with data. He was in constant touch with his people in and outside the wire. The radio net crackled slightly through the speakers. It was getting late and Gibbs had an important phone call to make.

"Hello?"

"Hello, son, Happy Birthday!" It was May 7. Richard Gibbs turned 16 that day.

"Hey, Dad, how's it going?"

"I'm good, how was your day? Did you get any good gifts?"

"Yah."

"And dinner?" Typical teenager. It took a bit of prying, especially from so far away.

"Pesto pasta." The colonel chuckled at the choice, a family favorite.

"Dessert?"

"You know, Dad."

He did know. The Gibbs family cheesecake recipe was standard issue.

"Enjoy the rest of your night, son. Put your mother on the phone, would you?"

"How did the other things go this week?" the colonel asked his wife, a little more soberly.

"We did okay, you know, it's getting—I hate to say—almost routine," she said.

It seemed to Nolly Gibbs that there were two or three memorials at Fort Riley per week. Hellish as it was for troops overseas, it was no picnic trying to console families back home. The casualties were nonstop. Eight hundred soldiers from their 4th Infantry Combat Brigade would be wounded during 18 months of the surge. One hundred and two would be killed.

"Yah, tough afternoon here, too" Colonel Gibbs sympathized with his wife. "The Jones kid. You know, he was adopted. Parents adored him. Really well liked by . . . "

"Patriot Security Detail has been hit!"

A voice blared through his laptop.

"Ricky what's going on? Who's hit?"

"I don't know," Gibbs half fibbed. "I gotta go." He abruptly hung up the phone. He could explain later. Hopefully it was nothing. Still, his heart pounded as he raced to the tactical operations center.

Lieutenant Colonel Frank could hear the stress tearing at their voices. Their words, tight; the comments, brief. But it was difficult for him to know, from the traffic coming over the radio in his office at FOB Falcon, who was injured and how badly. He listened intently as members of Delta Company 1st Battalion, 28th Infantry pulled their convoy of four Humvees up to the site of the explosion. These were his men. They had been patrolling a dangerous area near Route Jackson—one where IEDs were common roadway impediments. The Black Lions found their share of them, either by expertly trained eye or horrific accident. This time it was Gadson's security detail that made the horrible discovery. The Black Lions' immediate, instinctive response was to get to the scene to supply backup and help with casualties.

Frank could hear bits and pieces of conversations as platoon leaders organized security and the wounded. There were two. Maybe three casualties.

"Get him in the truck . . . " A loud scratchy voice. Something about a tourniquet. Then some shouting, swearing. Someone talked about blood. It did not sound good mostly because of what he did not hear: the voice of the battalion commander with whom, just a few minutes ago, he had been exchanging pleasantries about home.

The tactical operations center, or TOC, is a 24-hour central command, where live events are monitored, charted, graphed, reported, analyzed and when all hell breaks loose, sealed. Colonel Gibbs did not have to ask much. He could tell by the heightened buzz, the looks on the faces of the watch personnel gathered in the cave-like building, screens dancing with images overhead, the incident was escalating.

"Colonel Gadson's been hit, sir," one of the specialists confirmed.

"How bad?"

"We can't tell, sir. They're getting him transported back here now. They were only a few minutes away. They had a little trouble getting him into the truck. The 1-28th is just getting there."

"Has medical been notified?"

"Yes, sir."

Tonight, the stars aligned. It was Monday, which meant Army docs from all over the region were gathered for their weekly recreational video-game-athon at Falcon. "Counter-Strike" had appropriately been this evening's choice of on-screen annihilation. It was a rare occasion when the FOB had doctors and surgeons to spare.

In the TOC, Gibbs and the others listened incredulously, helplessly, as the driver and a Humvee full of security personnel, medic Eric Brown, and the gravely wounded Lieutenant Colonel Gadson raced toward the gate of FOB Falcon. The truck blew past base security and screeched to a halt as close to the troop medical clinic (TMC) as its wide berth would allow. Gibbs, along with his brigade sergeant major, Jim Champagne, raced out to meet it. The waiting crew had Gadson on a stretcher in no time. Gibbs and Champagne grabbed handles closest to the lieutenant colonel's head to help carry him in. That's when they knew. That's when they all knew they could lose him.

"Let me see my legs! There's something wrong with my legs!" Gadson began to thrash again as they moved toward the TMC.

"He keeps trying to sit up, sir!" Brown called to the colonel. Gibbs did his best to hold him back while helping to balance the gurney.

"Gadson. Stay down," Gibbs commanded. "We need you to stay *down!*"

"How bad am I? Just tell me!"

Gibbs glanced at Champagne. Champagne was tight with Gadson, having spent hours with him at Fort Riley, training a unit of 3,500 soldiers as infantrymen. Champagne was depending on some of those exercises to guide him now. He leaned in, nearly nose to nose with Gadson, trying to hold his gaze. But Gadson did not seem to see him.

"I'm losing it, guys! I'm losing it!" Gadson called out, feeling himself slip toward unconsciousness.

"You're not going anywhere!" hollered Champagne. Champagne and Gibbs kept yelling, their raw voices scraping together, desperate for the sound to save him.

They entered the medical unit. Gibbs held Gadson's head, trying to keep him still and focused on anything but his legs. Gibbs spoke continuously about his troops, his duties, the mission, any damned thing. He looked around the room. Brown looked stricken. Their eyes met for a second, Brown's brimmed with tears.

"Oh God, sir, I did what I thought—I didn't have anything else out there ..."

"You did good, Private," Gibbs interrupted. "You did all you could."

From inside the bubble of the TMC, Dr. Ross Witters could hear Gadson's screams, and took in a breath, preparing himself for yet another bloody tempest. Victims arrived daily, shot up by mortars or burned by bombs hurled inside the base. Others, like this one, were transported from Route One or "Thunder Road," as he had come to call it. FOB Falcon was sitting on some dangerous dirt.

Dr. Brian Derrick took the lead, while the rest of the docs split duties, one monitoring breathing, another taking charge of Gadson's right leg, Dr. Witters taking the left. Nurse Captain Eric Fourroux was responsible for administering meds and fluids.

Witters gasped at Gadson's wounds, more because of what was not there than what was. Skin, muscle and tissue no longer existed. All that hung from the bone was the sciatic nerve, or was it an artery? Witters could not even tell. There was blood oozing and gushing everywhere. He ripped at reams of gauze, pushing it hard into the back of the extremity, then desperately snatched spools of Kerlix bandage rolls, not bothering to unwind them, and packed a half dozen of them into what was left of the thigh. He was up to his elbow inside Gadson's leg, sopping up as much of the gush as possible, before drawing out his forearm and wrapping the packing with ace bandages. Witters knew his job there was just to buy the man some time.

Army Nurse Corps Captain Fourroux took his place alongside Witters. Their fevered motions were perfectly choreographed, their hands moving almost mechanically across Gadson's writhing body. They worked urgently, but with a businesslike air.

Fourroux doubled the tourniquets, smashing them up as close to the lieutenant colonel's groin as possible, knowing those limbs might be revived at the combat support hospital (CSH) a short medevac away. He grabbed shears and shredded Gadson's uniform from his body, working deftly to find a vein into which he could pump just enough fluid to keep the lieutenant colonel alive. Too much would exacerbate the bleeding. Fourroux looked up long enough to notice the TMC had flooded with rank. *Who is this guy?*

Fourroux did not know this patient from any other, except that he was the most "alive" IED survivor the nurse had ever seen. Most came in unconscious, their battle buddies pleading for miracles. Gadson, incredibly, seemed to be still in charge.

"I'm losing it, guys!" Gadson screamed again, commanding them to save his life.

Fourroux's latex gloves were covered in blood, making them too slippery to grasp anything. He tugged at Gadson's right arm, desperate to remove the lieutenant colonel's leather glove, but his own filmy glove would not grip. Gadson's screams were shrill. He was in excruciating agony.

"I need a fentanyl pop!" Dr. Witters called.

"I can't see!" Gadson yelled. "I'm fading!" His deep howls chilled their own blood.

Fourroux fixated on the lieutenant colonel's glove, grasping, sliding. That is when Gadson went silent. Then he turned to look Fourroux dead in the eyes.

"How in the fuck are you going to save my life if you can't get that glove off?" He delivered the line with the calm and panache of John Wayne, fingering his pistol grip.

Captain Fourroux froze. He was being dressed down by a senior officer, that much he understood, one who was currently dying. *This guy was some kinda badass.* Fourroux abruptly yanked the glove off, then found the accessory cephalic vein in the wounded officer's arm. Next there were narcotics. And oxygen. The lieutenant colonel calmed slightly. Fourroux was not sure, as the golden hour ticked closer to its end, if the calming was much comfort. He glanced at Gibbs, his own commanding officer. Gibbs' normally smooth, creaseless face was lined and furrowed. Their eyes met for an eighth of a second.

Gibbs' eyes flashed then focused back on Gadson. There was blood everywhere—had to be more outside the LTC's body than in. It had been a long time since Colonel Ricky Gibbs felt fear.

"We're proud of you, Greg," Gibbs said. "Everyone talks about what a great job you're doing up there. We need to keep you on that command, you know? The people who live there—those families—they're going to be pissed if you don't come back."

Gadson was his thinker, his unfailing team player, his solid "go-to" battalion commander. But now, Gadson was not taking orders. He would not stop moving. But at least he had stopped swinging. He was growing weaker, his blood pressure dropping. Still, he tried to push himself up on his elbows.

"You have to keep still. Stay *still!* Let these people work, Greg," Gibbs pleaded.

"I'll try. I'm trying. Just don't let me die in Iraq, Colonel," Gadson pleaded.

"You won't die here. You *won't*."

On the floor Gibbs saw a fresh red boot print, where someone had stepped in blood, leaving a morbid track. He wondered if he had just told a giant lie.

"Tell Kim I love her," Gadson said, as the sedative began to take hold.

"I will, Colonel."

Witters and the rest of the medical team, turned over custody, knowing their work was the best they could offer, the best the medical field could supply. If Gadson survived, he would be the most severely wounded person they had seen at Falcon to make it home.

Gadson, quieter now, was carried back outside and gingerly set inside a Blackhawk medevac helicopter. Colonel Gibbs stepped in and took a seat beside him. It was a 10-minute flight to the Green Zone, the most secure area of Iraq, heavily guarded by coalition troops. There was a small hospital there, staffed by American military doctors. Gibbs continued to talk, yelling over the noise of the chopper. If he made staying alive an order, Gadson might comply. Gibbs clasped his hand around Greg's and squeezed. Gadson squeezed back. He was still alive.

· · ·

First Sergeant Johnson and the remaining soldiers still out on Route Jackson were scrambling in the dark to be sure everyone had been accounted for, every scrap of gear, secure. For Captain Bandy, there was also the matter of how to tow the crumpled Humvee back to Falcon. They worked, averting their eyes from the foot-and-a-half deep hole, which spread 30 inches, now scarring Route Jackson. Explosive ordnance investigators were already there, reporting details of how the IED had been planted. Terrorists had used burning tires to loosen asphalt then planted explosives beneath it. A command wire ran from the device, through a hole in the fence, to a nearby building. The triggerman had waited, watching, timing the explosion as the convoy grew near, then had reeled in the wire after detonating the device.

The group of men was badly shaken. They had only been in Iraq for three months, but Gadson had been their battalion commander since 2006, back at Fort Riley. Bandy knew Gadson to be a soldier's soldier. When they went into a building, he went into a building. When they patrolled, he patrolled. He had the rank, the ability to instill fear in his troops. And he did, when he needed to. He could take a guy out with just a few well-timed words. But it was never vicious, or random. And he was always certain the lesson had been learned because he would come back later to be sure. He would try the guy out on the same task again.

Johnson sucked in some of the night air, then turned to face what was left of a broken detail. It was rare to lose a commander. Just did not happen, really. The security detail's job, its entire focus, was to keep the LTC safe. Now, the best Johnson could hope was that he was in a helicopter, fighting for his life, on his way to a hospital in Baghdad. The younger ones struggled with tears of anger and guilt. Their mission failed. Crumbled beneath the man to whom they had looked for direction, counsel, in fact, for their very lives.

Johnson needed to find the LTC's gun. He had gotten word it was missing. No need to arm the enemy. Besides, Gadson would want it back. Johnson knew the man. They had served together in the first Gulf War. Searching around the blast area, he fingered his swollen jaw. Luckily, he had never before given Gadson cause to throw a punch.

Modern warfighting is different from wars of the past, partly because there is no "front." Troops cannot advance to the front line, fight, then retreat to the rear to rest. It is often impossible to know where friendly territory ends and enemy lines begin. Some Iraqis were supportive of the American invasion. Others were trying to claim power for themselves. It was difficult to know friend from foe. You could be grabbing a chai in a marketplace, and the guy next to you might be wired with explosives. It was that kind of war.

A pair of headlights blazed into Johnson's peripheral vision, blinding him from the side and lighting up the scene. A little startled, Bandy looked up from his current project—fixing a tow bar to their new 10-ton albatross. Thanks to the 1-28th, the security perimeter was still in place. Still, with the personnel available, it was impossible to completely secure the entire road, a major thruway through the war-torn city.

A white Suburban, clearly Iraqi, approached. Bandy fingered his rifle. Just to be sure it was still there. They were vulnerable. Too many bodies. Not enough truck. Trying to clean up a failed mission in the middle of the Wild West. Perfect. Targets.

"Stop!" yelled a private, who had been manning one of the Humvee turrets.

The SUV did not stop, nor did it slow. It kept moving forward, directly toward them.

"*Stop your vehicle!*" the gunner yelled again, turning his machine gun toward the truck.

Damned idiot. Or enemy. Hard telling.

Johnson considered ordering the private to fire. He would wait another minute. Goddamn checkpoints. He could see the booth from where he stood. Like they did not fucking know the team was in trouble down here. Useless. Corrupt. But gunfire, especially tonight, was a last resort.

The truck slowed, then stopped. A man got out.

"*Stop where you are!*" yelled the gunner, poised, waiting for the fire command.

The man walked slowly toward them, seemingly unaware of the fire-power trained directly on his forehead.

One more step. The gunner felt his own pulse bursting in his trigger finger.

The man stopped.

Bandy held his breath.

The man said nothing. He turned around. He got back in his truck. And he drove away. The taillights gleamed back at them as the truck headed north, back up Route Jackson.

Bandy exhaled.

Johnson cursed. That gun had to be here somewhere.

CHAPTER THREE

"I want you to know I am here because your father is injured,
not because he is dying."
—Army Chaplain Brent Causey, Fort Riley, Kansas

Kim Gadson stretched her legs out in front of her on the wooden bench, enjoying a moment of tranquility. Glistening drops of water hung on the inside of the sauna windows. It was her custom to recover a bit from her afternoon workout at the Fort Riley gym. Good for the muscles. Good for the soul. She had only a short time before she had to get back home. Her daughter, Gabby was concocting some sort of experiment in the kitchen, which would be dinner for the kids. She had decided she would find something else to eat once she saw the new recipe called for shrimp. The texture made her wonder from what slimy crevice of the ocean they originated. She looked up for a moment and through the steamy windows, caught a glance of the brigade rear-detachment S1 adjutant officer, Major Christine Pacheco, walking out of the locker room. Strange time for her to be here in the gym, she half-noted. Rear detachment people deal in family support services. This would be a busy time of day for Pacheco. She inhaled one last breath of hot steam, feeling it seep through her sinuses, scouring her mind of the day's classroom stress. Relaxed now, she was ready to slip into parent mode. She glanced at her watch. There were shrimp to fry. Or something.

Kim grabbed her towel and looked up toward the locker room door again. This time, Nolly Gibbs, the brigade commander's wife, walked in. It was a sobering sight. As Nolly's gaze settled upon her, Kim realized she had been the target of Pacheco's search. And the commander's wife had zeroed in. Was it something about the Family Readiness Group she led? But something about the look on Nolly's face made Kim want to turn back time.

They met at the door.

"Greg is very much alive, but has been injured," came the kind, yet authoritative voice of the commander's wife, a little too quickly. The words echoed on the damp tile. The room shifted. Kim stood still, dripping, staring at Nolly, those deep, hot breaths turning to short gasps.

"We need you to go outside," Nolly nudged. "General Yarbrough is waiting to talk to you."

Obediently, Kim toweled off, shakily pulled on her sweats, and made her way out of the locker room, disheveled, and into the lobby of the gym, where the assistant division commander, Brigadier General James Yarbrough, Pacheco and the post family chaplain, Lieutenant Colonel Brent Causey, were waiting. Her stomach turned over at the sight of the general, the major and the Army chaplain, standing shoulder to shoulder, faces lined with concern. As a West Point cadet, she had always wanted to escape this sort of high-ranking attention. Now she felt the weight of their status poised to crash into her carefully constructed coping schemes, her day-to-day Army wife structure. She wished they would just come out with it, but her military training cautioned her to be calm, to respect their guidance. Pacheco had magically gathered Kim's things from the locker room. About 20 soldiers were loitering in the lobby, to see the commotion. They were getting ready for the evening unit basketball games.

Yarbrough motioned everyone outside, then turned to Kim.

"There was an explosion. An IED. Your husband's left leg has been severely damaged. The right leg is also injured but it's in better shape than the other." He told her Greg was being flown to a hospital in Baghdad's Green Zone, where he would undergo surgery. "We'll get him on the phone to you as soon as we can."

The phone, she thought, as the group walked toward the parking lot. If Greg could talk on the phone, Kim figured, it couldn't be that bad, could it? The loss of limbs—especially legs—was the sort of "expected" injury now in Iraq. Maybe that is why, she figured, the general meant her husband would lose his left leg, but not the right. Her own legs began to shake again as everyone huddled around her, Nolly to the right, the general to her left.

"Do you think I could sit down?" Kim asked. The group ushered her to the back of Nolly's Toyota Highlander. A rear detachment captain was already driving Kim's van back to the house. She fixated for a moment on how he could have gotten her keys.

"Who else was injured?" she asked the general as they made their way to the Gadsons' home on the base.

"We're not sure. We believe his interpreter, a, uh, Mike Oro, was hurt."

Greg had mentioned Oro. Oro was with him constantly during this deployment, as Greg was doing so much interfacing with the Iraqis.

"Badly?"

"He's got a fairly severe wound, but not as bad . . . "

"Where were they? What were they doing?" Kim asked.

"Route Jackson," the general replied. "It's a fairly well traveled road. They were headed back to Liberty after a memorial service at another base. It was dark."

"A memorial service?"

"Two KIA a few days ago. Younger guys—IEDs."

She wondered what the hell her husband was doing driving through Baghdad in the dark on the way back from something that seemed so *optional*. But it would not have been optional to him. He would have considered those soldiers part of the team. And *team* was everything to her husband.

"He's going to be so mad," Kim mused.

"How do you mean?" asked Pacheco.

"To lose that leg. He's going to be extremely pissed off."

No one answered.

The parade of Army brass marched into the Gadson family living room where Gabby lounged on the couch, having already wrapped up her shrimp thing in the kitchen. A few months back, Kim had given up arguing with Gabby about her wardrobe. Skin. It was what all the teenagers were wearing. Jaelen had called to say he was on his way home from track practice. It was obvious there had been no call from their father.

Kim wanted to tell both kids at once, but it is not every day the brigadier general brings their mother home from the gym. The sauna, no less. Yarbrough, feeling Gabby's nervous stare, took charge, explaining that her father was hurt. Taking a cue from her mother, she was calm and reserved. Finally, Jaelen burst through the door, but ran straight to the bathroom. No one at home knew, but he'd gotten into some trouble at school that day—enough to possibly warrant a call from his teacher. He'd come in through the kitchen door, missing all the commotion, hoping to buy some time before his mom dealt out the inevitable punishment, by hiding in the bathroom. When she called him a second time, he figured he'd better go face what was coming to him. Rounding the corner into the living room, he was relieved to see people in uniform, figuring the VIP visitors would delay any sort of castigation. But then he noticed his mom and sister looked as if they'd been crying.

"What's everyone doing here?" Jaelen asked no one in particular.

"Your father's been hurt. There was an explosion," Yarbrough started to explain.

Jaelen's boyish face immediately scrunched like soft playdough, tears brimming from the slits of his eyes. Kim pulled him toward her.

Jaelen and his dad had been at odds over the previous few months. In a way the youngest member of the Gadson family had been relieved to see his dad leave. *Finally he'll be off my back*, Jaelen had thought when his dad left for Iraq. He'd actually wished for his dad to leave and now wasn't sure he'd ever see him again. He was devastated.

Gabby, the elder, hung tough but after a few minutes disappeared up the stairs. Kim fought the urge to follow her, but she knew Gabby was headed to the attic, her "alone place" of choice. Staring at the phone, Kim nearly willed it to ring. Hearing their father's voice would reassure the kids—reassure them all. She struggled to find patience. And she asked for the Lord's strength.

Gabby, drawn back downstairs by the soft patter of comforting tones, slipped back into the room.

"Maybe Chaplain Causey would pray with us," Kim suggested to the kids. She wanted them to understand how much they needed God now and in facing whatever lay ahead. She wanted them to know if anything happened to their dad, they would always have the Lord.

The chaplain huddled with the three of them. He was familiar enough with the Gadson kids to understand their needs, what he might say that would provide support. And, unfortunately, this was not his first such counseling session at Fort Riley.

"First, I want you to know I am here because your father is injured. Not because he is dying." Both Gabby and Jaelen nodded. They bowed their heads, Jaelen, still teary.

Kim watched as Gabby prayed uncertainly. Her oldest knew instinctively there was a possibility her father could die. Gabby's brow furrowed, seemingly determined to push that darkness from her mind. Still, Kim knew her daughter would brace for the worst but expect the best. That is what she and Greg had always taught their children, but tonight it was an impossible combination.

"Let us pray to the Lord to guide the doctors to a quick diagnosis," the chaplain began. "We ask for your healing power for Lieutenant Colonel Gadson and for your strength for his family. And, Lord, we pray for a quick recovery." The chaplain checked himself. He did not want to specifically mention their father's legs. It would seem misleading to ask the Lord for something that may already be too far gone. "Bring Colonel Gadson back home to his family, Lord, where they can all heal more quickly and more powerfully, together. Amen."

"Amen," Kim and the kids answered together.

The prayer seemed to calm the children enough for them to go to the kitchen and sit down to eat their dinner. Thank goodness the shrimp gave Kim the excuse to sit this meal out rather than having to demonstrate any sort of normalcy by eating. Her stomach was in knots, but the promised phone call from the Baghdad hospital was giving her momentum. General Yarbrough was on and off the phone with other people in Baghdad, keeping tabs on where her husband was being treated. And soon she would be reassured by the sound of his voice. No need to panic his parents or their close friends. But she figured she had better call the local cavalry. She picked up the phone.

The one call she most wanted to make, she could not. Linda Anderson was her "go-to" friend and confidante. They had been friends for more than a dozen years—since Greg was a young officer in Major Rodney Anderson's command in 1993 at Fort Bragg in North Carolina. Anderson had noticed Greg walking down a hallway and invited him in for a personal counseling session. Greg figured Anderson had zeroed in on him because of his dark skin; Anderson was also Black. Kim and Linda became friends and not long after that session, Greg was burned severely enough to be hospitalized overnight in an accident with the Headquarters and Headquarters 82nd Command (HHC). When Linda found out, she chastised Kim for not calling. Now Kim desperately wanted to speak to her friend but knew she would be at her weekly unit coffee klatch. She felt inexplicably irritated. She dialed another number by rote.

Jennifer Frank was waiting for the call. The news of Greg's injury had traveled quickly outside the chain of command. She did not know if Kim had been notified and—by regulation and common sense—she was not the person to do it. Besides, she had no details. And the information she did have could be incorrect. Maybe Greg had not been hurt at all. Maybe it was someone else. Still, she had changed into something presentable. She took their puppy, Charlie, for a walk. She answered the phone on the first ring.

"Jennifer, it's Kim," the soft, low voice came over the phone. Jennifer knew what was coming. She tried to calm her own nerves with a few deep breaths. Kim's voice was shaking. "I need you. Please come down here." Jennifer calmly hung up the phone and walked down the street to the Gadson family home.

Gibbs, Pacheco and Yarbrough were all still there when Jennifer arrived. Jenn took a spot on the ottoman across from Kim and listened for updates. So far, there had been no call from Greg, but Kim had been told to expect one. And as the wife of a battalion commander, who led the Family Readiness Group at Fort Riley, Kim was worried about keeping the other families in the loop as much as possible. Rumors spread quickly on the base.

"How would you like to keep people informed, Kim?" Jennifer asked.

"That's why you're here," Kim said, gently. Jenn set about organizing phone communications, first to the Family Readiness Group, then with the dozens of people who were slowly getting the word about the attack.

The FRG, made up mostly of officers' wives, assembled in the Gadson home that night. Kim had run these meetings plenty of times before. These women were her peers, her support group through Greg's deployments, child rearing, work emergencies, everything. And she was always there for them. In the past she had told them to take care of their batteries, their units, and she would take care of them. Now, she said they would have to take care of each other. Like other families of wounded military, they would soon redeploy, to be near Greg, who she had learned would be headed, eventually, to Walter Reed Army Medical Center, in Washington, D.C. She did her best to prepare the other women for their new duties.

"They're moving Greg, as soon as he's stable enough, to D.C.," she told the group. "I'll meet him there. Once I leave for Washington, I won't be back for a while. When I do come back, it will probably be to pack up for a permanent move." The words came out like small rocks hitting concrete. Tick, tick, tick, precise in what she did not say. Everyone looked stricken, and worried, like they were waiting for her to collapse, or start wailing with grief. But she did not feel grief. She was just waiting for him to call her. He would soon.

"And I know," Kim added, "that Greg is going to walk again. I just know that." She wanted everyone to feel better. Not that she was sugar coating anything. She knew her husband would never tolerate being immobile. Or even slowing down. But she was not sure who was comforting whom. One by one, the women spoke to her alone, offering support, every sort of kindness. And as each one walked out the door she knew, despite their constant attention and love, this would be a lonesome journey.

The phone rang. Kim looked at it, longing for it to be her husband, but desperate not to speak to anyone else, not to tie up the phone line, not to have to go over, again and again, what little she knew. There were already so many people calling. She was humbled by their concern, their love for both her and Greg and the kids, but she could not pick up the phone. Jenn stepped in, notepad in hand. Kim sighed with relief. She still had calls to make herself: It was time to alert Greg's parents. And her own.

• • •

In the hours following Kim's notification, the house phone rang continuously. Jenn worked tirelessly, keeping meticulous notes of who called and when, filling several legal pads, which were stacking up in the kitchen. She earned the name "Pit Bull" for her protective watch over the phone and front door. Still, the constant ringing nearly brought tears to Kim's eyes. She so badly wanted to hear her husband's voice. Yarbrough had said he would call. He could call, she told herself. He was able.

She steadied herself enough to call Greg's parents. His mother had answered the phone. Patricia Gadson was a soft-spoken person and was quiet as Kim shared the news. She told them to expect an official notification call from the Army. And she promised to keep in close touch.

One tough task completed. Check. Kim took a quick inventory. Gabby was on the phone with her friends. That was her way of coping, for now. Jaelen was outside with some neighborhood boys, at their usual haunts. A neighbor was keeping an eye on them. Kim went to her bedroom, to make her final call of the night. There was one voice, aside from her husband's that she longed to hear.

"Linda?"

Kim could barely get the words out. It had been several hours since she'd been summoned from the sauna. Greg had never called. No one from Baghdad had called her directly. For the first time she felt fear rise up in her throat. Greg would live. She believed that. She had to believe. But he would be changed. And she so desperately needed to hear his voice.

Linda broke into a fevered prayer.

Kim heard the words and felt her own knees hit the carpet. She reached for her Bible.

The two women prayed and cried together. And they talked about when Linda would come. Her own husband was deployed in Afghanistan. They had three children. The women agreed it would be best to meet later in D.C.

"Jennifer Frank and the others are taking good care of me here," Kim assured Linda before saying goodbye. Kim turned back to her Bible.

Jenn cracked the bedroom door cautiously—the sight of her friend crumpled over her Bible in tearful prayer stopped her short. She did not want to interfere, but there was an important call on the other line. One she knew Kim would want to take. Kim picked up the receiver on the bedroom phone.

Greg's brigade commander, Colonel Ricky Gibbs, was straightforward.

"Kim, it's very serious. The backs of his legs are destroyed. I would say he has a 50-50 chance of pulling through this."

"Okay," Kim said quietly.

"He's strong, though and the team here at the hospital is the best."

Kim did not answer. She did not feel as if death were an option. It just was not on the table.

"Your husband wanted me to tell you that he loves you."

"Thank you, Colonel," she responded, holding her voice steady.

"He's headed into his second surgery now. The doctor will call you after, I promise."

Kim picked up her Bible and closed her eyes knowing that the next call from Baghdad would not be from her husband.

CHAPTER FOUR

"We arrived at Fort Dix—I had long hair parted in the middle.
We had no idea what we'd gotten into."
—Lieutenant Colonel Charles 'Chuck" Schretzman,
on his first day in the Army

Lieutenant Colonel Chuck Schretzman was scrolling through email when one sender caught his eye: Bert DeForest. Always good to hear from one of the boys, he thought, grinning, especially while he was deployed out of the country. Ottawa, Ontario, Canada, could hardly be called hardship duty. Still, he was away from his wife and kids. Chuck had fought alongside the Canadian Army in Afghanistan, but he missed being with his old unit—and with Americans. He clicked on the message, expecting a friendly football flashback. What he read set him back in his chair.

Sorry to hear about number 98.

His mind raced. Number 98 could only be one person: Greg Gadson. Greg had asked for the football jersey number after his mentor, Kurt Gutierrez, graduated, making 98 available. Greg wanted to live up to Kurt's strength on the field and his personal integrity. And Greg constantly strove for that. He was strong, always deceiving opponents who measured him only by physical size. Coach Jim Young would set the team up to scrimmage every day. And every day they fought for their lives on that field. He and Greg competed for the same position and Greg, shorter and lighter, most often won. Coach worked them so hard it made the real Saturday games seem like a vacation.

What happened? Chuck typed, his fingers quivering slightly.

He thought about Greg's knees, weakened by the constant impact on the gridiron and several surgeries. More than once, Chuck had played team medic, winding athletic adhesive around Greg's kneecaps. Maybe number 98 had just blown out an IT band or something. Maybe it was as simple as that.

IED, DeForest responded.

Chuck stared at the screen, feeling slightly lightheaded. His mouth went dry. Greg's strength, he knew, would be that West Point football had prepared him for the Army. Chuck believed the 100-year-old home of the Black Knights, Michie Stadium, was a virtual leadership lab. The players were smaller and slower than other teams who were not facing the same academic and military standards. But Army players were tough, mentally and physically. They had all taken their hits. No team was going to beat them because they were smarter or tougher. No team. No enemy.

Twenty-three years earlier, on the very first day of practice at Fort Monmouth, the West Point prep school, Chuck had broken his wrist. It was one of Greg's stories that would ring in his ears forever.

"So I'm walking across the field and there's this guy and he's holding his wrist like *this*," Greg would say, grabbing his left, limp wrist and flapping the attached hand in the air. "And he's wearing his huge helmet, it's a different color from everyone else's, cuz his head was so big they had to send out for a special one. He looked like a Martian!"

The story never failed to get lots of laughs. He had been a pretty big dork, Chuck conceded. But his reasons for choosing West Point were fairly sophisticated for a shaggy-haired Philly kid. He knew he needed to stop running the streets of his blue-collar neighborhood and get into a supportive school. One of five children of a Philadelphia firefighter, he had called his father the morning after he wrapped his wrist in magazines and tape, asking to come home. His dad, however, had four other kids to worry about.

"You're at school, right? A prep school," Charles Schretzman Sr. had said.

"Yeah, Dad, please I'm in so much pain!"

"They'll take care of you," he said, and hung up. Tough love was a big part of his somewhat hard-knocks upbringing.

Greg's parents had both graduated from Howard University in the early '70s, Willie Gadson becoming a pharmacist and Patricia, a schoolteacher, in Chesapeake, Va., where Greg grew up with his brother and sister. He was a quiet kid who would fall asleep at parties because he had gotten up well before the sun to deliver newspapers.

So, when the smallish, low-key young Black man from a little town in the south and the blonde, scruffy-haired inner-city kid from Philly each learned they would be competing for the same position on the football team, there would been some mutual sizing up. It did not take long, though, for their differences to dissolve into the turf. When one wore himself sick, the other powered through for two. When one felt the heavy hand of military discipline, the other stood tall in his place. When one fell in love, the other played Cupid. When one night in a Philadelphia bar, Greg was taunted by a horrible racial slur, they both felt the sting. And when one was injured . . .

Chuck blinked at the email and squared his shoulders. He took a deep breath, then dialed the Gadson home at Fort Riley.

An unfamiliar voice had answered the phone. "Gadson residence."

"Hello, this is Lieutenant Colonel Chuck Schretzman," he said, following formality with formality.

"Chuck Schretzman?" He had the sense he was being screened. There was a pause, then Kim got on the phone.

"Kim, it's Chuck."

"Chuck, I . . . " He could hear her throat tighten. He knew Kim to be always the quiet professional, but she was struggling to maintain that now. Kim, Greg, Chuck and his wife Stacy all had a pretty solid grip on the roots of each other's lives. They had all come together at West Point, the men first in Fort Monmouth, N.J., at the U.S. Military Academy Preparatory School, knocking into each other initially on the football field. Kim was a West Point grad. Stacy and Chuck had met at summer school. Chuck was best man at Kim and Greg's wedding. When they were both majors at Fort Leavenworth, Kansas, in 2000, they lived about 150 feet from each other.

He broke into her ragged breathing.

"What do you hear from Baghdad?" Chuck asked.

The question snapped her back into a military posture. "Greg is unconscious still. He's had two surgeries. They're working on his leg. He might lose . . . " Her voice caught. "They're flying him to a hospital in Baghdad now, then bringing him to Walter Reed in D.C., hopefully in a couple of days."

"I'm meeting you there." Chuck hung up the phone and looked around for his car keys. He thought about all the ribbings he had taken from the cocky linebacker over the years. But this was not about tape. Or friendly competition. This would reach into the belly of the brotherhood, and his link in that chain would be unyielding.

CHAPTER FIVE

"I would not have put a dying person on a helicopter.
They don't get any healthier on there."
—Dr. Brad Woods, Staff Surgeon General,
Combat Support Hospital, Baghdad

Sometimes Dr. Bradley Woods wondered why they even had an "on-call" system, since he always wound up in the operating room anyway. Table hours, the military called them. He glanced at his watch. It was a little after 9 p.m. He turned the beeping pager off and jogged lightly from his office to the emergency room of the 10th Combat Support Hospital in Baghdad's Green Zone.

The 10th CSH is a mobile hospital, with more than 80 beds, an emergency unit, two intensive care units and an operating room equipped with two tables. It's made of temper tents—soft-walled, modular, aluminum-framed canvas, designed to be configured to accommodate heat and air conditioning as needed. Once inside, the "mobile" aspect is barely noticeable. It looks and functions like a brick and mortar Army medical unit back in the States, where it was first conceptualized during World War II.

"Guy's a battalion commander," someone said to Woods as he walked toward the gurney. The patient was babbling something in a big, scratchy voice, but the doctor could not make it out. The tourniquets were still in place—as high up on each thigh as they would go. Both legs lay limp and blood-soaked below.

"Oh, God," Woods heard himself mumble.

Doctors at the Baghdad hospital saw on average 10 to 20 patients a day. Some days there were maybe five. But on some long, long days into nights as many as 25 patients with wounds, some fairly minor—a finger that held on to a flash-bang too long, or a gunshot graze to the abdomen, the part of the upper body the IBA (Interceptor Body Armor) does not protect—came through the doors. But shredded limbs resulting from IEDs, either walked over or triggered by a tire, were sadly the norm.

People say you get used to things, Woods thought. *Sometimes people are wrong.* The doctor snapped on a pair of protective rubber gloves.

"Blood pressure's 40," a nurse reported. It was not unusual to bring the young ones back from such a shallow heart rate. But this guy looked older to Woods. And big. Dude's thighs were the size of his own torso. He was conscious but in shock, well on his way to dying.

"That's Greg Gadson!" came the surprised voice of another surgeon, Dr. Al Beekley. "I used to scrimmage against him at West Point. Guy could put a *hurt* on me."

So he had been an athlete, in the day, at his very own alma mater, Woods thought. Would not have wanted to mess with him. He was *thick.* Thick all over.

"Let's go," said Woods. Medical staff wheeled the gurney, overtaken by 210 pounds of agitated, bleeding mass, barely cornering the turn into the cluttered operating room. Medical equipment hung, balanced or otherwise taking up room along every inch of the beige walls and floors. It looked as if everything that vacuumed, monitored or sliced needed to be within arm's reach, because anything could happen, always. This was not the first such surgery for anyone there but each patient brought with them a *déjà vu* which could quickly turn into something uncharted.

They quickly intubated Gadson, so the chore of breathing was no longer his.

First the team had to get the commander's blood pressure back up. Dr. Woods called for dozens of units of packed red blood cells. No platelets or plasma. The packed cells would better carry oxygen. Next, the nurse anesthetist began to administer Versed, a sedative which would also cloud his memory—a prescribed amnesia. Soldiers are better off not remembering details of this sort of trauma. The Versed was combined with fentanyl, a narcotic painkiller, much more powerful than morphine. It took only a few moments for the lieutenant colonel to lapse into a controlled, carefully monitored oblivion.

Like other IED wounds Woods had seen, Gadson's had collected a lot of the detritus the enemy had packed into the weapon, plus whatever the force of the explosion carried with it. The doctor picked through bits of clothing, metal splinters and dirt, cleaning between pieces of charred flesh as best he could, to find the veins severed in the left leg. The nerve in the right leg hung exposed, with no flesh left to protect it. It was obviously damaged but, amazingly, not severed. It was hard to know if it was beyond repair—if the leg would ever work again. Either leg, really. Woods quickly decided he would try to save them both, for now. If taking one leg would have meant saving his life right there, that is what he would have done. But both were so torn up there was no quick solution. There was no time for a permanent repair. That would take a while. Gadson did not have a while.

The surgeon managed to locate both ends of the vein in the left leg and insert a hard, plastic straw-like tube—a shunt—between them, making a connection so blood could get to the lieutenant colonel's lower legs. He did the same with the vein, so blood could get back to his heart. The massive loss of fluid he had in the field resulted in a drop in body temperature, so his own blood would not clot properly. But clean, fresh red cells continued to flow into his system through an oversized IV—70 or 80 units in all—about eight times the man's total volume. Woods washed out the right leg, removing as much dead tissue as he could. It was not the tears in vein that worried him. It was the fact that there was little flesh or skin left to hold them in place.

Once the surgeon had all the pieces he could find aligned and matched up as best he could, the orthopedist, or the "bone guy," stepped in. His weapons were menacing: long metal rods with screws and bolts sticking out like those on Frankenstein's neck, forming round oblong cages. They looked harder and colder than a metal coffin, more threatening than rusty barbed wire. The orthopedic specialist went about his business of drilling rods of the "external fixators" perpendicular to whatever solid bit of bone he could find, close to the hip at the top. He struggled to find much solid anchorage near the feet, but he managed. The fixators would keep the bone fragments between the ends from flopping about, causing more tissue damage.

All the king's horses and all the king's men. Woods figured the lieutenant colonel was put back together as well as anyone could do for now. He and the nurses pulled the tubes and drips out of the way and began wheeling the gurney gingerly out of the operating room, toward the ICU. They monitored every number that a body could possibly generate. That is how they knew they were about to lose him.

"Blood pressure, dropping . . . fast . . . 30!" a nurse called out as they entered the hallway.

Shit.

Dr. Woods and the nurses broke into a trot, bouncing bags and tubes to the ICU where they could attempt to stabilize their newest and most volatile patient. More blood—packed red cells and plasma—appeared from nowhere. Expert hands moved over his crashing body, looking for any opportunity to force life back into his system. The breathing machine kept up its good work, pumping amped-up oxygen into his blood. Reserved for dire occasions is the drug epinephrine—known also as "Adrenaline" for its ability to induce a higher heart rate. A nurse filled a syringe with the very potent, yet very temporary medicine and shot it into a vein.

Woods figured the artery and vein in the legs would hold through the commotion of jump-starting his heart. The legs could not move because of the fixators. Even if his patient regained consciousness and started to thrash, the legs were not going anywhere. *Former football player. Battalion commander. Prefers to take control.* Woods figured Gadson for a thrasher. If his heart could survive the trauma, if they could get enough oxygen back into the blood stream . . .

"BP 40."

Okay. It was moving in the right direction. Everyone worked furiously.

"BP 60." *Now we're talkin'.* Woods sighed, stretching his shoulders back, trying to relieve the pinch in his shoulder blades. It was midnight before anyone in the ICU could take a breather. Soon fresh staff would take over their vigil. In all, Gadson had taken 129 units of blood products—70 were actual pints of blood—to replace what he had lost since the attack on Route Jackson.

Dr. Woods pulled off his bloody gloves and scrubs. The goal here in Baghdad was to get the patient stable enough to move to the city of Balad, where more American medical personnel could better treat his injuries. Woods was proud of his work here. Grueling, gut-wrenching, soul-crushing and gloriously rewarding all at once, it was the best and worst job he had ever had.

"Ground Hog Days" they sometimes called them, after the hit movie. Everything seemed to keep happening, the same missing arms, fingers and legs, gunshot wounds to the neck and gut, it hardly varied, day after day after day and night. This case was a close one. By no means was the lieutenant colonel clear, but he had a chance. A pretty good one, now. Sometimes that was all he could give people.

Tired, the doctor felt his pager on his belt to be sure he had not lost it in all the juggling around. He was hoping for a few hours of shut-eye.

. . .

A few hours of sleep cleared Colonel Ricky Gibbs' head slightly. It was early morning and no one had been in his guest room at the 10th CSH to wake him. Gadson must have had made it through the night. The commander fingered the Purple Heart medal in his pocket, glad at least he'd had the presence of mind late the day before to have it sent over from Falcon. He made his way over to the ICU where the medal's unknowing recipient was lying eerily quiet. Gibbs pulled the medal from his pocket and pinned it to Gadson's chest. Then he leaned over and whispered in his ear, "It's your Purple Heart, Lieutenant Colonel Gadson. You have sure as hell earned it."

It had been a fast night for Dr. Woods, too. The surgeon woke and went directly to the ICU to check on his newest patient. He knew Gadson would need more work before he could put him on a chopper, if he'd survived the night. He suspected he had, or that pager would have gone off. Expecting to find the patient asleep and alone, Woods was surprised to find a slow, steady parade of visitors had quietly made their way in and out of the unit. Word traveled fast. Colonel Gibbs, whom he had seen briefly the night before, was standing over Gadson. Another guy, dressed in desert fatigues, looked a little familiar.

"Major William Huff." Huff offered his hand. The surgeon shook it.

"Bradley Woods. I'm Lieutenant Colonel Gadson's surgeon."

"West Point?" asked Huff.

" Ninety-one," said the doctor.

" Ninety-one! Me, too," said Huff, momentarily sidetracked by the serendipity of the impromptu mini-class reunion.

"I was a sophomore when Gadson was a senior," explained Woods. "I didn't know him back then. You?"

"I was on the football team with Greg, at West Point—he's a brother, he and Kim . . ."

For several years, Huff's and Gadson's football lockers were three feet apart. They killed a lot of time in a little space, sharing their team's ups and downs and more than a few laughs. When Huff heard that Gadson was hurt, he had commandeered a helicopter from his office at Camp Victory. Thirty minutes later he arrived at the combat hospital in Baghdad's Green Zone.

"Listen, Doc, I came in this morning on a chopper as soon as I heard. My intelligence analyst told me about the hit and I caught the next flight. I'm staying as long as I can. What's his situation?"

Dr. Woods quickly summed up the injuries, and the previous night's surgery. He explained that Gadson had remained stable through the night, or the rest of it. So much so that Woods felt he would easily survive a "wash out," a surgical procedure to further clean out the wounds, and a better fix on that vein and artery. Could be, he said, that they would get him to Balad, about 50 miles north, that afternoon. But no promises.

"I'd like for him to have an escort and I can't go," Gibbs interrupted, taking charge. "I have to get back to the base." Gibbs said, looking at Huff.

"I'll go, of course, sir. I can stay. I'll go with him all the way to Germany."

"Very good, Major. You'll stay in touch."

"Yes, sir," Huff answered, honored by the task.

Back in the operating room, things went a little more smoothly. Woods gingerly went back into the left leg and removed the plastic shunts, then set about making permanent repairs to the vein and artery. Blood pressure, heart rate, breathing—everything remained stable. It all boded well. He was not ready for a super long flight, but he would make it to Balad, the doctor was pretty sure of it.

The short night was beginning to catch up to Woods as he walked with the gurney back to ICU. But it was clear there would be no rest. Brigadier General Dana Pittard, the assistant division commander, was there waiting.

"General, good to see you," said Dr. Woods by way of introduction.

"Doctor, I would like you to call Mrs. Gadson."

Woods was unused to such requests. Medical staff was not normally part of notification or even updating conditions. But it was clear General Pittard wanted this one handled personally by the person who could best explain the injuries. He sensed the general had some sort of bond with Gadson. General Pittard was one of the few Black generals in the Army.

"Of course, General," he answered. "Right away." He sorted through time zones in his mind, figuring he'd best just carry out the general's request as soon as he could find a quiet place to talk. He wound up back in his office.

It was about 3:00 a.m. in Kansas, but it might as well have been noon, when the phone rang again in Fort Riley. Kim lunged for it.

"Mrs. Gadson? This is Dr. Woods in Baghdad."

"Yes," answered Kim, all composure. The *doctor* is calling?

"Your husband is a very sick man. He's lost a lot of blood. But so far, we're not taking his legs."

"So far," said Kim. *Does he know Greg?*

"They may be able to save them once he gets back to the States."

"So it's *both* legs?"

"Both are in pretty bad shape, Mrs. Gadson. General Pittard asked me to call."

"Oh, now I see," she said, letting her guard down a bit. "I thought it was mostly his left leg."

"No, ma'am. I just finished doing repairs to both legs. I'm fairly certain they'll hold." He always found it difficult to explain details to loved ones. How much does a wife want to hear about his yanking and tugging on those important blood supplies?

"We were able to restore the vein and artery in the left leg and repair nerve damage in the right. We're just holding steady right now but he's stable."

Holding steady. So things were worse than she had understood. The doctor's voice was so grave. And it was clear that Greg was not conscious, unable to speak directly to her. If she could just talk to him it would make things okay, or at least a little better. She tried to picture him, laying still. It was an impossible image.

"Thank you, doctor, thank you so much for calling."

She hung up the phone and only then, alone, allowed the grief she'd been avoiding, to consume her.

She wept herself to exhaustion, then finally sleep.

She awakened just a few hours later, the events of the last day (or was it two?) rushing over her, pummeling her back under the covers. It was May 9. Kim pushed away the paralyzing fear and forced her mind toward the task of the day: packing and leaving for Washington, D.C.

. . .

Alone in the ICU, Huff committed now to escorting his old teammate, watched Gadson for a moment—the Purple Heart rising and falling with each intubated breath. How strange it was to see the former West Point linebacker lying so still. Huff knew Greg Gadson to be almost always in motion. But heavy doses of medication were keeping him quiet. Huff sat down next to his friend and took his hand. It was bloated, he guessed from the transfusions, or maybe the drugs.

"Hey. Gadson. You're a little quiet today. Not to mention a little puffy." Huff spoke as if Greg might, at any moment, laugh or even answer him. He studied his face. It was not restful or peaceful or any of the other euphemisms people use when someone is near death. It was ready. Ready to wake up. Ready to move on. Like maybe he was going to sit up and give a command.

"Yo!" Huff said, a little louder. He was pretty sure Greg did not know he was there and maybe never would know. Still, he felt the sound of his voice might somehow help soothe him. Or inspire some unconscious memories of better days. The days on the gridiron. The days that had helped to mold Greg into the officer he was today—the officer Huff had witnessed only a week ago.

Part of Major Huff's job with the Army's Asymmetric Warfare Group was to check in with troops on the ground in Iraq. He would regularly embed with various units to share lessons learned during warfare and pass them on to incoming soldiers. The overall strategy was no longer mainly about killing terrorists. Their mission now was to protect the people. So, on May 2 he bunked in with the 2nd Battalion, 32nd Field Artillery, or 2-32, in Mansour. What he discovered was if there was a battalion commander naturally fit to carry out the Petraeus/Odierno doctrine, it was, not surprisingly, Greg Gadson.

General Raymond Odierno, commander of the multi-national force in Iraq, followed General Petraeus once Petraeus moved on to Central Command. Odierno had been a football player himself. He understood teamwork and he well knew Greg's work. So did the Iraqis. Greg was particularly popular with the local Sunnis, Huff realized, when he spent two days patrolling with Gadson and his unit. Huff stepped back while the lieutenant colonel befriended family after family, consuming gallons of chai tea, a staple of Iraqi hospitality. The dark, thick texture of Greg's skin made him look slightly local. Maybe that was part of it. But Gadson was welcome in almost any home. Still, they had to be wary. Not every Sunni household appreciated the American presence. Greg also worked with Iraqi police, which sometimes raised suspicions. The key, Huff learned, was to understand what the Iraqis wanted, which was little more than most people want: security and well-being. They saw Lieutenant Colonel Gadson as a means to that end. And Gadson was not merely a foot soldier. He truly believed taking the message of friendship, democracy, understanding and diplomacy directly to the people was the way to win the war. Huff remembered the telling comment his friend made as they trudged from house to house like some sort of evangelical recruiting team.

"You know, Huff," Gadson had said, "The way we're doing things, just walking around out here, may get me killed or maimed but it's the only way we're going to get this place secured." Huff did not think he was talking about being taken out by an IED. He thought an attack might be more personal because of the work he was doing. Maybe it had been.

. . .

Two days at the medical facility in Balad brought not much change, at least from Huff's perspective. The medical staff there bowled him over, though. There was almost a maternal quality about them, he thought. Maybe it was because they were taking care of their own. The fact that Gadson was still alive was testimony to their constant vigil.

"Though I lay me down to bleed a while, I will rise to fight with you again." Huff chanted their mantra out loud to Greg several times over the next few days. It was on a plaque that hung in the West Point football team locker room. Coach Jim Young had hung it there to encourage teamwork in the face of adversity. Now, Huff knew Gadson would rise again. He believed.

Meantime, Huff blathered on. Earlier, he had spent some time with the Gadson family at Fort Riley, right before the 2-32 deployed. At the time he thought Kim was most gracious, but over the next several days through their conversations on the phone, he came to better understand her. Them. He got it. He was the warrior. The tough guy. The leader. The thick and thin guy. She was exactly the same, but quieter, more subtle, preferring the wings to the stage. He knew she loved her husband fiercely but without the drama of a younger, less-seasoned military wife. She was shaken, to be sure, not in a self-pitying sort of way, but more with a "Well, let's figure out what we do next" demeanor. Huff shared those conversations with Kim as part of his ongoing monologue—letting Greg know too, how the kids were doing. There was no way of knowing, but he figured some of his babbling had to be sinking in somehow. Sometimes, though, he just ran out of things to say.

When it was finally time to put Greg on the 3.5-hour flight from Balad to Landstuhl, Germany, he had undergone several surgeries. There was talk he would keep his legs. Huff was more skeptical. The Army medical team lined up on either side of the gurney. A miniature village of appliances and blinking lights surrounded his bandaged and caged body, making for a heavy load. Some of those boxes and tubes would keep him alive, others would tell medical staff that the boxes and tubes were working. It looked like a small construction site with an unconscious man strapped down in the middle. The weight put a strain on the staff and as they lifted with a final heave-ho it was too much for one of the smaller staffers to handle. Huff watched in horror as she lost her grip and the gurney lurched toward her. The village bobbled like it had been nearly upended by an earthquake. Huff dove the 10 yards between himself and the gurney to try to stop the crash. But the slide subsided before he got there. The stronger parts of the lineup managed to recover. It all worked like a football play, Huff thought, one team member backing up another.

The C-17 was reserved for medical staff only, but no one questioned Huff as he boarded. He wrapped his hand around Greg's. It was still swollen. Again, for a moment, Huff recalled better times, when team members held hands on the field. It was a show of unity. The guy calling the play would be in front. Everyone else was palm to palm. And here they were once more, in a handshake of solidarity, counting on a winning play.

• • •

Twenty-four hours after Dr. Woods' phone call, Kim set about casting off the last of her Fort Riley support system. Jennifer Frank helped load her luggage into the car and drove her to the airport in Kansas City. They walked together to the security checkpoint, where Kim slid behind the glass window, dividing friends and family from ticket holders. And there she stood. Normally she did not mind a little solitude, but suddenly there was just a little too much space, too much air. She put her hand on the glass and looked back at Jennifer.

"This sucks," she mouthed.

"I should have come with you," Jenn said, only somewhat aware that Kim could not hear her. After all the planning and comforting, they had not figured on this moment. Kim, for the first time since that blurred, sweaty moment in the sauna, would be on her own. *Shake it off*, she told herself. She picked up her bag and headed for the gate. A pretty short flight, she figured. It would only be a few hours before Linda Anderson would meet her at Ronald Reagan Washington National Airport. Representatives from the Army would be there, too. Then Chuck Schretzman would meet her at Walter Reed. She could tough it out. And after that, she would see her husband. Maybe he would even see her.

CHAPTER SIX

"Upon the friendly fields of strife are sown the seeds that on other days, on other fields, will bear the fruits of victory."
—Gen. Douglas MacArthur, Superintendent, USMA, 1919-1922

The *Virginian-Pilot* landed with a hollow thud as it made its 5 a.m. arrival on an expectant reader's driveway. The noise was satisfying to Greg—it meant an accurate pass. He and his little brother, Patrick, did the drive-and-toss drill through the tree-lined streets of Chesapeake, Virginia, each morning, landing nearly 300 newspapers squarely where their custom-ers could easily find them in the chill before dawn. Patrick, seven years younger and smaller than Greg, couldn't throw as far, but helped keep pace by wrapping each paper with a rubber band. He also handled all the "porch specials"- which meant getting out of the car to be sure the *Pilot* landed squarely on those customers' front stoops. There were three routes combined—the last one was mostly apartments, so the Gadson brothers did that one on foot. After that they'd dash home for a quick breakfast and maybe a discussion with their dad. Willie James Gadson liked to engage Greg in conversations about current events—when he had time between his two pharmacist jobs: he was chief pharmacist at Norfolk Community Hospital as well as a staff pharmacist at Chesapeake General. After that, Greg would head off to Indian River High School, the "Home of the Braves." He was 16 years old.

Academics weren't all that challenging to Greg—he just wasn't very interested. School was something he did between the paper route and football practices. He'd discovered his love of the game in the autumn of sixth grade, after moving into a new neighborhood where a different league provided more opportunities to get on the field. By the time he'd graduated from Sparrow Road Intermediate School, his obsession with the game that had shut him out when he was younger was in full bloom. Looking back on his first couple of years on the field, he couldn't fathom why he hadn't given up the game completely. He'd been small, nearly two years younger than the other boys, barely ever getting to play. Two seasons in a row they'd lost the league championship game. That second year he'd broken down in tears of frustration at never having gotten off the bench. He'd been mortified but came back and worked hard. Now the practices started after school and ended just before dinner time. He squeezed his homework in before bed, barely feeling his head graze the pillow before 300 more bundled *Virginian-Pilots* plopped onto a nearby corner, awaiting his and Patrick's attention.

The money he made delivering newspapers went toward buying his first car—a 1973 Camaro Rally Sport. He bought the decade-old car for $1,200, or really, half that. His dad paid the rest along with the insurance, no small sum considering his age and the "sports car" designation. While the lines were sleek, the color was an understated gray and perhaps less of a target for police looking to hand out speeding tickets.

His 4:30 a.m. alarm clock made a charade of his social life. If he ever did get out to an evening party, he'd find himself snoring on the couch by 10 p.m., much to the amusement of his friends. He was shy, too. Even the notion of starting a conversation with a girl left a pit in his stomach. Plenty of them caught his eye, but looking was easier than speaking. It just seemed easier to keep his focus on football. Besides, he was getting bigger, more robust and muscular—better at holding the line, defending his teammates. A few colleges began making inquiries, so it seemed a football scholarship, if not inevitable, might be on the horizon.

Greg's dream was to play professional football. And the path to the pros was what was then known as a Division 1-A college, where he was convinced he'd be a standout. He considered dozens. Staying near his family would mean a lot to his parents, but he was ready to go wherever he could step out of his high school small-town player status and make a nationwide impression. He narrowed his list of possible schools to William and Mary, James Madison and the University of Virginia. It was UVA which seemed the most promising.

In the fall of 1983, Greg got the invitation to visit Charlottesville. He watched the Cavaliers lose to the University of North Carolina during his visit that weekend. Cavaliers Assistant Coach Tom O'Brien, a US Naval Academy graduate, was doing the recruiting. O'Brien had coached for his alma mater for a couple of years and the connection wasn't lost on Greg. Chesapeake is in the very southern part of Virginia, near Norfolk, the largest Navy base in the world. That makes it a Navy town, and would naturally put USNA in Annapolis, Maryland, on Greg's list of schools to visit. But he barely took note of his blue and gold surroundings and didn't even bother to keep track of the Navy football season until each winter, when "Go Navy Beat Army" signs made it impossible to ignore.

It was head coach George Welsh's first year at UVA and there was a lot of hype. By the end of Greg's visit, O'Brien had pretty well guaranteed Greg would get an offer, possibly a full ride. Greg went home happy and relaxed, planning to coast to the end of his senior year. He'd choreographed the perfect play, he thought, a career in the NFL. He would dominate Division-1 football in his own home state.

Greg wasn't cocky but his confidence grew as he matured along with the team. Indian River was strong—not the best in the state but it had gotten some recognition. Recruiters came and went. He felt lucky on those days that he didn't have to suffer the jitters some of his teammates had when they were being studied, filmed even. He played his best, tried to support his colleagues, and every few days, checked the mail for the offer from Virginia.

News didn't come in an envelope, though. It came on the phone.

"There are only just so many scholarships, Greg," O'Brien explained. "It's limited." Greg cringed, drawing in a deep breath. "The staff just felt uncomfortable with your size," O'Brien went on. "You're not as big as a lot of the other guys."

A wave of unease crashed over Greg. It was near the end of the signing season. He'd been planning on, no, *counting* on UVA. By now, there was nowhere else to go.

"What I can offer you," O'Brien went on, "is the opportunity to walk on. We'd get you some scholarship money later."

"No, no, no," Greg heard himself murmur. Walking on would mean attending UVA with no guarantee of making the team. If it didn't work out, he'd be stuck there as a student with no chance of playing football. He suddenly felt like a man without a country. All the other schools, where he might have gotten an invitation, had already selected their recruits. He figured he'd go to college one way or another, but football was the only thing that mattered to him. It was the only clear path to his future. He didn't see another. Graduation was only five months away and the University of Virginia had formed an impenetrable line of defense.

His parents didn't seem to get it.

"Something will reveal itself," his mother said in her always unflappable way. "You know, I always say you travel with angels." Her faith, her belief that God would see her and her family through, seemed to float Patricia Gadson over the rough spots. His dad was a man of faith, too, but he didn't have much at all to say about the "big no." They were both so dang calm. Too calm. It was irksome. His life had come to a screeching halt and they were just going on about their jobs and chores as if nothing had happened.

Determined to mimic their annoying disengagement, he put on his stoic face, strode into his bedroom closet, slid to the floor, and wept.

The football season at Indian River had ended. As he dragged himself into the two-story white brick building each day, he had to rationalize the reason. The individual goal, the prize, was foggy. It was wrestling season now, but his time on the mat didn't ignite any sort of fire or passion. At 176 pounds, he was in the highest weight class. His dad was more a fan of individual sports than Greg. Greg preferred a real team effort—a coordinated execution of strength and talent.

Greg had heard some football recruiters were coming to Indian River to talk to one of his football teammates, Tracy Branch. Just looking for scraps, Greg thought, filling in gaps on freshman teams. He'd missed his shot and he still hadn't figured out how to recover. On the day the recruiters showed up, he couldn't imagine why Indian River Football Coach John Dukes called him into his office.

"Greg, this is Coach Ted Gill. He's from West Point." Greg and Gill shook hands squarely. *What the heck was West Point? A marina?* He felt it'd be impolite to ask and he didn't want to seem ignorant, but his face must have betrayed him.

"The U.S. Military Academy at West Point, New York," Gill offered.

"Good to meet you, Sir," Greg said, broadening his shoulders, taking Gill's hand. He looked Gill in the eye, expectantly.

"Mr. Gadson, we think you might make a nice addition to our team at the Academy. Have you ever been to Michie Stadium?"

"No, Sir."

"Would you like to come to visit?"

A *military* academy? Good Lord. Was this the team Navy was always going on about beating? This couldn't be God's big reveal.

"Yes, I would," he heard his mouth say, but he wasn't sure he agreed. It would be a free trip, though. He'd only used four of the allotted five. And he'd hang out with some football players, probably. That'd be fun.

"We know, Greg, your SAT scores aren't quite on par with the sort of student we normally recruit," Gill said. Greg nodded. This wasn't the first time those test scores had put some friction into his future.

"But we can help with that. We have a prep school. And we offer more than that. We offer a lifetime of opportunity. When you attend West Point, you're part of the U.S. Army. When you graduate, you'll become a commissioned officer."

Whoa.

"And you can choose to stay in the Army after your commitment is over. Pursue just about any job you want. It's a real plan for your future."

Commitment?

It was intriguing. And terrifying. Nice to be wanted, but this was obviously no path to the NFL. No way was he going to school there. The Army? Didn't they shave their heads and wear uniforms? Some of the local Navy guys he knew. He'd seen them around so he sort of got that. Ships and sails and the ocean. But running around and rolling in dirt and all that G.I. Joe stuff? As a career?

"It's a lot to think about, son. I'd like for you to talk it over with your folks," Gill said. "We'll be in touch."

"That's enough of a break, Gadson. Get back to work." Coach Dukes sent him on to wrestling practice. But his head wasn't on the mat—it had turned back to the turf, the grueling squat-thrusts, the running, the tackle drills.

Running around and rolling in the dirt—as a career. He chuckled to himself. Maybe it wasn't such a stretch after all.

• • •

"The Long Gray Line"—they called it. It was a college famous for its lineage. "The key to the continent," George Washington had deemed West Point, during the Revolutionary War. The nation's future first president believed the real estate was perfectly positioned, and used it as his headquarters for several months. West Point is the longest serving garrison—created or "stood up" by the United States Congress in 1800. Benedict Arnold once tried to pass off plans for the garrison to the British. The class of 1915, referred to as "the class that stars fell on," would produce 59 generals serving in World War II. One of them was Dwight D. Eisenhower. General Douglas MacArthur attended West Point and went on to become the most decorated soldier in American history. When MacArthur returned to West Point as superintendent, he incorporated the physical rigors of war into the curriculum. "Every cadet an athlete" became his code. For a student who wasn't so much about academics, this was a pleasing anthem.

Greg was touched by the history. The massive stone gray and granite maze absorbed and fascinated him. The more he took in, the more he understood the importance of the place—the critical role it would play in America's future. Something like pride began to melt the steel of his skepticism. Now humbled by the invitation, he marveled at the massive stone architecture, the bridges, the view of the Hudson River. A college career dedicated to representing his country, in a way, on the athletic field was becoming more appealing, if not slightly overwhelming. Gradually, as he walked "The Plain," the grassy area of the college overlooking the water, he felt his dreams of athletic dominance meld with a newly formed sense of duty. A higher sense of purpose was salve to the sting of the UVA rejection. Maybe his mom's faith was yielding fruit.

In choosing West Point he could attend Fort Monmouth in New Jersey for a year, playing football, while also working to get his grades up. He would have to commit to five years, academically—one at the prep school then four at the academy. When he graduated, he'd do five years of service in the Army. He'd come out of college as a second lieutenant—not bad, he thought. Some people spent 20 years paying off student loans. Five years of service seemed a small price for four years of education. He imagined walking the same halls as the men he'd been learning about: MacArthur, Eisenhower, and General George S. Patton. West Point had also been the nation's first engineering school, and he'd thought at times he'd pursue something along those lines—maybe electrical engineering. Despite his distracted study habits, he did like history. The key to understanding, he thought. Looking back provided unmatched insights into the view ahead. Being a part of West Point's past would give him the chance to be catapulted into a promising future.

He accepted the offer.

He had only one moment of doubt, stemming, as so often it does, from his first love, the University of Virginia.

"Greg, how are you, I'm just checking in to see where you wound up," Tom O'Brien's voice came over the phone. "I'm going to West Point," Greg answered, "I'll play there."

"Well, UVA has a spot for you on the team now, but you wouldn't be eligible for a scholarship."

Too little, too late.

"I've already accepted the West Point appointment, coach."

"Would you be interested in playing for Navy?" Greg was uncertain- it was all a little confusing. When, at O'Brien's prompting the USNA admissions called offering a spot, he sought some advice.

"Chesapeake is a Navy town, maybe it's my calling," he told his dad. "Maybe I'm meant to go to Annapolis."

"Greg, you're meant to keep your word. And you've given it to West Point. Your word is your honor. Sometimes that's all you have. Don't waste it."

Greg entered the US Military Academy Preparatory School (USMAPS) in the summer of 1984 having no notion, as he stepped onto the Long Gray Line, how it would draw him up expeditiously, catapult him into vast desolation then ultimately wrap him in a protective life-saving cocoon.

• • •

That July, Greg found himself riding comfortably slumped on a bus, "smokin' and jokin'" with a bunch of other cadet candidates. As they passed by the red brick archways marking the base entrance, they all had pretty much the same attitude—it was just a prep school, after all, not the real thing. Some had endured plenty of bruising football practices back home, so they were less intimidated by the threat of grueling physical workouts. Personally, he counted the UVA rejection as a major life disappointment from which he was recovering and developing some emotional calluses. What more could "pre-Army" do? As he stepped off the bus onto the grounds at Fort Monmouth, the reality of Cadet Candidate Basic Training struck him like the scream of a thousand angry feral cats. First was the bellowing cacophony of seasoned drill sergeants in their state-trooper-style hats, who could goose-bump the back of a guy's neck with a glare. The sounds of their voices jump-started Greg into doubletime. He tried to move at a stealthy clip, but it was tough to stay under their radar while catching mesmerizing glimpses of their veins popping out of their necks at the slightest offense: unruly hair (there was plenty of that), disrespectful posture, or, heaven forbid, a smirk. Each "CC," including Greg, was uniformed and shorn, barely leaving any identifying marks. They were being reduced to nobodies.

Physical training began daily at 5:30 a.m. with warmups and continuous cardio and strength training for about an hour. But most of the harassment revolved around drill and ceremony. His feet, more accustomed to cleats, hammered the concrete in dress shoes, "falling in," then "falling out," then back in again. He balled his fists and puffed his chest to "attention," measured space between his fellow cadets' squared shoulders to perfect arm's length and practiced the about-face pirouette for hours each day. Even the "at ease" command didn't mean he could relax. He learned who to salute and how, where he was permitted to walk versus where senior cadets could trod. Before each meal there were pull-ups. Greetings, proper uniform, bed making—every aspect of his and his fellow cadets' lives were subject to drill sergeant scrutiny.

Greg, who'd been taught at home that it was cruel to make fun of people, was surprised, then amused, by the nicknames drill sergeants would come up with for various cadets. One poor guy seemed to always have his mouth open, so he was dubbed "Venus Fly Trap." Another cadet's last name was "Fly" so of course he became "McFly," after the wimpy version of the father figure in the 1985's hit movie "Back to the Future." Hapless cadets were often ordered to drop and do on-the-spot push-ups for alleged violations. Protests were not tolerated.

"Sir, I—," a cadet would attempt to explain the alleged offense.

"No shit, Sherlock!!" the sergeant would scream back, no matter if it made any sense.

Academic instruction was designed specifically to raise ACT and SAT scores, so all of Greg's classes were either English or math-oriented. They routinely practiced the admissions tests. Over the course of the year Greg increased his test scores from 920 to 1060, bringing him to just over average, in the 51st percentile. It was good enough to eventually get him over the admissions hump.

Greg found the training and the academic schedule at first relentless, but soon more or less settled into a routine. He found he could study and do well in school. And the physical nature of the trainings provided an outlet. In between all of that he played football. There were about a half dozen prep schoolers who were headed for the official roster. Among them were Chuck Schretzman and another player who would become a lifelong brother, Troy Lingley.

So far, Greg had overcome two major hurdles—he'd improved his grades and he'd proven that despite his smaller size he could play football. Sometimes hurdles come in threes. His third came when, after earning a number of meals by satisfying the pull-up requirement, his elbow swelled to the point he couldn't bend it. He was forced to go to sick call and to undergo an X-ray which revealed an old injury. He'd dislocated it back at Indian River when he easily survived a tackle, then leaned one arm back to brace himself as he got back to his feet. That's when two guys landed on it, knocking the joint inside-out. Now the injury had come back to form another cloud over his future. The fact that the area of dislocation had shown up in radiology was not surprising. What nearly did him in, though, was a letter from the Department of Defense Medical Examination Review Board, declaring him ineligible to serve. No service, no school. No school, no football. Again, he was devastated.

It didn't take long, however for school administrators to correct the problem. By then Greg was proving to be a valuable asset, so West Point chief of orthopedics Jack Ryan[2] wrote a medical waiver to let him play, and stay in school.

Greg wasn't aware of it, but he was being closely watched as a plebe player. One of his most critical monitors was West Point Assistant Coach Tim Kish. Coach Kish watched film after film of Greg on the field.

"I just saw this skinny guy who played so hard," Kish told me later. "He wasn't intimidated. I've seen players from all over the country. I saw something in him."

There wasn't much of a break between prep school and becoming a plebe. Greg began his official West Point education in August 1985.

The pace of being a plebe wasn't too much more difficult than that of a CC. So, in that regard, the prep school had lived up to its name. All the running, marching, assembling, memorizing, and generally being harassed

---

2 Ryan, who was a team doctor, would later perform three knee surgeries on Greg during his college football career, and eventually write another medical waiver which allowed Greg to serve as a field artillery officer.

by upper classmen didn't bother him so much as it did others. To him, the overall mission was bigger than the day-to-day hassles. There was a higher purpose. So long as one could accept authority—not necessarily embrace it, but swallow it along with the awful mess meals, there was always a way through to the next task. In many ways football went hand-in-hand with that. There were lots of parallels. Being ordered to line up, run through drills, jump through whatever hoops coaches laid down, or held up; it all was goal-oriented. There were days when Greg thought they were going easy on him. He'd see his classmates getting their faces chewed off, while he was mostly left alone. Maybe it was a race thing. Or maybe it was his own version of "resting bitch face," that played a part. Either way, he managed to stay out of everyone's crosshairs.

On the field it was a different story. At 183 pounds, he thought he would wind up a defensive back. When he was given the linebacker position, he was sure he was being set up to fail. He didn't think his body could hold up so close to the crush of the competition. Again, he felt threatened. All the other linebackers had about 40 pounds on him. And if he broke down, if he couldn't hold the line, if he failed, it would all be over. He'd be sent back to Chesapeake, Virginia, head and helmet in hand. His mind and body kicked into survival mode, drawing on pure instinct to adapt and stay alive. He took a daily pounding. He waited to be cut. He wasn't.

There were other things driving him. Greg still harbored a little anger about being rejected by a Division 1 school. When he first arrived at Fort Monmouth and landed on the practice field at Michie Stadium, he was pissed. But he was also still shy and introverted. When he made the travel squad freshman year, West Point Coach Robertson roomed Greg with one of his star players—Kurt Gutierrez. Gutierrez, a senior, or "firsty," played first string. Greg was fifth or sixth on the depth chart. As Robertson planned, Gutierrez' maturity and drive rubbed off on the younger player. By the end of freshman year training camp, Greg had made his peace by moving up to third string. Gutierrez would remain a mentor, then later, a business partner with Greg long after they'd both retired from the Army.

"You have to channel that negative energy," Greg would tell me later. "You need to find peace or that energy will destroy you."

As an outside linebacker Greg was responsible for containment—securing the perimeter and keeping everyone on the inside. Freshman year there were six or seven players vying for the position and two were sophomores. When it came time for the first game of the season against Syracuse, a second-string linebacker got himself into some sort of trouble and was suspended. That left a hole for Greg to move up. He couldn't believe his luck when he got to play in that game. He remembered taking his position, and inevitably getting hit. It wasn't half as bad as it was in practice, he thought. Practices were much more intense than actual games. The next week, when the Black Knights played Western Michigan, the coach sent him in again, an even stronger, more confident player. West Point won that one at home, 48-6. The season ended well: 9 and 3. Greg was one of a handful of freshmen who lettered that year. He'd dressed for every game.

By his sophomore year he was a regular first-string player. Two guys ahead of him were graduating. One guy was right behind him: his Fort Monmouth buddy, Chuck Schretzman. Schretzman was bigger, but Greg managed to stay ahead of him. Despite the competition they became friends, practicing and playing together for hours, analyzing plays, telling stories. They pushed each other on and off the field.

Greg had five starts under his belt when one afternoon he and Chuck went into Coach Al Stevenson's meeting room for a routine gathering. Greg thought it odd that Lou Dainty, a senior, was sitting near Stevenson.

"Greg," Coach said, "Lou here is going to be starting this week." Had he heard him right? Was this some sort of experiment? He stared at Stevenson, unable to process the coach's pronouncement.

Greg felt like he'd been blind-sided by an 18-wheeler. What had he done wrong? He wracked his brain, trying to understand how the position for which he'd been sacrificing every fiber of his body and sometimes his very well-being was being yanked away with no explanation. In his own mind he'd been doing well. But he knew better than to argue or even question. He was being fired, with no notice, no warning, no . . .

"That's it, Greg. See you at practice." Stevenson's voice snapped him back into the room.

Greg left, bewildered and crushed. It didn't make any sense. Had Lou somehow talked the coach into this? Did the senior player want to start that bad? He was angry and so was Chuck, but in the end, he knew he only had himself to blame. Maybe he hadn't worked as hard as he could physically.

"What can we do?" he asked Chuck.

"I'm not sure. It's really unfair, the way he brought Lou out of nowhere. Honestly, I'd have thought he'd at least try me or one of the younger guys."

When Greg really took a step back, he realized that while he had many great moments on the field, he was inconsistent. He and Chuck made a pact to work even harder.

Not only did Greg learn a lesson in fallibility on the field that year, he learned that same lesson in the classroom. He chose Arabic as his language, figuring it was the next frontier of war. Schretzman took Chinese. Neither was exactly an "easy A." At the same time Greg also took chemistry and calculus. In all he was carrying 22 credit hours. Counselors told him to defer some of the hours to summer, but he had a certain amount of pride in being able to "do it all." He puffed up his chest and carried on. At least that's what he meant to do. What he did was fail calculus. So began the academic thread upon which he'd hang for the rest of his time at the United States Military Academy.

He'd been so proud his plebe year, earning a 3.2 grade point and lettering in football and apparently getting slightly cocky. Now he'd gotten fired from his slot on the football team and he flunked a class. He was barely hanging on in Arabic. He decided to ask for help, but not without an ulterior motive.

Another cadet, Kim Thomas, had caught his eye. Blonde and blue eyed, the Lee's Summit, Missouri, native was quietly disciplined. And she was the better student of the very vexing language. Kim agreed to a study meeting with the linebacker. But she didn't seem impressed by his football prowess, or anything else, for that matter. And when Greg, cleverly, he thought, uttered the words *ana muejab bik* which translates to "I like you" in English, she stood ramrod straight, and bolted from the room.

Just a Missouri hillbilly, Greg thought, dismissively. *Probably doesn't take well to Black men.*

Truth was, Kim was not a fan of pretense. She'd agreed to help Greg as an act of good will, not romance. If he could articulate "I like you" in Arabic, he probably didn't need her help. She found the ruse annoying. And there was a shade of truth to Greg's observations. She knew her parents would never approve of her dating a Black man. Turning herself from a small-town young woman into a West Point cadet brought plenty of challenges in itself. She didn't need to be tangling with her parents just now.

So went sophomore year for Greg. His lost football position was surpassed in misery only by his nearly negative grade point average. And now he'd struck out with Kim Thomas. There would be no vacation and definitely no girlfriend that summer. He stayed at West Point to retake the calculus class. And he worked out. A lot.

Slowly, in his junior year, things began to turn around on the field. But he continued to stir a burn in the hearts of his coaches every time an officer representative came around. ORs were responsible for notifying football personnel when a player was in academic or some other disciplinary jeopardy.

"Greg was the best player I had, but he was on academic probation the entire time he was at West Point." Kish, the assistant coach, laughs about it now. But at the time Greg's lack of academic focus threatened the team, the season, his own reputation. Greg had to move into the academic barracks where even more rules and restrictions bound up his already impossible schedule. There were tutors. There were counselors. It essentially took a separate support team to keep Greg on the football team.

"He was my meanest, toughest player, though," the now retired Kish reflected, as we sat one afternoon in the warm Tucson sun.

"Meanest? Really?" I'd often thought of Greg as tough, badass, even. But mean?

"He might never admit this, but one time I overheard him talking to his opponent over the line of scrimmage. He says to the guy, 'It's going to be a very long day for you. I hope you packed a lunch.'"

. . .

"You're a bag of tape," Schretzman observed one day, as Greg was working on his latest limp. Three years of hits on a collegiate field full of bigger guys were taking a toll on his comparatively small frame. The injuries were mounting. Still, he was playing better. And knocking out the calculus class over the summer cleared the way for a slightly more academically successful semester.

It was October 17, 1988, when the Black Knights took on Colgate University. Greg's parents, for the first time ever, came all the way from Chesapeake to watch Greg play. Kish chose Bobby Wagner to start, but Wagner was having a tough game. So, Kish put Greg in, despite a foot injury. Greg almost immediately got a 15-yard penalty and found himself back on the sideline. They lost the game 22-20, and his parents barely saw him play. The three of them went to dinner, then his parents headed home. He was sitting in his dorm room, feeling dejected, when a woman named Julie, who he knew to be Kim Thomas' roommate, knocked on the door.

"Hey Greg, tough game," she offered.

"Yeah, overall, not a great night."

"The Principle" is playing at the theater in town. Wanna go? There's a group of us—we'll pick you up." Turned out when he got in the back seat of the car, there was Kim Thomas sitting on the other side. They had managed to avoid each other for a whole year, which took some maneuvering since they were in the same company.

What the hell is she doing here? As if this day couldn't get any worse.

He slid into the seat and maintained his focus straight ahead, shoulder snugged as close to the door as he could get it. He'd moved on from their Arabic encounter and was in no mood for that sort of rejection again. Before the movie they stopped for some Chinese food.

"I've never had Chinese food before," Kim confessed to the group. While others coached her on what to order, Greg stayed silent, thinking, again, she'd had a backwards upbringing. Then, somehow, they wound up sitting next to each other during the movie. Sometime between James Belushi's arrival at the raucous, fictitious Brandel High School, and Louis Gossett Junior's pledge to back him up, Greg began to get a different vibe from his former crush. By the time they were headed back to the dorm, they had more contact with each other than with their respective car doors.

Back on the field, Greg was named the team's best defensive lineman. He had three knee operations and during his senior year he hardly practiced, saving his knees and other body parts for the games. "I was always accused of playing favorites," says Kish, "because I didn't make Greg practice all the time. But it was the only way to keep him in the game." It was just one of many saves Kish would execute for Greg over the next 30 or so years.

Two summers spent at West Point making up first calculus then a failed English class, along with other volunteer leadership trainings, meant he'd had very little time off and hadn't been home for months. And there was an important errand he wanted to run with his dad. Time, as usual, was tight.

"Hey coach, I gotta get a few days at home before the season starts," he told Kish the August before his senior year.

"You've got to be kidding, Greg, I can't let you go home right now. I need you here. The season's starting!"

"C'mon coach, I need to get an engagement ring. I want to ask Kim to marry me."

Coach Kish softened. "I get it, but I can't 'okay' that. You're going to have to talk to Coach Young."

Greg paused. Head Coach Jim Young was tough—one of the few people who could cause him to pause. But this was a high-priority item. He needed to close the circle. Eventually Young approved the time off.

Ring weekend at West Point celebrates the accomplishments and the potential of those cadets who've made it to their senior year. In a ceremony marking the connection each student had made with the corps, and to their duty, honor and country, students receive their class rings. It's a poignant time. Greg thought he'd ride the wave of relative solemnity the morning after the gala. Still sanguine from the celebrations, Greg pulled out the diamond ring he and his father had selected.

"Kim, I'm only giving you this ring if you take it now. I don't want to be worried about this during football season."

Back in Missouri, things had changed some for Kim. Her parents had divorced. The turmoil of the split had shaken the foundations upon which she was raised. But the quake had also rattled her free of certain childhood rules and norms. Does every girl dream of quickly accepting a marriage proposal under a football season deadline? Probably not. But she'd fallen in love with Greg. She accepted the ring.

During his last semester, Greg was named regimental executive officer, which meant he assisted in day-to-day management of an entire regiment of cadets—about 1,000 young men and women. Normally the higher ups at

West Point chose those dean's listers or team captains for those jobs. His own GPA hovered in the lower 2's. And while he was named "best defensive lineman" again, he was never a part of the official team leadership. Still, for reasons he couldn't imagine, he felt he was being groomed to lead.

The final football game his senior year was the Sun Bowl. Kish battled from the sidelines, guiding his best, and by now one of his favorite "kids," as he took on the 6'5", 250+ pound tight end, Howard Cross, from the University of Alabama. Cross would soon be drafted by the New York Giants, where he would play 13 seasons. Cross's weight and size should have crushed Greg. But "Greg kicked his ass," says Kish. "He played above his ability that day."

West Point lost by a single point. The Black Knights finished the season 9-3. If they'd have won that Sun Bowl game, they would have finished with 10 wins. No Army team had ever finished with 10 wins. Greg received the Army Athletic Association Leadership Award upon graduating from West Point in May of 1989. There were around 1,000 in his graduating class. Academically, he finished somewhere in the upper 900s.

Greg and Kim were married three days after graduation, at Fort Story in Virginia Beach. The location was a matter of convenience. A West Point wedding was out of the question—that chapel was booked years in advance. Greg's mother made Kim's dress and the bridesmaid dresses. Chuck was the best man. They were too broke for a honeymoon, but they did have two months of free time to enjoy before they deployed into the real Army.

CHAPTER SEVEN

"The Long Gray Line—as a cadet you can't wrap your head
around it and I didn't really until I was wounded. Army icons like
Petraeus and Odierno all wrap their arms around you and lift you
up in a way you didn't understand before."
—Col. Greg Gadson (Ret.), August, 2022

Even as Greg prepared for his first deployment, he didn't think he'd make a career of the Army. Kim was much more gung-ho, scolding him for the lack of shine on his shoes and what she saw as his less than professional attitude. But like Greg, she hadn't planned on West Point. A recruiter had come to her high school and Kim had left a pamphlet on the kitchen table at home. Her father, an Army veteran, coerced her into applying. She wound up loving the Army, although it split up the newlyweds for their first six months. Kim, as a signal officer, managed communication and computer networks. She was assigned to Fort Gordon in Georgia. Greg, who'd studied not only the language but the culture and history of the Middle East, was aiming for Fort Stewart in Georgia where the 24th Infantry had a rapid deployment force. A rapid deployment force is just as it sounds—everyone is poised, ready to fight. Greg figured with the 24th he'd ride the tip of the spear in the event of a confrontation. But assignments are based upon class rank, which did not bear out his tip of the spear aspirations. His second choice was Fort Sill in Oklahoma, where he could join a unit supporting the rapid deployment force. So, after studying the language, customs and communities of the Arab world, he wound up in the center of America's breadbasket, studying basic artillery.

That January Greg found himself with a bunch of other West Point graduates on "temporary duty," or "TDY," in airborne school at Ft. Benning. After completing ground training, where soldiers learn to land properly in a gravel pit, they advance to tower school where they jump from a mere 250 feet. No one jumps from an actual Lockheed C-130 Hercules until the third week, when each airborne candidate must complete five jumps, four in daylight and one night jump. Greg completed his first jump along with his old friend Troy Lingley. Neither of them shared in the adrenaline-induced euphoria that swelled up around them.

"I'm thinking this is not something I'd, uh, pursue, in the future," Greg said to Troy after their first step into the empty air.

Lingley agreed.

Their mutual hesitation would be cemented to near paralysis just before their fourth jump, when it was clear something had gone horribly wrong somewhere on the massive Fryar Field drop zone. There was a sudden up-tempo buzz, followed by a loudspeaker blunder, where someone could be heard asking about "the guy with no pulse." It was the first fatality at the jump school in many years. The tragedy not only saddened the soldiers, it cast a foreboding shadow on their final efforts. Plenty nervous for their final jumps, both Greg and Troy landed safely. Lingley deployed to Germany and Greg returned to Fort Sill, where Kim could finally join him. (Kim had completed her required jumps at West Point, but football players were not permitted to participate in training activities which risked injury.) And it wasn't long after that Greg's cultural foresight became a current event. Iraq invaded Kuwait in August of 1990.

The Army's National Training Center—home to mock battlefields and makeshift "towns" where soldiers get a taste of real-life desert and urban war situations—is in Fort Irwin, California. That's where Greg was, again on temporary duty, when Saddam Hussein invaded the small, oil rich country. Greg went back to Fort Sill for a couple of months before deploying to Saudi Arabia. It only took a few days for Saddam Hussein to take control of Kuwait and its oil fields, giving Saddam control of most of the world's energy resources. Multilateral diplomatic negotiations and condemnations went unheeded so in January what had become known as Operation Desert Shield became Operation Desert Storm: the US launched an aerial and naval attack on Baghdad. The ground war began in February. 2nd Lt. Gadson led the 60 or so soldiers of 2nd platoon, Charlie Battery, 5th Battalion, 18th field artillery (one of the battalions of the 75th Field Artillery Brigade) to occupy an assigned area in Kuwait. Upon arrival they discovered enemy bunkers still littered with unexploded ordnance. He radioed command, asking if there was another area they could hold.

"Request denied, Lieutenant. Proceed as assigned," a voice squawked back at him. So, he and his soldiers began using an aiming circle, a device which measures the horizon and various angles, to position their 28-ton M110 A2 Howitzers. They maneuvered around a bunker, still hot with explosives, popping noises drumming their senses into hyper-alertness. As the fourth and final gun was set, Lt. Gadson looked up just in time to see Sgt. Bruce Wayne True hit the ground like a sack. Greg rushed to his side, but it was impossible to determine how seriously True had been wounded. He pulled out his bayonet, and sliced True's pantleg open. There was blood, but True remained conscious and in reasonably good spirits.

"Medic!" Greg yelled. A combat "lifesaver" appeared and snugged a tourniquet above the wound. True stabilized, but writhing about among hot munitions didn't seem to be a proper prescription. The sergeant was eventually medevacked out of the desert and on to Landstuhl in Germany.

The ground war in Kuwait lasted 100 hours. What should have felt like a glorious, rip-roaring tar and feathering of Hussein's Republican Guard impacted Greg more poignantly than he'd expected. Instead of basking in victory, he felt he'd personally delivered a lackluster leadership performance. It wasn't noted by anyone but himself—a small gnawing in the back of his mind. As Greg packed up his gear in Doha before heading back to the States, he pulled his bayonet from the scabbard. It was still bloody. He stared at it a moment, recalling those moments in Kuwait and the man whose blood still coated the knife. True was a Vietnam veteran who'd done his early wartime years in the Navy, then later joined up as a soldier. He was the most senior section chief in the platoon, setting a stoic example when he was wounded, even getting a few laughs by asking if his "family jewels" were still intact. But what Greg remembered most about that day was not the initial shock of the explosion or the rush to save a man's life. What struck him was that he, as the person responsible for the unit, had been unprepared. Isolated and charged with holding disputed territory, they hadn't reacted quickly enough, they weren't on the rapid-fire auto-pilot needed to execute a proper emergency reaction to an event that shouldn't have caught them off guard. Instead of waiting for a command, his team should have been on top of True. They'd seemed dazed rather than proactive. It wasn't the sort of response Greg wanted in his team. If the battlefield had been a football field, coach would have lit up. True was lucky. He'd lived. But in that moment, Greg vowed he'd never again go into combat without properly oiling the machine. His soldiers would always have the rapid reaction necessary to accomplish the mission as well as take care of themselves. More sobering was the war itself. He'd left Fort Sill eager to prove himself. He returned thinking war, even as a last resort, was the saddest remedy to any diplomatic issue. Through those few days of cruising by burned-out, blackened enemy vehicles, still smoldering with their dead, he couldn't help but grieve the lives lost. What were their final thoughts? Did they know they were going to die?

"People think of war as a noble endeavor," he told me years later, "but there is nothing glorious about killing someone."

. . .

Back in the states, happier moments buoyed Greg and Kim. On August 30, 1992, Kim's own birthday, she and Greg welcomed Gabriella Gadson into the world. From the beginning, Gabby was a girl who knew what she wanted. She was, and continues to be, a gale force whirlwind swirling about her parental pillars. Like in many Army families, her dad was away a lot. Still, she grew to love and respect his duties and his way of looking at the world. Soon after becoming a father, Greg was promoted to 1st Lieutenant. Then it was time for the small family to move on.

They next went to Fort Bragg, North Carolina, where Kim and Greg provided 18-month-old Gabby with a little brother. Jaelen Gadson was born on February 21, two days after Greg turned 24. It was almost as if Jaelen was waiting for his father to mature a bit—he came into the world two weeks after he was expected. Gabby found that her little brother was worth waiting for—he fell in line perfectly when she felt she needed to take charge. Greg thought of his first-born's bossy tendencies as "leadership presence." As Jaelen grew, though, he developed his own quiet confidence, more prone to analysis when confronted with tasks and relationships. Less than a year later Greg's own leadership presence was rewarded with another promotion, now to captain.

Adding children into the mix was complicating their Army life, so Kim, having fulfilled her five-year commitment, made the tough call to get out. Of course, the Army was never far away. She remained an active spouse, while at the same time caring for toddlers and launching her own teaching career. Teaching was portable, which allowed her to leave decisions about assignments and deployments up to Greg, figuring if he was happy, they'd all be happy.

It was at Fort Bragg where Greg met a man who would hold influence over him for the rest of his life. Major Rodney Anderson called Greg out one day as he walked through a building on base.

"Captain, come to my office. I'd like to speak with you," Anderson extended the vague invitation. Greg had no idea what it could be about. But Anderson outranked him, so of course he complied. It took a few moments for Greg to relax into a chair across from the major, who had recognized something in Greg and wanted to be sure he didn't lose it. The older soldier pulled out a 5x7 card and gradually sketched out a path—a series of waypoints for Greg to follow—if he in fact wanted to make a career of the Army. Greg kept those notes close and would hold on to that card as his career advanced, through deployments, injuries, and crisis, well past his own and the future major general's retirement.

Anderson, after being promoted to lieutenant colonel, gave Greg a company battery command of his own. He would be responsible for Charlie Battery, 3rd Battalion, 3/19 field artillery regiment, which meant he would be accountable for ensuring his soldiers complied with the Uniform Code of Military Justice, and for all government property used under his command.

Captain Gadson began to find a rhythm to his duties. It felt familiar. There was the physical part, the jumping out of airplanes, (the reluctant airborne student, some 60 jumps later, completed Jumpmaster school, and was even recognized as the Distinguished Honor Grad from the program which had an intimidatingly low pass rate of 30%) the rigorous workouts, all for a larger purpose. Then there was the camaraderie, the routine that bonded him to his soldiers, the leadership and to the organization of the United States Army. It was a whole lot like being an integral member of a football team.

Greg's next command opportunity was at the division's Headquarters & Headquarters Company, also at Ft. Bragg. HQ & HQ is where the Army leadership lives. He reported to a two-star general, a couple of one-stars and managed around 400 staff, who were all supporting the top brass. One day during a fueling exercise a soldier tried to refuel a kerosene heater while it was still on. It fell over, the flames shooting out toward Greg as he turned toward the commotion. He wound up hospitalized overnight with second-degree burns on his wrist and shoulder and first-degree singes on his face. Other than that single incident, he was settling into a certain comfortability, looking more for internal pathways rather than a way out.

The Gadsons' third move was to Alexandria, Virginia, to the Human Resources command where they served two years, then on to Fort Leavenworth, Kansas, where Greg was promoted to major. He attended Command and General Staff College, a graduate school for officers where future leaders were taught exactly how the Army functioned as an organization, how all the moving parts fit together. It was critical knowledge for any soldier expecting to command at larger and more complex levels. At the same time Greg also got a Master of Business Administration degree from Webster University, specializing in computer resources and information management. He was, perhaps even sometimes subconsciously, preparing for what he suspected would be the next front, the possible conflict between the Christian West and the Islamic East. The new millennium was dawning upon the world, but few people recognized the terror threat that loomed over America.

Greg, Kim, Gabby and Jaelen had made their fifth move, this time to Hawaii, where Greg was assigned to the Pacific Command. It was 3:30 a.m. there when Greg took a call from Dennis Kirby, his good friend and fellow West Point alum.

"Turn on your television," ordered Kirby.

"What channel?" Greg asked, groggily.

"Doesn't matter," Dennis answered. "It's everywhere."

He watched, mesmerized, as a second airplane rammed the World Trade Center in New York City.

"I didn't know what to make of it initially, but we all quickly realized we were under attack," Greg recalls. At the time he was part of a three-star general's staff, so he was included in briefings that began within a week at the US Army War College in Carlyle, Pennsylvania.

As the war machine was spinning up, Greg became a late add to the team working in Bosnia. He deployed to Operation Joint Forge even as forces were lining up to invade Afghanistan. Greg saw his work as chief of operations for the 25th infantry as prescient. "It was the battle between the Christians and the Muslims- that fault line between the East and the West," he told me years later. He was part of the dividing line, the multinational task force division north, whose job it was to maintain peace and stability between conflicting factions in a war-torn country. He was in Bosnia for six months. By the time he returned to Hawaii it was 2002. The United States had been engaged in Operation Enduring Freedom for several months. There was no sign of any impending invasion of Iraq.

By June of 2004 Greg was in Afghanistan. He was the division artillery executive officer reporting to then Colonel Gary Cheek at FOB Salerno. The base, close to the border with Pakistan where hundreds of Al Qaeda were presumed to be encamped, came under occasional rocket attack. The launches were fairly predictable, based on the lunar cycle. When light was low they would listen for the expected intel chatter, then prepare to be fired upon. Greg's initial visit to the camp—his pre-deployment site survey—had been uneventful, but for the fact that the remains of a football player, Corporal Pat Tillman, the Arizona Cardinals defensive back, who, it would later be discovered had been killed by friendly fire, was also on his plane headed back to Germany.

He spent most of his time in Afghanistan on the FOB. He was responsible for managing personnel and logistics for about three thousand soldiers. Their mission was mostly counter-insurgency against Al-Qaeda-backed organizations. But for one rocket, which scared the bejezus out of him when it exploded about 25 meters away from where he was working, he wasn't close to much combat. While there were some casualties and hardships,

Afghanistan in no way prepared him for what was to come in Iraq.

He was selected for promotion to lieutenant colonel near the end of his time in Afghanistan. He was also selected for battalion command. He knew that meant another move—what the military calls a "permanent change of station," or PCS.

He made a call to his former teammates at the Human Resources Command.

"I'm coming home from Afghanistan, and I wanted to check to see how soon it would be before I PCS—I'd like to be able to prepare my family."

"Oh, you won't be moving for another six months or so," they told him. "Plenty of time."

"That's great, thanks. I need another knee operation and I'd rather get it over with before we move."

"Fine, sir, you should be good."

Greg was promoted to lieutenant colonel on July 1, 2005. There was a family vacation, then the surgery on July 8.

Major General Dennis Hardy, his new commander, called to congratulate him on his new rank.

"Well, I can officially congratulate you and tell you you're coming to Fort Riley."

"Good sir, when do I report?"

"ASAP."

"What??"

"We need you immediately."

"Yes, sir."

Greg hung up the phone, incredulous and pissed off. He'd only been home from Afghanistan for two months and he was on crutches. He'd be on them for another six to eight weeks. As he hobbled into the Fort Riley community, he knew he would have to prepare to deploy but he didn't know to where or how long he would have to essentially create a unit which, when he arrived, consisted of about five people. He'd be starting from scratch. His job would be to fulfill an authorization document ordering him to build the unit. He would be the recipient of soldiers from other units and organizations from all over America, some fresh from school—and charged with sculpting them into a cohesive unit—a team. He would create operating procedures, policies, and the rules under which they would all live—and keep each other alive.

They eventually learned that their destination would be Iraq, so they prepared for the heat, studied the battle space, the enemy, and they learned about killing. Mostly, they were instilled with one of Greg's most important lessons from his time on the football field: Nothing was more important than the guy next to you. The team always would come first.

Casualties in Iraq were mounting. President George W. Bush was talking about a surge of US troops. They learned they would be part of that surge in November 2006. The 32nd Field Artillery prepared to go to war. Will Huff, one of Greg's closest West Point football teammates, would also be part of the same deployment. So, when Huff came to Fort Riley to meet with his counterparts he visited the Gadsons at their home there. Both men knew they would meet in the field, somehow, under less pleasant circumstances. The West Point brotherhood was beginning to take shape in ways that dug deeper into their beings than school, military drills and even the Black Knight football family had instilled.

Long before Greg said goodbye to Kim, Gabby and Jaelen, he called a few other folks to let them know he was headed to the war zone. One call was to a West Point teammate. Mike Sullivan was now a coach with the New York Giants. It was an accomplishment that made Greg proud, so he called Sully to tell him so. Sully seemed surprised that with such pressing matters before him, he'd be on Greg's call list. It was a good conversation. Both men said their farewells, somehow knowing their paths would soon again entwine along the Long Gray Line.

CHAPTER EIGHT

"He hit me once jokingly. I had a bruise for a week."
—Dr. Paul Pasquina, Chief of Integrated Department
of Orthopedics, Walter Reed Army Medical Center,
and former West Point teammate

The expansive lobby of Walter Reed Army Medical Center was tinged with all that is rumored and written about military medical facilities. On the morning of May 11, it was inundated. People sat slumped or stretched out, some reading newspapers or eating clumpy Subway sandwiches, purchased from the sandwich shop in the front corner. The lighting was dim, as if there were a collective migraine. Everyone looked as though they had been there for a long time.

It was a long way, emotionally and aesthetically from Canada where LTC Chuck Schretzman had handed over his duties temporarily, a few very long hours ago. He stood with Kim now in the midst of the filmy crowd, wondering where they fit in, or how long it would be before they blended. Their appointed hospital family liaison said Greg would arrive via bus from Andrews Air Force Base at 5 o'clock. They would be waiting for a few hours.

Chuck found a couple of empty seats together in a middle row. A tanned and well-groomed receptionist, who looked a little like Al Franken's Stuart Smalley, efficiently handled a steady stream of incoming calls and walk-up questions. Their hospital point-of-contact bustled off to talk with some administrative people in an office down the hall. There was always this vacuum now, whenever someone left the room, hung up the phone or even stopped talking—the space too soon filled with fear or doubt. Neither of them could be reassured of Greg's condition until they saw for themselves.

"Do you want something to eat?" Chuck asked Kim, glancing over at the Subway. There was a Dunkin' Donuts, too. "A coffee or something?"

"No, thanks." Nothing sounded good to Kim. Her phone buzzed. It was Gabby calling from Fort Riley, where she and Jaelen were staying with the Weaver family who lived on base.

"Have you seen Dad yet?" she asked.

"No, he won't get here for a few more hours. They're flying from Germany now. Did I tell you Major Huff was with your dad on the plane from Iraq to Landstuhl? So—"

"He wasn't alone," Gabby finished her sentence.

"Yeah. So that's really good. What are you up to?"

"Nothing, just school."

"Everything okay there?" *Nothing* was never reassuring. But it was not an unusual response from her teenager.

"Everything's good, Mom. We're okay. I'm studying. It's a little hard having to take our tests early."

"I know but it's best if you get here as soon as you can. Your dad will want to see all of us together. Keep your spirits up, Gabby, as much as you can." What was it her own mom used to say about being in two places at once?

"We'll get through it, mom," Gabby did her best to sound upbeat.

Gabby said goodbye and hung up the phone, grateful for the one-on-one talk with her mom. Gabby would not tell her mom this, but the truth was, academics were the least of the problem. School work, she could handle. It was everyone in the school knowing about what happened to her dad. She did not want to think about it. She kept trying to put it out of her mind, but people kept asking. Sometimes it was all she could do to hold back the tears when people asked about him. How was she supposed to answer? She tried to be polite and respectful but saying things out loud just made them more real. Mrs. Weaver was really cool, but she missed her mom too. She just needed to make it through the next couple of days. She and her brother needed to stay in school until May 15, in order to complete their respective school years. Soon her freshman year would be behind her. Complicating things a little further was the fact that she had just gotten out of a cast herself. A soccer injury had laid her up and packed on about 40 pounds. The gift baskets that kept arriving were not helping. Then again, she figured she should be grateful for a couple of things. The school was allowing her and her brother to wrap things up early. And her dad was still alive.

The smell of mayonnaise on wax paper wafted over Kim as she slid back in the cushioned lobby chair and looked at her phone, buzzing again already. She glanced at it and, not recognizing the number, let it go to her voice mail, which probably was getting close to full again. The phone had rung several times just in the last hour. She had spoken with Greg's family. His parents were headed up from Southern Virginia and his sister was flying in from Texas. Her D.C. support system was building. But still there was that gaping hole.

"I can't handle all this," she said, holding the face of her phone up so Chuck could see all the missed calls. "I don't mean to be rude. Greg would be really upset if he knew all these old friends and teammates were calling and . . . "

"No problem, Kim. That's no problem. I think I can set something up on the web. We'll make a place, a page, where everyone can go and I'll put updates about how he's doing there. The crush of calls is only going to get worse, or better, depending on how you look at it. You know the 'brotherhood.'"

Kim nodded. "That would be a big help." Her phone buzzed again. She checked it, then tossed it into her purse.

They watched the crowd. People read newspapers. Some dozed off. One better prepared woman was working her way through a crossword puzzle book. It was not like a regular hospital where at least some of the people were happy. Where this place was not sad, it was just grumpy.

Occasionally a soldier or Marine using a crutch or walking on a prosthetic leg would walk between the rows of seats. Kim and Chuck studied the machinery, the hinges and hydraulics at work. Some patients seemed to swing quickly along with only a limp or small clip to their gait. Others were more labored. Seemed like most of the double amputees they saw were in wheelchairs. Neither Chuck nor Kim could picture that sort of confinement for Greg. But neither of them spoke aloud their thoughts.

Chuck's mind drifted back to the early 1980s. Was it two? Or was it three knee surgeries Greg endured at West Point? Chuck's forehead creased with the memory. He remembered Greg on crutches a lot. Seemed almost every year he would run out of cartilage in one knee or the other and he would go back under the knife, then to rehab, before once again taking the field at Michie Stadium. Crunch. Slice. Heal. Repeat. Greg had stamina, all right, he thought, but without knowing the extent of his current injuries, it was hard to tell how much deeper he would have to dig this time.

The "click, click, click" of their appointed escort's high heels on the linoleum announced her return. They both stood.

"Okay, as we know, your husband is en route," she said, addressing mostly Kim. "He's stable. They will land at Andrews Air Force Base this afternoon. There are several other patients on the plane. If anyone needs a break—any sort of treatment—there is medical staff standing by there. But no worries, okay, because we have lots of medical staff and state of the art equipment on the plane and at the base, so he's constantly being monitored."

Kim nodded a lie. Of course, she was worried.

The woman continued. "From there they'll put him on a bus. That's fully equipped with beds and monitors and medical personnel too. And they'll be in constant contact with us here at the hospital. It's about a 45-minute drive from Andrews to our front door." She gestured toward the front of the lobby.

"When can I see him?" Kim asked.

"As soon as he arrives. We'll take you upstairs, to a big room right above us, it's actually our second-floor lobby. The bus will pull into the oval there. That's how we bring in all our patients from Andrews. So, you'll see him right away."

"Now," she continued, "Depending on the diagnosis, you may be here a while." Kim nodded, thinking only vaguely of their apparent next deployment.

"So, let me introduce you around. We have all sorts of family support services and people who can help you."

"Okay, good, let's go," Kim answered, wondering if she would remember any of it. The women walked through the throng, toward the back of the lobby. Chuck settled back into his seat.

"Is your friend coming in on the 5 o'clock bus?" a woman sitting across from him asked.

"Yes, he is. Lieutenant Colonel Gadson?"

"I don't know the name. My son is here. I'm just visiting. I noticed you're new."

"Yeah, I just found out a couple of days ago Greg was hit. I'm here with his wife. She's . . . "

" . . . being introduced," the woman said.

"Yeah," Chuck smiled. "You've been around the block here."

"I've been here for almost a year. My son was injured last June. Plus, I'm pretty familiar with the way the military works. He went to West Point."

"No kidding! What year? I went there, so did the guy I'm waiting for, Greg."

"My son graduated in '99."

"Well, we both got out in '89," Chuck said. Her son was so young, only eight years since commissioning. Chuck had always harbored great hopes for his own son, Zach, to become a cadet himself in a few years. But now...

"It's easy to get lost in this place. Would you like a walkabout?"

"Absolutely," Chuck said, thankful for the latest West Point connection and, albeit temporary, solid plan and a place to go. They wound through the crowd, then down a hall, ending up at the doors of a giant cafeteria, where everyone—the staff, the doctors, and the patients ate.

"Lines get long at lunchtime, so you want to avoid obvious eating times," she advised. They kept walking.

"This is probably where he'll go first," she waved at the door of the intensive care unit. They walked through a few hallways, turning right across a glass gangway. Colorful paintings portrayed soldiers in various states of glorified rehabilitation. They stopped in front of another glass wall.

"That's going to be the new rehab facility. I forget what they're calling it, but it's going to have all state-of-the-art equipment, especially for, um—the amputees." She stopped.

"Has your friend . . . ?" she asked.

"He still has two—for now."

She nodded. "So many lose legs or arms that they needed more space and equipment to accommodate." They stood for a moment looking through the glass at the pristine gym, where workers were installing a walking track, stationary bicycles, and short platforms with raised bars on each side for leaning. The shining weight machines took Chuck back to the college gym for a minute, where he was always egging Greg on to go heavier. Now he was still just hoping to see his friend through the front door.

• • •

Walter Reed Army Medical Center had been known as the jewel of the military's health care system for almost 100 years but a recent tarnishing of its reputation had affected perceptions. Doctors first began treating patients there in 1909. Greg Gadson's own uncle—his father's brother—had been assigned there in the 1960s. There was a long list of distinguished doctors, administrators and patients who had helped advance military medicine, battlefield applications and care of the wounded, who called WRAMC home. The center was named for Major Walter Reed, whose most noted contribution was his discovery that yellow fever was transmitted by mosquitoes, rather than through human contact. That revelation had major implications for biomedicine and, as a practical matter, the construction of the Panama Canal.

But in the winter of 2007, *The Washington Post* unleashed a scandal that would shake the base to its core, drawing the ire of President George W. Bush, Secretary of Defense Robert Gates and much of the leadership at the Department of Defense. A two-part series, entitled, "The Other Walter Reed," told stories of patient neglect, mismanagement and horrific health care. Within days, two base commanders as well as Army Secretary Francis Harvey were asked to resign.

The Post series told of dirty, moldy cockroach-infested base housing, and administrative disorganization that ran so deep patients were sometimes lost, forgotten about, and left to sort out their own care. Hospital workers were demoralized. The series focused on a few extreme cases. Certainly, there were many more who were treated with great care and healed well. But how could the care of even a few of those who were so bravely serving the nation have slipped so radically?

It may have been a simple fact of war. It had been more than 10 years since doctors, nurses, and other staff had dealt with actual war wounded, even longer since they were incoming at this pace. Before 2001, patients checked in to WRAMC for various reasons: sickness, injury, and health maintenance. They were mostly veterans and their families. But Operation

Enduring Freedom in 2001 and the addition of Operation Iraqi Freedom in 2003 increased the patient load tremendously and unexpectedly.

The stress of the increased flow of patients was complicated by the catastrophic nature of the wounds—a good news story, actually. Modern battlefield medicine increased survival rates dramatically. If an injured soldier made it to a theater hospital, he or she had a 95 percent to 98 percent chance of survival. But in many cases, survival meant living with lost limbs, large area burns, and brain injuries. WRAMC staff were suddenly tasked with a major surge in incoming soldiers who needed acute care, rehabilitation, housing and family support. They responded, but the call may have been greater than they anticipated, greater than they were equipped, physically and administratively, to handle. And patients who had multiple injuries, requiring any number of separate specialists, therapies, and medications, were buried by paperwork, staff shortfalls and arcane military requirements.

To the credit of the U.S. Army and those it chose to put in place there, the scandal served as a wake-up call. Commander of the North Atlantic Regional Medical Command and Walter Reed Lieutenant General Eric Schoomaker oversaw a restructuring of warrior care including the establishment of Warrior Transition Units and the Army Wounded Warrior Program. (Schoomaker would later become the Surgeon General of the Army.) Colonel Patricia Horoho[3] took over command of the Walter Reed Health Care System. It was a massive effort geared toward correcting months of administrative confusion. The new leadership engineered a fairly fast response, establishing new guidelines, putting in place what they called a "Triad of Care," a system whereby each injured soldier was assigned a case manager. The case manager's duties included making sure

---

3 Colonel Patricia Horoho was later promoted to Lieutenant General then became the first female Nurse Corps officer to be appointed Army Surgeon General and serve a full term. She is also a U.S. Army Women's Foundation Hall of Fame inductee.

the patient was making and keeping various appointments, was obtaining and ingesting the appropriate medications, and was dealing with the necessary crush of paperwork. Four months of press conferences, management changes, congressional hearings and media scrutiny had left the hospital scandal-weary. But the staff was rallying.

. . .

Close to 5 p.m. that evening the bus carrying wounded patients from Andrews Air Force Base pulled into the circular drive in front of the hospital. Chuck found himself alone in the second-floor lobby—Kim was with friends back in the Soldier Family Support Center. He stood close to the glass as Greg, bundled in white linens and strapped to a gurney, was pulled horizontally from the bus and wheeled up the covered brick entryway. Nurses and staff hovered about, prepping their patient for transfer, even as the gurney rolled towards him. He stared at his friend's swaddled body.

He heard Kim bursting through the lobby's huge wooden doors behind him, running toward Chuck.

"Is that him?" she asked.

"Think so," answered Chuck. "Hard to ... " He caught a glimpse of rough, dark skin. "Yeah, yeah, it is."

Greg's medical escorts kept working, even as they came inside, stepping back only slightly to allow Kim and Chuck a view. Kim gazed silently at her husband for a moment. It was disturbing to see him so still, so removed. Her eyes glanced down his body, toward his feet for a second, but she wanted to hold his gaze if he woke, if his eyes even flickered. She wondered if he had any idea where he was, of what had happened.

"Greg, it's Chuck," Schretzman tried.

Greg's face was still puffy with medication and trauma. The flight nurse told Kim he had not regained consciousness on the plane. And, as far as she knew, he never really came to during his time in Landstuhl, but he was stable and had remained so during the flight. He was heavily sedated. The damage to the back sides of his legs was severe from the knee down. Evacuation personnel were moving him directly to the ICU.

And then he was gone again. *There was that vacuum.*

It was another hour before they were allowed into the ICU. They stayed as near as hospital personnel would allow, until about 10 o'clock that night. To an outsider, Greg's arrival may have seemed anticlimactic. Greg never even stirred, let alone tried to speak. But to Kim, there was much solace in seeing her husband's face and knowing where, exactly, he was, even if she could not talk with him. Finally, she headed over to the Mologne House, the base housing for families of wounded soldiers, called the kids, then said some silent prayers of thanks. Chuck went back to the Marriott Hotel in nearby Silver Spring, Maryland. ICU nurses assured them they would call if Colonel Gadson woke up. It was nearing the end of the week, when most other places in Washington slowed down.

. . .

Friday morning did not often mean the end of the work week for Dr. Paul Pasquina. His small office in the medical center was becoming more of a changing room than a place of business. Off came the flawlessly fitted and pressed navy blue suit jacket. On went the starched, white coat with the hospital insignia stitched above the pocket, where he slid two identical blue pens, caps up, aligned like soldiers. He clipped his ID onto the pocket opening, square with the seams.

Pasquina served as chief of the Orthopedics and Rehabilitation Department at Walter Reed. This war had raised the bar, virtually exploding his duties. The rate of incoming cases and complications had forced the department into overdrive. Pasquina essentially tasked himself with making sure every wounded soldier was offered the best technology available and sometimes that meant innovating, quickly. Every day the wounded streamed into the hospital, each case with its own complications. He also had a young daughter at home. Sometimes, he was not sure which job was more relentless.

His desk was no reflection of the pace, though. The spotless, generic wood was broken up only by the most relevant, neat stacks of notes, records and requests. There was one gleaming family photo of himself with his wife. They looked so much like models his visitors sometimes thought he had forgotten to remove the fake photo that came with the frame.

A single yellow sticky note disturbed the uniformity. It read, "LTC Gadson, ICU." He pulled the note off the desk and studied it closely. Then he left his office, turned down the hallway, and calmly maintained his gait, toward the intensive care unit. *Of all people.*

Difficult to imagine Gadson was severely wounded, he thought, as he made his way through the hallways, absently greeting staffers. Two years apart at West Point, Pasquina was a small quarterback, and Gadson was not much bigger. But Gadson was deceiving. Pasquina avoided the defensive lineman's grip at all cost. Getting hit by Gadson in a drill or practice meant several days of soreness. He would knock you down, then help you up; He would make sure you were okay. There was something spiritual about him, something Zen. The thought made him smile slightly, elongating the creases on either side of his mouth. He imagined Greg Gadson would not be long for the ICU.

The doctor stepped into Greg's bay in the ICU, his professional gaze resting on his friend's still, sterile body. He lifted the blanket, surveying the metal cages. Not as good as he had hoped but he had seen worse. A nurse handed him a couple of X-rays in a large envelope. As he pulled them out, he noticed a big, blond guy sitting in a chair in the corner. It took him a few seconds to flash back, once again, to the West Point gridiron.

The big, blond guy spoke. "Hey, Paul? It's Chuck."

"Schretzman, yes, God, man, good to see you." Paul and Chuck shared a fast back-smacking man hug. Paul remembered—Greg and Chuck had played the same position, the two were constantly together. Here in the cramped room, Chuck towered over Paul, as he had in 1985 on the field. Now, the lineman's forehead was knitted, fear and worry graying his face, so changed from the days when the intensity of practice, anticipation of the next play, set his skin and eyes glowing.

Chuck watched Pasquina. A fine doctor, he had heard and believed. He knew if that if he was the one lying there tubed and caged, he would want Paul on his case. Now they would once again be teammates, Paul carrying the ball. Paul would be his lead, his best source in matters of life and death, going forward. It tickled him, though, somewhere in the back of his mind, that there was a war on and, still, Paul Pasquina had not a hair out of place.

• • •

Since the actual wounds were bound up in bandages and braces, pictures of Greg's legs, taken back in Baghdad, were the best way to get an idea of what was going on. Standing in the ICU, Dr. Pasquina and Kim and Chuck went over the X-rays a few times. The doctor explained the damaged arteries and nerves. He clinically explained why each leg may or may not be functional again. It depended on whether or not the veins and arteries could handle the blood flow and on whether the flesh would regenerate enough to hold the insides in place. So much depended on Greg's remaining strength and endurance.

Pasquina had examined hundreds of lower limb X-rays over the past several years, most of the time having no personal ties to their owners. But in this case, he had been a direct witness to Gadson's physicality. Gadson had been a linebacker. Once he got his hands on you, you were a goner. He was an incredibly strong, determined, yet gracious athlete. Would rip your head off, then smile, with a sincerity that made you forget how much you hurt. As a battalion commander, he knew Greg thrived on adversity and challenges. In America, Pasquina thought, we celebrate rock stars and athletes, independent of character. But Gadson was well known as an athlete and as a leader. Five years of war had sent many a true hero through the doors of this hospital and under his care—living examples of the words "duty" and "honor." He knew Greg took those words very seriously. And it was that for which Greg was most celebrated. If there was a candidate to mentally tough this out, it was Greg Gadson.

He looked at the photos and charts again. The legs were mangled, essentially shattered from the lower thigh down. Muscles and bones were completely separated. One band was folded at a 90-degree angle. It would take many, many surgeries and months to even present the possibility of restoring functionality to either limb.

The philosophy of the medical staff at Walter Reed is to generally remain objective as possible regarding limb salvage. It should be a decision for the patient to make, that is, if there is much deciding to do. Sometimes legs had to be removed to save a life. So far, it did not seem as if either leg was an imminent threat. But the pictures were graphic indicators of the extraordinary healing that would have to take place if his legs were to remain intact. The caretakers' ability to keep infection away was also critical. As a doctor, Pasquina thought it unlikely Greg would keep both legs. As a friend, and former teammate, he wanted the decision to be Greg's. He knew he would be asked for a lot of advice by family, friends and teammates. The brotherhood had already started calling. For now, it was important to keep Greg quiet and allow him enough healing so they could begin to determine, in addition to the physical injuries, what mental or emotional trauma had occurred.

Still huddled in the ICU, Paul reviewed the medical events of the last several days. Greg had already undergone several surgeries. The two surgeries Dr. Brad Woods conducted in Baghdad were just the beginning if he were to keep both limbs. Every day, sometimes more than once, doctors performed "wound debridements," which are commonly known as "wash-outs." Debridements were chiefly to prevent infection by clearing out contaminants picked up in the field or somehow contracted locally. In the end they normally speed healing. But the process, where they essentially swab the inside of the wound, was excruciating. So far, the LTC had been unconscious for the treatments. On this day, he would undergo a major exploratory procedure where the vascular doctor, the plastic surgeon and Dr. Pasquina would all get a look. After that, docs were planning to take him off sedation. Kim and Chuck stood by, either standing in the unit or in the nearby waiting room, until Greg was wheeled into surgery.

That night, after another day of intense listening, learning, comforting and questioning, Chuck went back to the Marriott Hotel and, keeping his promise to Kim, began an open online journal for friends and family, but mostly for the men who formed the brotherhood of the gridiron at West Point. He was hearing from many distant alums, to say nothing of those who had already been "hands on." Dr. Brad Woods, Dr. Al Beekley, Brigadier General Dana Pittard, Major Will Huff, and Dr. Paul Pasquina had all begun their service at the United States Military Academy. It was a rolling stone, gathering some mighty moss. He made his first entry:

Men,

Today was a very long day for Greg in the operating room—over 8 hours . . . He is still under sedation/ intubated and has not been able to speak with Kim. The doctors will bring him off sedation tomorrow sometime in the morning. Kim will be right by his side when he wakes up! She is so strong and wants to say thanks to everyone for their support. The doctors have been magnificent over the last 48 hours and he is in capable hands.

CHAPTER NINE

"The Word of the Lord is really what he hears. Once you speak
His words to Him they do not come back void."
—Damaris Coles, Greg Gadson's sister

Everyone kept asking him the same questions over and over. "Where are you?" Do you know where you are?" Greg told them. Again and again.

"Bosnia," he would answer. *Why wouldn't they just let him sleep?*

"Colonel. Tell me where you are," a nurse tested, or a doctor demanded. It was really pissing him off.

"Iraq!" *For crying out loud. Of course, that is where he was. He had been there for weeks. This was exhausting. There were tubes running into his arms. He guessed he was hurt. But how? What had happened?*

"You're at Walter Reed Army Medical Center," a familiar voice would say. Was that Chuck?

No. I am in Iraq. This guy, whoever he was, was lying. He needed to be silenced. He started to draw his shoulder and arm back to throw the punch. But he could not move it. What the . . . ?

Plastic bands pinched the skin inside his elbows and disappeared behind him. His legs were bound with steel bands. He had somehow become a prisoner.

"Agh!" he yelled in frustration, fighting the restraints, clenching his fists. How had he been captured? He strained, trying to remember where he'd been. Then blackness engulfed him. He braced, waiting for his captors to begin their torture—the relentless questioning, the beatings. The first punch would probably come to his head. He braced, then faded back to blackness.

Kim and Chuck had been warned about the hallucinations and the confusion Greg would feel as they worked to bring him out of sedation. Still, it was alarming to see him so wild, so strung out. Dr. Pasquina had suggested that they read aloud some of the many letters that were arriving from teammates, to try to soothe him, but he was too agitated at the moment to hear a word.

Greg's eyes flew open again. There were people standing around him, working at something or talking. One woman was squeezing a bag of liquid, hanging over his head. *She must be mixing the poison.* He struggled against the straps again, calling for reinforcements. *Johnson!* Where the hell was Fredrick Johnson? Didn't the first sergeant know he was supposed to be protecting him? He looked around the room again. Odd thing was all of these people looked American. Not a drop of chai in sight. Their demeanor seemed fairly nonthreatening, actually, and it appeared they were listening to him but not understanding what he was saying, as though they did not speak English. Where was Oro his interpreter? Maybe he could make some sense to these folks. One woman looked suspiciously like his wife, Kim, right down to her blonde, layered flip hair style and wire-rimmed glasses. Very cunning, he thought. He pulled his hand up as far as he could, considering the bondage his enemies wrought, and pointed his index finger at the woman with the poison.

Bang! He drew back his hand in disbelief. He had not meant to shoot. He did not even know for sure now if these people *needed* to be shot. Who were they?

Bang! Bang! Bang! He could not stop the bullets from flying out the tip of his finger.

Bang! There went another. If he did not stop, someone was going to be hurt or even killed. He flinched as bullets whistled through the air, ricocheting off the walls.

"Get down!" he yelled, "I can't stop them!" He had become some sort of science fiction creature. He hid his hands under the blanket, hoping to prevent their willful violent rampage. So far no one was hit. No one was even trying to get away. People were just gaping at him, smirking even. Did they not understand he was dangerous? He fired several rounds straight from his index finger, at close range, but luckily, he had missed everyone. Better get some range practice in, he thought. His aim was failing. He looked down at his dangerous digits. He was sleepy. Certainly, all of this called for a nap. He nodded off into a deep Dilaudid-induced sleep. It was late afternoon, May 13—day two in the ICU at Walter Reed Army Medical Center.

Time passed, or did not in Greg's mind. Might have been an hour. Might have been a day. The voices were quieter now, hushed even, like at a funeral home. He stirred at the notion. A funeral gathering would definitely be bad news. But there was also a certain energy. There was bustling, business, something was going on. A hum. He opened his eyes to see what it was. Yep, he was dead. Because right there in front of him was his wife, Kim, and a very fuzzy-looking Chuck, just as dorky as he was in military prep school. Fort Monmouth. 1984. West Point. Football. Coach Young. Chuck was saying something about Coach Young. Greg tried to make a joke. Neither Kim nor Chuck laughed. They were staring intently at him. I am right *here*, he thought. *Talking* to you.

Chuck stopped reading the letter from Coach Young. He watched Greg's lips twitching, struggling to form syllables still stuck in his brain.

"Kim, he's trying to say something for real, I think," Chuck said.

"It's like his mind is all scrambled and he can't assemble the words," Kim said. They both leaned closer to the bed. Even if Greg was not putting together intelligible syllables, at least he was trying to communicate in a somewhat rational manner. This was not the hysterical babble that had been setting them on edge for the last several hours. Chuck had seen actual recognition in Greg's eyes. He seemed to know both of them. All good news.

Chuck tossed the coach's letter on a nearby food tray. He kept his gaze trained on his friend. Greg seemed to stop his mental struggle for a moment, obviously exasperated with their inability to understand him. Greg sighed. For a moment he seemed to gather his strength, then blurted, "Be on time!" Chuck shrugged and shook his head. Who knows what that meant? But Greg had managed to string three words into an almost-sentence. That seemed like progress. Maybe.

Then in a low voice, Greg said, very slowly, "The Goooolden Roool."

"Ah!" Chuck snatched up the letter. "Right! Golden Rule! Coach Young! I was just reading an email to him from Coach Young—our football coach at West Point. Golden Rule was Young's mantra, remember, Kim? He would always say, 'The Golden Rule: If nothing else, be on time!'" Chuck beamed. His friend had put together an actual coherent thought. The trigger seemed to be football. He watched the lines that had been so deeply etched in Kim's face fade into exhilaration.

"Hey, I got an email from Coach Kish, too," Chuck said to Greg. "You know who that is?" Greg smiled a little. He was finding his voice.

"Yah, Charlie, you gotta punch." Greg had not referred to Chuck as Charlie in years—maybe since college.

"Ha, that's great! You gotta punch!" He turned to Kim. "There was this board," he explained, "that we had to punch, all of us, before practice. It was Kish's thing, to make us jump up and do that on our way onto the field." Kim nodded. She was sure she had heard of the punch-board drill before, but it had blended into the back of her brain with dozens of other West Point football stories. She wished she could remember some of them now. Chuck kept going, staying with the coach theme.

"Remember Robertson?"

"Jesus Christ, Christian, you move like two old ladies." The sentences were slow but deliberate and clear.

"Ha, right! Mike Christian from the scout team. That's what Coach Robertson would always say to Christian when he was moving too slowly."

Gradually, Kim felt fear and strain physically release from her shoulders, as she listened to her husband accurately answer question after question—quickly piecing together jokes and memories made with West Point football players and coaches. Some of it she understood. Some of it only a fellow teammate would get. Kim's own father had suffered a brain injury. While he could not recall his own wife's name, he could talk with an old friend and co-worker about his 30 years as a truck driver, handing out detailed maintenance tips and directions to anywhere in Kansas City. Her husband's recollection process seemed similar. So, she watched with both delight and trepidation as Chuck exploited this new phenomenon. He paused, temporarily out of West Point trivia.

Kim wondered if the parameters of these exchanges would extend beyond sports.

"Babe, do you know where you are?" Kim asked. Greg frowned. He hated this question.

"No." he said, matter-of-factly.

"It's okay—you're at Walter Reed Army Medical Center, in Washington, D.C. You were in an explosion." He took this in as if it were new information, although he had been told many times.

"Can you see the clock up there?"

"Yes."

"What time is it?"

He looked for a moment. "I don't know. What does it matter?"

"It doesn't. It's nighttime. You've been here two days."

"Okay. If you say so," he said.

The football conversation seemed to have worn him out and he started to fall back into a restful state, a relief from all the jerking about and violent episodes. Kim wondered aloud to Chuck if soon those bands could come off his arms. It was disturbing for her to see him tied down, her gentle husband, father of two, an 18-year career military man, who did not even really like guns.

He stirred a bit. "Kim? Are you still here?"

"Yeah, babe?" She answered, hoping he might have remembered something besides a football stat.

"I've been shooting at people in here. Could you keep everyone out of the room so no one gets hurt?" She and Chuck exchanged glances. He had seemed so lucid only a few minutes ago.

"Yeah, I'll do that," she answered. "Don't worry. Get some rest."

That night, Chuck made this entry in the online journal:

Status as of 2100, 13 May 2007

Gentleman,

Greg was taken off intubation at about 11AM. He spent a majority of the day with Kim and his Mom and Dad. Greg was able to start speaking coherently at approx 1900. As I read some of your emails to him and brought up stories about Army Football Greg's expressions became animated. I told him that Jim Young sent a message. He plainly said out loud, "The Golden Rule! BE ON TIME!" Kim and I almost fell on the floor. We talked about Swarming the football etc and after several moments of Army Football talk . . . he replied, "One thing about our guys . . . our team . . . WE NEVER QUIT!" I will read more emails tomorrow as I know it will continue to help him fight. As a true warrior, he has already expressed a need to be back with his battalion. Tomorrow he is scheduled for follow-on surgery. He is excited to see the kids on Thursday. Kim feels he may be ready to see visitors in about a week or so. We will keep you updated on this. Everybody keep praying . . . Your emails are helping . . . LTC Chuck Schretzman '89

. . .

Something about always waking up in the same place, the ICU, made tracking his own existence impossible. Dreams and reality blended then collided, jerking Greg from restless sleep. He often called out for his troops, searching for a weapon, his children. He saw snowy mountain scenes or seascapes through the lens of his camera, which would blur, then steam over until he could not breathe. He seemed a hostage determined to outsmart his captors. But it was impossible to know if it was day or night. He sometimes saw his wife, then he would hear his sister, Damaris, praying a psalm he recognized.

"... He will command his angels concerning you to guard you in all your ways. They will lift you up in their hands ..."

The room grew warmer one evening as the sun turned the sky outside his window red, then hot as a desert road. Before him stood Satan himself, wielding fiery spears, plunging toward him. His chest seared as the crimson rods plunged into his soul. The very pit of evil emerged before him. Now the Devil tied Greg's arms behind him then held his gaze forward, forcing Greg to watch each member of his beloved family be savagely tortured. He saw Kim and Gabby and Jaelen suffering mightily for his own sins. He knew he truly had reached the depths of Hell. He flailed, lurching for his wife, his children. He had to save them. He had to save them all.

A loud noise—maybe the door of the ICU slamming shut—pierced his sleep, forcing him back to his own being. The images now intertwined with his subconscious memory of a white-hot light, obliterating noise, people and shapes and the vague notion of inexplicable loss. It all lasted for minutes, then dragged on for days until light and dark finally seemed to part, and emerging realities made him yearn for blackness.

. . .

When the phone rang at 5 a.m. in Kim's Mologne House apartment, it no longer alarmed her. It could be anyone. In fact, a few people knew this was a good time to reach her. So when it jingled her awake in the early morning of May 14, Kim rolled over and calmly answered.

"Mrs. Gadson?"

"Yes." In the span of a week, she had never been addressed as "Mrs. Gadson" quite so often.

"Lieutenant Colonel Gadson is asking for you."

"Oh!" Adrenaline rushed through her body. "Of course, I'll be right there!" She hung up the phone, euphoric. Her husband was *asking* for her. He knew who she was and knew she was nearby. That must mean he knew where he was—this was huge. She ran under the shower then raced across the base. She could not wait to talk to him, for real, about things. The kids, the impending move to D.C. from Fort Riley, his loving friends who called incessantly, there was so much to discuss. She had missed him and it sounded like, maybe, he was back.

The folks in the sterile ICU smiled when she slammed through the door. They were as happy to deliver the news as she was to get it. He was still in a state of trauma, they cautioned. The aroma of absolute sterility helped tap down her expectations. She calmed herself before stepping into the beige blur of his bay.

"Hey. Welcome back," she said quietly, expecting the softened look of her husband's glance settling on her familiar face.

"Kim."

"I got here as quickly as I could. I'm staying at an apartment where families of, um, injured soldiers stay, just across . . ."

"Kim. Listen." His voice was rigid, his words clipped. "You know Ricky Gibbs?"

Of course, she did. Gibbs was his commanding officer in Iraq. She had heard he had personally helped carry her husband from the medevac helicopter at FOB Falcon, where he was first transported. And his wife, Nolly, had first told her that Greg was hurt, only days ago in the sauna at Fort Riley. It all seemed in the distant past.

"He's trying to kill us," Greg said.

"No, no," she protested, not wanting him to be like this. She wanted him back. This was not back.

"Kim, Gibbs is planning to assassinate our whole family. We need to hide."

"Greg, Colonel Gibbs helped you. He was there when you almost died." *Was she supposed to say that? Was he supposed to know he had nearly not made it back?*

"He's dangerous. He'll take all of us. Gabby, Jaelen, you, me. And my dad. I saw my dad here!" His eyes widened.

"Your dad *is* here. And your mom. And your sister."

"We have to find a place to stay—away from here."

It was clear he did not know where "here" was. And she felt alone in nowhere. She tried to talk football but she needed Chuck, who had been called back to Canada. Despite the numerous times she had heard the stories, she was vague on details. She talked about past family vacations, about scuba diving together—anything that might jar his way-back memory. Sometimes it seemed like he was following. But he would eventually launch into some paranoid warning about their lives being at stake, or how someone was trying to kill them. Adding to her frustration was the fact that he seemed almost normal when no one else was around. But left alone with her, he would start the crazy talk. Worried that the episodes might indicate a brain injury, she explained to the nurse what was happening. She nodded sympathetically. It happened to a lot of patients who were fighting infections, the nurse told her. The fevers and the meds make folks a little crazy. Kim tried to apply this intellectually, but it was impossible to separate it from her emotions. No one could understand this. Her husband of 18 years, as many in the Army, a combatant commander, had become Johnny Depp's Jack Sparrow or some Shakespearean lunatic. And to further complicate matters, the kids would be here in a few days. It would be upsetting for them to see their father acting like this.

. . .

Willie James Gadson stared hard at the crinkled black and white photo he had held onto for so many years. It was his own grandmother, great-grandmother to Greg. She was an inspiration to the whole family and she was called upon from time to time. He set the picture on the stand next to Greg's bed. *Work your magic*, he thought. A small shrine had sprouted up around his son. He knew the prayer Greg's sister, Damaris, had taped to the rail of the bed, by heart, but he read it anyway.

"I *will say of the LORD, 'He is my refuge and my fortress, my God, in whom I trust.'"*

Psalm 91. He was more of a Proverbs man. But the psalm seemed appropriate. He tried to remember a few lines from Proverbs. Patricia was so much better at that. He knew the gist, always, but was not great at recalling quotes.

Impatience tugged at him. Proverbs. Maybe he should read his Bible. But it was hard to concentrate. If he had just gotten here a few minutes earlier, he might have been able to speak with his son. Kim warned him of the "crazy talk." But the sound of his voice would have been some reassurance. He glanced at his wife. She was so even, so balanced. They both were, usually.

Willie Gadson was born in Walterboro, South Carolina. He got a southern elementary and high school education, but wanted to see a bit more of the world, so he migrated north, living with his sister in Baltimore for a few months. His older brother, Sammie Gadson, joined the service and was stationed at Walter Reed. So, he spent more time there, eventually moving in with Sammie. So as a young man, he saw his share of the inside of WRAMC. At the time, the hospital was filling up with Vietnam War wounded. His brother worked as a medic, telling stories of lost limbs, head traumas, lost souls. The patients called the orthopedic wing the "snake pit."

Willie worked and saved, then went to school at Howard University in Washington, D.C.—one of the nation's highest ranked historically Black colleges. It was 1965. He was given a 1A status for the draft, meaning he was considered by the government to be a potential soldier. Later he received word that he would get a student deferment. In 1966, he married his longtime friend and love, Patricia.

Greg was their first son. He showed signs early on of a certain zest for life, arriving slightly prematurely as Patricia enjoyed a visit with her sister in Oklahoma City that February. Her mother was there too, so when one Saturday Willie got the call that his wife had gone into labor he was not so panicked as he might have been. She was with family. He did not see his son for the first time until days later, when the baby and his wife were recovered enough to travel.

They set up a home in part of a house in northwest Washington, in what would become a vibrant area close to Silver Spring, Maryland. Playtime for Greg was in the backyard of that home, where a fence backed up to Walter Reed.

After graduating from Howard with a degree in pharmacy, Willie accepted a job at the Strong Memorial Hospital, which was part of the University of Rochester. By now there were two children. Damaris arrived two years after Greg. It was not until he had been working for the Eli Lilly Company out of Buffalo, and the birth of his second son, Patrick, that his oldest remarked on the weather. It was a weekend and he was enjoying a little downtime with his son outside.

"Daddy, when is it going to warm up?" the four year-old Greg had asked. Seemed like maybe it was time for a change. So, in the spring of 1975 they moved to Tidewater, Virginia, then settled in a small town called Chesapeake. It had the most pleasant temperatures in the world, he thought. Perfect for his chill-challenged son. It was a good community, where the children could find plenty of activities. That is where Greg started playing football. That is where the children all had a paper route. He thought it was important to teach them to fend for themselves, to work, to earn, and to spend wisely. It taught them responsibility, too. They only had one day off per year—Christmas Day. And every month they had to go door-to-door to collect payments. That was the toughest part for them. But it taught them persistence—gave them that "never-give-up" attitude that people sometimes need in life. Maybe that was helping his oldest now. Maybe it was helping all of them.

. . .

Greg's view in the ICU never changed. The sameness made him feel as if he missed whole days. Other times he seemed to be living in the same minute for hours. Again, he thought he had seen his parents in the room, and his sister, Damaris. And Satan was making regular appearances—delivering some sort of message, but Greg was not sure of the point. When he would wake up and they would all be gone. Maybe he was just dreaming them up. Oddly, there was no pain in his legs, even where the metal prongs pierced his flesh. Still, there were constant visits by doctors and nurses. More tubes, and questions. The damned questions. *Didn't anyone at this place write anything down?*

Gradually, things began making more sense. Patriot Six, "*sitrep*," he thought. His own situation report: day stayed light, night remained dark. He had been struck by an IED. Everyone in his security detail was okay, except for Oro, but he would be back on his feet soon. Greg knew he was at Walter Reed Army Medical Center in Washington. And, like so many others who had served in Iraq, his legs were messed up. Over. But not out.

. . .

Kim had told him the kids were coming but it was still a surprise when they walked into his room on Thursday afternoon. Sergeant Major William Huffin, Greg's senior enlisted, had escorted them on the flight from Fort Riley, Kansas.

"Hi, Dad!" both kids called, trying to sound as nonchalant as possible. They shared their parents' confidence, their easy, polite way with strangers, their respect for family and authority. Gabrielle was tall and athletic, her long curls softening her, her skin a perfect smooth blend of dark and light. Jaelen, at 13, was thin and still looked like a boy, but ready for this sudden onslaught of manhood. Kim had told them a little about what to expect, so they were prepared.

"Hi, Jaelen," Greg said, enthusiastically. Jaelen's shoulders squared with pride. He knew his dad's brain was still suffering aftershocks and names didn't always come easily. He'd not been on good terms with his dad. The worry was crippling. But the sound of his own name in his dad's voice was a soothing remedy.

Then Greg looked at Gabby strangely.

"Esther?"

"No, Dad, it's Gabby. Your daughter?" She flashed him a hopeful smile.

"Esther," Greg repeated.

Kim saw the sudden tears burning Gabby's eyes, her throat tightening. Greg did not seem to recognize his own daughter. Gabby looked at Jaelen, then Kim, her eyes brimming. After all they had been through.

"He knows you, honey," Kim said, "Don't you, Greg? It's Gabby." She turned to her daughter.

"Sometimes your Dad's words get scrambled or he can't find the right one." Then turning to her husband she playfully admonished, "Who's Esther, anyway?"

"What did I say—Esther?" He laughed a little, partly at his mistake and partly to soothe his daughter. He was learning to acknowledge that his brain was a little like a jumbled Scrabble board.

"Oh, I don't know who Esther is. I think I have an Aunt Esther, or something."

He held his hand out toward her.

"Gabby," he said, reinforcing her name in both of their minds. "I might be a little nutty but it's okay to touch me. I won't bite. At least I think I won't!" The match of her name with the sound of his voice made her want to cry even more, and she did a little, but it was a good cry.

Jaelen was quiet, taking it all in. Just seeing his father made him feel like everything, while still chaotic, was going to be okay. He asked if he could see his dad's legs. Kim gingerly pulled the white blanket back so they could see how their father was being treated, how he was healing. Both legs were in the fixators and wrapped with gauze. What could be seen of the tops of his legs looked almost normal. There were hoses and sponges connected beneath, and the skin there was dark, making the wounds difficult to discern. Still, Gabby looked away.

"You guys probably need to head over to the Mologne House to get sorted out," Kim said, opening an escape hatch. She knew these would be some tough moments and wanted to keep the visit brief. The kids nodded and said their goodbyes. But Gabby wanted to be sure of him.

"Bye, Dad. See you tomorrow."

"Okay, Gabby," he said forcefully, taking the cue.

"You guys listen to your mom," he added, almost absent mindedly, like he had said a million times before. Kim watched the door close behind them. Normal was a long way off.

CHAPTER TEN

*"After we saw him, I felt this peace about everything else.
I thought everything was going to be okay."*
—Jaelen Gadson

It was early on Friday, May 18th, when Greg woke up feeling like something was very wrong. Not that lying in intensive care with your legs all mummified and caged like coalmine parakeets was all hunky-dory. But he had a feeling something was about to get worse. There was discomfort, but he could not call it pain.

"Something's not right," he told the nurse. "My leg, on the left side, it's, it seems like there's something..." The nurse glanced down at the bandages where Greg had pulled back the sheet.

"I'll call the doctor," she said, almost breezily. She did not like what she saw, but there was no need to panic the patient.

Being on call at Walter Reed meant you spent your days and nights in the hospital. Gone were the days of phoning in a prescription. Best you could do was phone home to tell the family you were not leaving for a while. Dr. Donald Gajewski had already been called to a number of bedsides by the time he got to LTC Greg Gadson that morning. He knew all too well how this was likely going to go. And it was going to go quickly.

"Hello, Colonel, I'm Dr. Gajewski," he said as he entered the room.

"Hey, Doctor. You know, I'm not sure what's going on."

Gajewski looked at the VAC, the vacuum-assisted closure device, which was attached to Greg's left leg. "We're probably going to need to take you to surgery, Greg. We don't have much time to talk." Dr. Gajewski nodded at the nurse, who called the OR. The VAC was filled with blood. The system, essentially a sponge with a suction attached, is designed to keep an open wound clean. It continually pulls bacteria and other fluids away from the wound and helps prevent infection. Normally a VAC pump will fill within a couple of days. But this morning it had taken only about 10 minutes for it to fill with a crimson colored liquid. There was too much blood. The artery that had been so painstakingly saved by Dr. Brad Woods in Baghdad and heavily guarded by Major Will Huff through Balad, then on to Landstuhl, Germany, had given way. Gadson was bleeding to death. He would in a matter of minutes either lose his leg or lose his life.

"Here we go," Gajewski said half out loud as Gadson's eyes flickered into a restless unconsciousness.

"Have we called his NOK?" His next of kin was Kim, who was still asleep at the Mologne House.

Over the last few years, the Iraq War had created many experts in limb removal. Dr. Gajewski had performed enough amputations to have them categorized loosely in his mind, for his own organizational necessity. There were the soldiers who came in with no legs. They had been removed in the field, either by a violent blast or in field surgery. They routinely just needed follow-up surgeries. Stub smoothing. Washes. Clutter removal. And lots of psych, but that was another department. Next were the guys who were offered options. They came in with limbs, then made the decision—given the likelihood or percentage of predicted function, and general wear-and-tear it would take to restore it, or them— to have them removed. Those surgeries were planned, methodical even. The decisions were heavily weighed and left ultimately to the patient. The third category was emergency removal. In other words, it was the leg or a life. This was the rarest of situations, but it happened. In the fourth category were the patients who came back for amputations later. They would spend months, years even, enduring surgery after surgery, painful therapies, infection—then finally they would surrender. Their resolve was diminished and maturity had set in. Usually it was the right decision. A barely functional limb often served as not much more than an albatross. The attempt at something closer to normalcy was often abandoned for functionality. Eventually. Gadson had arrived at Walter Reed as a category two. Things were changing quickly.

Dr. Gajewski was a fan of the limb. He preferred his patients to leave with them. And he would do anything possible, as many times as necessary, to accommodate his own hopes, as well as the hopes of his patients. In fact, all the doctors and staff at Walter Reed wanted to leave decisions regarding amputation to the patient. They preferred to stabilize, assess, then let the patient decide, given predictions for recovery and how much use the limb would have, and in some cases, how much danger the limb presented, whether or not to simply eliminate the problem. This patient, however, was about to lose his opportunity to weigh in.

It took only about 15 minutes for Kim to get from the Mologne House to the ICU. The kids had not been awakened by the phone, so she decided to let them sleep. She could travel more quickly solo. By the time she got to the hospital the operation was underway. She waited only a short time before a doctor she had never seen before came out of the operating room. There was a little blood on his scrubs, which she did her best to ignore. One just never knows if that is a sign of life, or a sign of death.

"Kim? Are you Kim, Lieutenant Colonel Gadson's wife?" asked Dr. Gajewski.

"Yes."

"Good. Well your husband is doing fine. Fairly stable. But we had to take the left leg."

"You removed it," Kim confirmed.

"Yes. There was nothing else we could do. That artery, I presume you've seen X-rays?"

Kim nodded.

"That artery that was repaired overseas gave way and he was near to bleeding to death. The only way to stop the problem this time was to go in above the injury and just remove it."

It all actually seemed logical to her. She *had* seen the pictures. They had talked about the possibilities with Dr. Pasquina. In fact, she had almost assumed that her husband would become a single-leg amputee. No one had counseled her in any direction. Everyone wanted it to be up to Greg and his family. She guessed instead it had been up to God.

"He's strong—he's an athlete," Dr. Gajewski continued. He'd played football for Harvard himself. "He'll come out of this okay." Kim nodded again, this time in agreement.

"He will," she told the doctor. She silently thanked the Lord for saving her husband's life, if not limb. She was sure He had a plan.

"When can I see him?"

"He's still out cold. We'll come and get you when he wakes up. It'll be a bit of a shock for him, so. . . ."

"Not as big as you might think, Doctor. I think he was getting ready for this. And thank you. Thank you so much for coming out."

The loss of the limb had seemed inevitable for a week now, what with the constant infection and fever. Her husband had become a statistic of Operation Iraqi Freedom: he was one of thousands of men and women who'd lost limbs to the cunning war-fighting ability of the enemy. She had seen other amputees at Walter Reed undergoing extensive rehabilitation. It seemed grueling, learning to walk on metal poles and hinges, knowing that for the rest of your life you will be dependent on some sort of mechanical device to get from one place to another, even to stand. She murmured a quick prayer, then searched in her bag for her phone. She needed to brief the kids.

Back in the ICU waiting room, she had an odd sensation of starting over. But she was more hopeful this time. She waited, again, for Greg to come to. She called the apartment at the Mologne House. Gabby answered.

"Mom, where are you?"

"I'm over at the hospital. Your dad had an emergency surgery." She paused. "The main artery in his left leg collapsed and . . ." She took a breath. "They had to remove it."

"His whole leg?"

"Yes. Or he would have bled to death."

Gabby was silent for a moment. "So, he's okay though? Should I come over there?"

"The doctor says he's going to be fine. He's still asleep, but we'll all plan to be here after he wakes up. They're going to be able to fit him with a prosthetic leg, so he'll be able to walk, eventually." Kim hung up the phone, wondering for a moment if she should go be with the kids.

Gabby hung up the phone and, taking a breath to calm the fear rising in her own chest, carefully shared the news with her brother. Her mom had been so calm. She tried to be the same but she was having a hard time steadying herself. What about their camping trips? Could her dad still come to her soccer games? Could he still manage their home? Her dad was now a *disabled* person. What did that mean? Their lives were going to be so different. They already were. She missed her friends. She and Jaelen had become joined at the hip and they were getting on each other's nerves. She wanted to go home.

. . .

"What happened?" Greg asked Kim when he began to come out of the anesthesia.

"You had to have an emergency surgery."

"What was the emergency?" he asked groggily.

Kim was not sure how much to tell him. But she also assumed a person could not go very long without noticing their own leg was missing.

"They took your leg, Greg. It's gone."

"No, it's still there," Greg argued. He moved his left hip, as if to prove it.

"That's normal," the nurse who was writing something on the erasable board with a quick dry pen, butted in. "People who lose limbs often have the sensation that it's still there. It's like the rest of the body hasn't been informed."

Greg went quiet. It was a lot to take in. And still, it was so hard to simply stay awake.

"Just don't get up and try walking around here in the middle of the night, like the guy down the hall." the nurse dead-panned. "Made for quite a clatter," she called back over her shoulder as she moved along to the next room.

Greg fell back into a restless sleep, awakening only to a vague memory of being wheeled into an elevator on his way to the OR earlier that day. Lying on the transport bed, he had at first sensed a presence, then the physical sensation of someone taking his hands and holding them firmly. On his right he saw his father, Willie, smiling, nodding reassurance. On his left was Brigadier General Rodney Anderson, his longtime military mentor, lifting him above the confusion, the dread of impending loss. Both General Anderson and Willie Gadson stood over Greg for a moment, then disappeared into a sweet dusky night. He rested more quietly then, as Dr. Gajewski and his team did their work.

Meantime, Kim called Patricia and Willie, who were actually at home in Chesapeake, Virginia., and her own parents. Then she called Ottawa, so Chuck could update the online journal.

Status 18 May, 2007

Not good news on Greg's left leg. It started bleeding more than they could control and they had to amputate it earlier this morning. Just above the left knee from what I understand.

Hopefully his right leg will be able to recover better. . . .

Greg did not fully awaken again until the next morning, when he felt that similar discomfort, now in his right leg. A surge of panic clenched his gut. It was a nasty bit of déjà vu.

Within minutes, the same doctor who operated the day before appeared in the ICU. The VAC on the right leg was filled with blood. Dr. Gajewski looked at the fresh amputee.

"We'll see what we can do to keep this one, Colonel," he said.

"Don't try too hard, doc," Greg responded, before once again, the anesthesia took hold.

Everyone knew the surgeries were taking a mental and physical toll. The emergency procedures were not the only ones he had endured. There were the "washes," the scouring of the wounds. Infection was the show-stopper in most catastrophic injury cases. An out-of-control infection meant certain amputation, even death. Greg knew too, even in the fog of his occasional delirium, the more operations it took to save the leg and get it working again, the longer it would be before he was out of there. He had heard of guys who spent more than a year in rehab at Walter Reed. It had been just 11 days since the explosion in Baghdad. And he was already itching to get out of there. If he had to leave another limb on his way out the door, so be it.

The phone was becoming more of a reliable alarm clock than a means to communicate. At 5 a.m. again, Saturday, it awakened her.

"Mrs. Gadson?"

"Yes?"

"Lieutenant Colonel Gadson is on his way to the operating room. The doctor says to tell you the artery behind his knee on his right leg has collapsed."

"The *right* one?" *How could this be happening again?*

"Yes, ma'am."

Kim bolted into instant replay, only this time when she got to the hospital, she was directed to the OR waiting room. If she had to wait anywhere, this would be her choice. The recliners were awesome. She selected the same one she had in the past—the one in the corner where she wouldn't be bothered by passers-by or families of patients having knee replacement surgery. She settled in for another wait. She tried not to watch the clock, but as a half an hour grew to an hour, then another, it became apparent this surgery was not like the last. Whatever it was, it must be more complicated. If things had turned bad, someone would have . . .

A man was talking to her. She drew into her focus a tall—very tall—blond man. He was pale and spoke with a slight brogue.

She shook her head, trying to clear her mind. "I'm sorry, I was sort of drifting off. What were you saying?" she asked him.

"I'm Mike Corcoran. I'm a prosthetist here at Walter Reed." *A prosthetist. Already?*

"Mrs. Gadson, I just wanted to introduce myself. I got word from Mark House." Kim recognized the name but was not sure of the connection. There had been so many people calling.

"He's a classmate of yours and your husband's from West Point."

"Oh, right, oh good!" she remembered. *How in the heck?*

"House is an old friend of another prosthetist here and, well I just wanted to say he'd called and I will do my best with your husband."

"Your best. Well, thank you," Kim said, a little bewildered.

"We're here, and we'll get it right," said Mike. "We'll get him walking." *Walking.*

"I'm not sure if he's—he's in surgery now. I don't know, you know, if . . ."

"When you're ready Mrs. Gadson, when you're both ready. Of course, we'll see how it goes in there now, then we'll begin to make a plan."

"He's going to want a plan right away."

"I've heard that about him." Mike smiled. He was looking forward to working with his new charge.

She watched the Irishman walk out of the waiting room. Who *didn't* know her husband? Or know someone who knows her husband? It was difficult to catalogue who was who and through what connection they knew him or had heard about him. It was not just teammates calling. West Point football players from back in the 1960s were phoning in their concerns. Former mentors who had become general officers were calling from theaters all over the world, requesting information on Greg's condition. Each day the Pentagon sent a soldier by Greg's room, for a face-to-face check-in. His peers were all now colonels or lieutenant colonels and former subordinates were often now non-commissioned officers or command sergeant majors. But no matter the rank of the caller, the hospital could not release any information without her approval. The operator at Walter Reed was being overrun. Twenty years of popularity was funneling into one very long week at an Army hospital, where the recipient was often nearly comatose. He would have loved hearing from all these people himself. As it was, designated recipients were told to keep to a script, releasing only his exact condition, and keeping quiet about his mental status. No one needed to know about the crazy talk.

One former West Point football player's call did funnel through to Kim as she sat in "her" chair.

"Hello, Mrs. Gadson. This is Ray Odierno."

Kim nearly dropped her phone. Odierno was a three-star general. He was also the commander of Multi-National Corps–Iraq (MNC-I). His was as close to a household name as Petraeus. Odierno would later become chief of staff of the Army.

"General, hello."

"How is Colonel Gadson doing?"

"He's hanging in there, sir. He's having a lot of surgeries, trying to keep the infection down." She felt like she was outside her body listening in to her own conversation with the general who was pretty much running the war.

"Well, my wife and I know about that. Our son, Tony—he's recovering now—but he lost his arm back in 2004. It was a rocket propelled grenade that struck their vehicle here in Iraq."

"Yes, General, I'm sorry. So, you understand . . . "

"Kim, we spent a lot of time there at Walter Reed with him. Tremendous people there. It was hell on everyone watching him go through those washouts, though. It was like a fresh step back in his recovery every time. Just really so painful, and all you can do is support. You feel a little helpless. I can empathize."

Kim had so far managed to keep her emotions in check while talking to the brass. But not today. There was something about his demeanor, his reassuring tone in the midst of so much chaos, and his candor. His call humbled her to her core. Despite the distance in rank and geography, she felt he was the only person in the world who understood. The impermeable wall she had been holding up for the past week, all at once, seemed to crumble. Crushed under its unmanageable weight, she involuntarily let out a sob. *Why now? Why when I'm talking to this general?*

Kim tried with brutal self-discipline to finish the conversation as gracefully as possible, and made a note to send the general a letter later. She needed to thank him for the call. And although no one else would have expected it, being a West Point graduate herself, she felt she needed to somehow explain her tears.

The sight of the vascular surgeon walking into the waiting room yanked Kim back to the present. She remembered him from briefings the week before but could not lock in on his name. She never knew whether to wave these guys down or pretend they did not exist. Who knows if they are looking for her? His eyes panned the room then rested on Kim.

"Oh, Mrs. Gadson, there you are."

"Hello, Doctor." He seemed in good spirits.

"We were able to save the leg this time." She felt some relief. Losing two legs in two days would have been too much of a shock.

"What happened, was that artery that was repaired in Baghdad? It gave way. It's the artery that runs behind the knee. It couldn't be repaired, but there's enough flesh, you know, the meaty part of the leg, there was enough there to allow us to replace the damaged artery with one that can handle blood flow." *Replace it?*

"We took a vein from his left arm and bypassed the damaged part."

Criminy.

"So now his arm?"

"He doesn't really need that vein in his arm."

She wondered why the Lord put it there, then. And if anyone asked her, she might have objected to taking a perfectly good body part and sticking it in an area of known chaos and infection.

"It will hold, for now," the doctor said. *For now.*

"Will you be here at the hospital for the rest of the day?" *Because who knows how long "for now" is.*

"Oh, no, I'm on my way out. My wife has plans for me and a utility shelf that needs hanging at home." It was the weekend, after all, family day for many. Her too. She needed to call the kids. Again.

"Thank you, Doctor. I'll see you Monday, then?"

"Yes, of course, Mrs. Gadson. We'll see you tomorrow. He'll pull through this just fine."

Kim pushed herself as far back as she could into the giant recliner. One leg is better than no legs, she guessed. And he had survived. Again. For the second time in as many days her husband had cheated death. But was it cheating, really? Seemed to her he had won, fair and square.

. . .

It was a few days later, back in a regular hospital room, when Greg began to process his most recent visits to the OR. He stared down at his lopsided lower half. Pretty damned weird, if you asked him. One day you are chatting up Sunnis and sipping tea. Two weeks later, you are laid up and down a leg. What is worse, the other one has become a bit of an anchor. So now, you are pondering whether or not to further dismantle yourself. From what he could gather, the artery bypass which saved his right leg was something he may not have voted for, if he had not been so busy nearly bleeding to death. Tomorrow he was scheduled for another washout. Despite those efforts to clean out the wounds, he continued to spike fevers, a sure sign invasive microbes were attacking with such voracity that even massive doses of antibiotics dripping into his bloodstream could not control them. They were slowing his recovery and, apparently, making him a little kooky. He needed to work through his options with his wife. But first, he had an odd question for her.

"Hey Kim," Greg asked, "Over the last couple of days, did Rodney visit?"

"No, why?"

"What about my dad? Was he here?"

"He's been in and out. What?"

"Oh, never mind. I just thought I saw them on my way to surgery."

"Probably a dream," she answered. "You're still on a lot of drugs. They do strange things to your head."

He knew it was not the drugs. It was the palpable presence of his family and friends lifting him up. But he did not argue. He needed to look ahead.

"These guys, these doctors—the surgeons—they're all about salvage.

I'm not sure it's the right thing," he told Kim. "If it gets to a point again, where it doesn't look good, tell them to take it off."

"It's too soon, Greg. No one knows yet. You might be able to save it. You don't want to jump to any conclusions. This is the rest of your life we're talking about."

"And I need to get on with it: my life."

"Let's just see how this one goes," Kim said. "Let them have another look. We'll pray. We'll ask for guidance."

Greg fingered the silver cross that hung around his neck. A chaplain, somewhere along the way, had bestowed it. Greg saw no reason to take it off. Ever.

Monday's surgery was attended by several specialists—nerve, ortho-pedics, and vascular. All of them reported to Greg that the arm artery was adjusting to life in his other limb well. But the patient was not convinced. And doctors, including his friend and former teammate Paul Pasquina, would not just *tell* him what to do. They all seemed to be dancing around the decision. It was frustrating.

The discussions were becoming like tribunals. Kim and Dr. Paul Pasquina sat in wide wooden chairs. Greg presided, propped on pillows, from his hospital bed.

Pasquina took the lead. "We're not ready to recommend that you have it taken off, Greg."

Greg understood, intellectually, it was not protocol to tell a patient what to do in this situation. The docs were there to do all they could to keep as many parts as they could, attached. He could see it was an emotional time for Paul. On one hand, Greg knew his was just another case like so many the doctor had seen. On the other, they had been teammates in a sport that made extreme demands on their physicality. He thought Paul perhaps wanted to help save some dimension, some aspect of that past. Paul wanted them to wait, to see where the medical world could take him. At the same time, he knew the doctor recognized he was suffering like a thoroughbred horse in the gate of a big race. It was time for the gun.

Kim tried to be gentle.

"Babe, if you *elect* to take that leg off, what happens to your health benefits? If doctors say it could have been saved, and you choose to take it off, what happens to our coverage?"

"I just don't think that's a concern, Kim."

"It's not. Your insurance will support." Pasquina confirmed.

"You need to take your time with this," Kim said.

"This has already taken enough time. They cleaned it out again today. I still have a fever. I can't get out of this bed. And I won't be able to while *that* leg is *this* sick." He gestured down at the bandaged limb as if it were already no longer a part of him.

Kim was not sure how to respond. It was not a conversation she could have planned for.

Pasquina went back to the facts. "The sciatic damage is something you need to consider. It's difficult to know if it will ever heal—whether you'll have any function in that leg."

"It's too soon to know, right?" asked Kim.

"Right. But that artery could blow again," Pasquina said.

"But doctors say it looks good," Kim countered.

"It does," agreed Pasquina. "It's working." But, he thought, he has almost died three, maybe four times. "There is the possibility—we have to consider—if that repair doesn't hold we may not get him back again."

"If that collapses, I could bleed to death," said Greg.

"Just like the last two times," answered the doctor.

"How many lives do you think I have, Paul?" Greg joked, then seriously asked, "How many more surgeries would it take before I could walk on this leg?"

"There's really no way to know. Some patients have as many as thirty or forty. Even after that, you may never be able to walk on that leg."

"So, I could be in here for months. And never even get the leg back, I mean, really get the leg back."

"That's possible. But some patients find it's easier to get around with one real leg and one prosthetic, rather than two."

"But the damage to this leg, it sounds like a fake leg would work better than this one ever will," Greg continued to argue. The word "prosthetic" was not yet an easy part of his vocabulary.

"Possibly." He paused.

"Probably," answered Pasquina.

He turned to Kim. "It's a sort of time bomb, as far as I can see. I can tell you—I know I will be better, faster if we just take this thing off."

Kim and Paul were silent.

"You talked with Gabby and Jaelen about this?" Greg asked Kim. He wanted to be sure it was a family decision.

"I did last night. They just want you to get healthy," Kim said. "You know they'll do anything for you."

Greg nodded. "Look, I need to get the uphill behind me."

Kim and Paul both felt the rope slipping out of their hands. They were losing the tug-of-war. And it was not that Greg was making a bad decision. It was just an extremely difficult one.

"We'll make it through this," said Greg, trying to pivot them to his side of the struggle. "We've made it this far, right?" Kim was ready to turn it over, to her husband, and to God.

"We'll do it your way, Greg."

Greg nodded. "Okay then. We're moving on. Let's get it on the books."

Pasquina leaned back, with some relief. At least they had a plan. As he made his way back to his office through the tunnel of white spackled walls and grey marble floors, he shook his head. The one who had the most to lose had become everyone else's source of comfort.

Status 22 May 2007 2200

Gentlemen,

Greg and Kim have made a very difficult decision today. After consulting the lead doctors, Greg has decided to have his right leg amputated above the knee. He is scheduled for surgery tomorrow—

Wednesday.

I spoke with Greg on the phone and he was excited about moving ahead and getting healthy. Greg has always faced adversity with a smile and let's get it done. He told me he could still run faster than me on his hands . . . I have no doubt about that.

VR,

Schretz

CHAPTER ELEVEN

"Most are motivated. Some you have to prod along.
Greg emerged as the most driven."
—Michael Corcoran, Prosthetist, WRAMC

Moving on came at a high price. And the view from Ward 57, the orthopedic wing at Walter Reed Army Medical Center, was already getting old. Ward 57 was where amputees and other war wounded landed, after being paroled from ICU. Most soldiers there were missing one body part or another and stood to also lose his or her mind. To Greg and a few others, it became known as "the Land of the Misfit Toys," a reference to the Island of Misfit Toys in the holiday classic "Rudolph the Red-Nosed Reindeer." Greg fancied himself something like the blue choo-choo train, made with square wheels on its caboose.

The move from the ICU to the ward was not without incident. Nothing was, anymore. After about 24 hours in his new quarters, he began spiking fevers as high as 104 degrees, only to discover that a PICC (peripherally inserted central catheter) line had been left inserted in his chest. PICC lines are used to give doctors and nurses better access when delivering medicine and other fluids. Now it had delivered a raging infection, which temporarily delayed other necessary treatments. Removal of the line and a few days of heavy antibiotics cleared it. But removal of the line also meant he was no longer receiving meds—the narcotic Dilaudid, specifically—intravenously. It was only then he realized his body had become addicted. For about 24 hours he felt flu-ish, but worse, he was shaking and agitated, sweating, then damp and cold. He felt like a street-drug addict on the wacky television series "Cops." Luckily, his withdrawal only lasted about 24 hours but he swore he would never touch the drug again.

The temporary drug dependence only fueled his determination to leave the hospital. And he knew any attempt to keep that right leg would have meant more downtime. Greg was sure he had made the right decision in casting it off. He was absolutely positive, until he looked straight down. His glance reached the end of his body much more quickly than it used to. His former 5-foot-11-inch frame once filled the bed, his toes resting at its foot. Now his stumps stopped about three-quarters of the way down the mattress, each looking like a baby mummy. The sheets and blanket stayed neatly tucked at the bottom corners, where his size 12 feet once would once have kicked them loose.

"I'm half of me," he thought. He wondered, again, if he was dreaming. "Nightmare-ing." But looking out his window as the scattered oaks cast their long, steamy July shadows across the landscaped lawn, it all seemed too real. Kim, the doctors and hospital staff were all flesh and blood. If it was a dream it would have been a *very* long night. The only thing that seemed highly improbable was the void at the end of his thighs. He rubbed his hands over the scars at the ends of his stumps. They were a little sore, and thinner than they had once been. He had always had remarkably thick quads. Someone told him when they had first brought him into the medical tent in Baghdad, that the doctor, Dr. Brad Woods, had commented, "Man, thick legs!" Al Beekley, another West Point doc, had commented, too, someone told him. Those legs had pushed him through many a defensive play for the Black Knights. He wondered how far he could push through the rest of his life without them. Once a source of strength, they were now sapping his emotional energy.

He had lost a lot of body weight over the last week or two, fighting fevers and infections. He reached up to his face with his left hand. The stubble from not shaving regularly felt soft in the hollows of his cheeks. His right arm was still nearly useless. The upper part had been broken along with the elbow, something no one even realized at first. Three 130 mm shells of explosives do not set you down gently. His hand was swollen and parts of it were numb. It was Stacy Schretzman who had figured out something was wrong with his arm. She and Chuck were visiting—trying to be supportive—on the day of the scheduled amputation. Everyone stood around the bed, staring, words hanging in the air like wasps looking for a landing zone.

Stacy's gaze fell to his elbow.

"Hey, I think there's something wrong with his arm," she announced as if the guy attached to it could not hear.

A nurse who was prepping him looked up. "That's just the IV, he has to have . . ."

"No, look, how it's bent funny."

"It is swollen," the nurse noted. Then sometime between having one leg and none, there was an X-ray taken, showing the break. He guessed that when there is a four-alarm fire burning about your legs it's easy to overlook a broken arm. But in a lot of ways, losing arm function was potentially even more devastating than losing both legs. Now more than ever, he would need his arm as a tripod, to balance one of his favorite windows on the world.

It was not that he kept it a secret, but second to his gun, his camera was his most guarded piece of equipment in the field. He'd used his high school graduation gift money to order his first camera, a Nikon FG, 35mm, from B&H, through the mail. He loved playing the role of observer, taking in, and preserving life in its most candid moments. The lens could see inside people. It could tell their stories. More than people, he loved landscapes. God's art. As technology evolved he could be instantly digitally gratified.

The arm bone break was the sort that could not be put in a cast, so surgeons had to implant a plate and some screws to keep it in place to heal properly. The operation seemed to go smoothly until he tried to move his wrist. At first everyone passed it off as residual numbness, but after a few days it became apparent that somehow the insertion of a steel plate had damaged his radial nerve. His right arm and hand were nearly useless. Not only could he no longer walk or stand, he couldn't get a fork to his mouth, a brush to his teeth or wrap that arm around his backside to wipe himself. He had been left with one functional limb—his left arm. Greg was right-handed.

Now it was unclear how much function he would get back. He would probably be able to take basic shots with a lighter camera, but could he lift his heavier DSLR camera? Could he steady his shot? Could he even move to get a certain angle, capture the lights and shadows on his wife's face? He shook his head like a dog flapping his ears. Why was he even thinking of this right now? He was a man in his 40s, his prime. He had been strapping, muscled, handsome even. He had been a force, a powerful one, for his unit and his family. His strength was in making things happen. Now his whole badass persona was dissolving into a bedpan. He wondered what he looked like to other people. To his kids. To women. He used to turn heads in admiration. Now people would look away in sorrow, pity. He had taken on an entirely different shape, from head to: *stump*.

He could not imagine what Kim and the kids were truly thinking. Not what Kim had signed up for, specifically. Oh, sure, she had signed up for Army life, but who ever really thinks they are going to wind up with an invalid spouse? Or dad? He had not been much with a lacrosse stick before he was wounded, but now there would be no hope in training with Jaelen, who'd recently taken up the field sport. And Gabby—what if she got married? *Who would walk her down the aisle?*

In the military, waypoints were guides on a map which would lead you in or out of a location like a rendezvous point. They were used to execute missions or to simply provide direction. For the first time in his adult life he was not sure of the way ahead. There were no waypoints. Direction was sure something he could use right now.

From his room in Ward 57, Greg could watch the shadows on the lawn disappear into darkness. Greg was not certain if his dinner tray had come and gone—he did not eat. It was hard for him to stay awake for long. One minute he would be talking to a nurse or Kim or the kids, then the narcolepsy would kick in and the next minute he was waking up, alone and confused. Then reality would slam into his consciousness—where he was, who was there, what the hell had happened. Shadowy ghosts from Baghdad hovered. He wished they would explain a thing or two. Like, why had he lived? Why had he survived, just to be dropped into what was becoming more like hell than he'd anticipated? Why was he being punished? He had been over there trying to help, trying to do some good in that country. He could not even help himself now. Maybe it would be best if he died right now, be done with it. Give everyone a clean slate, a fresh start. The despair caught in his throat, the panic choking him. There was no escaping this reality, these tortured years that lay ahead.

On this night, the blackness settled over him, the very hue of doom. Greg's stomach clenched. He saw a jagged mountain path ahead careening skyward, incredibly, insurmountably. He could not climb that sort of incline. He imagined crawling, dragging his wounded limbs uphill, the chopped ends scraping against rocks and gravel. His chest began to heave under the sheets and blankets. He gasped loudly, shocking himself, arching backwards, then crunching forward. His face felt slimy and wet. He could hardly breathe for the sorrow pressing the air from his body. His torso tightened, again and again, tighter, then softer as he searched for air. The room darkened, then was lighter. He saw Kim's creased face, and ordered her to retreat. No one could see him like this. No one could know that he died, not of wounds but of suffocating self-pity. He would never shame his family with pills. He would will himself dead. He tried to stop breathing. But involuntary sobs pounded oxygen in and out of his lungs. He could not stop. But he did not care. For hours and then days, he existed only to cry for what was lost and past and given.

His subconscious dragged him deep into a tunnel now, black as his mother's Bible. He searched for a way out, flailing, arms still pinned back, then spiraling forward. Then, for an instant he thought he could make out a white pin prick, a miniscule opening ahead. His arms broke free and swam through the thick air, tearing at the light, stretching the hole bigger. It grew brighter, so bright he could barely keep his eyes open. The blinding whiteness engulfed him in warmth, then became dimmer, milky, even soothing. Light bathed him in salvation. He listened for the Lord's words, his guidance. Perhaps the love of the Lord, his family and everyone he had touched through his life could repair him, make his soul whole. The room cooled, the bright light fading to the earth's dawn. He slept.

It was probably midafternoon when he awakened, wracked, and parched. His tongue grazed the crust on his lower lip. He felt like he had vomited a monster. Exhaustion cupped his body where the sorrow had left it limp.

Greg blinked, remembering the visions clearly. First, back in the ICU: The blasted visit from the devil. And how the devil had worked his soul. He knew now the Lord had been drawing back the curtain on hell because he, a mere man, had questioned Him. He had doubted the path ahead. But God himself had presented an epiphany. He had handed him hope. Greg knew now that he was to put his trust in the Lord. God would provide the waypoints.

He looked around the sterile room. The devil had left no evidence. Damn, he was hungry. And he was mad. He called Chuck in Canada. He needed a positive, a throwback to their glorious comeback.

"You know, when we were playing football, it was like, life or death. It seemed like we were fighting for our lives," Greg told Chuck.

"It was, man. Michie Stadium was like a laboratory for leadership," said Chuck.

"It got us ready for deployments."

"Got us ready for life."

"Yeah, like now," said Greg. "Remember sophomore year?"

"When you got cut."

"We had that great freshman year," Greg recited the history they had both invoked through their careers. "I'm first string, and two seniors were graduating. We both thought I was a shoo-in to keep that defensive line position until we graduated, and you were ready, right behind me."

"Yeah," Chuck joined the play-by-play. "You were already starting—how many?"

"Five!" Greg held five fingers up in the air. "Five games I started. And we both get called into coach's office."

"Oh my God. Oh my God, yeah. Lou Dainty."

"Coach says Lou Dainty is going to start!"

"We both got thrown out," Chuck half laughed. A bitter memory, but long ago. "We were mad."

"I was devastated!" Greg was yelling now, pushing to the story's new crescendo.

"You were . . . " Chuck paused. He sensed a different ending.

"Remember what we learned? How we came back?"

"Oh my God, yeah." Chuck heard a parable coming.

"I wasn't performing. I wasn't meeting their expectations, their standards. My academics were suffering. I took too many classes: calculus, economics, chemistry, physics and Arabic."

"You got cocky."

"Failed calculus."

"But you turned it around, Greg, you got it together."

"I did, Chuck. We did. We studied and worked out like crazy and I got that position back."

"Oh, man, oh my God, we both worked like crazy, man. We were *insane*."

"Maniacal." They both chuckled. Chuck waited.

"Well, it's like that now. I'm mad. I need to fix this. I need to get my life back."

"You're gonna do it, man," Chuck said. "You're gonna get that position. You're gonna start. We're all here. Your whole team—me, Stace, Kim, the kids and West Point—the brotherhood. You're gonna kill it, Greg."

• • •

Kim slid back into the yellow vinyl chair by the side of the bed. It was starting to take the shape of her behind, she joked to herself. Finally, her husband was resting, mostly peacefully. The restless jerking, endless night sweats, fevered mumblings had taken a toll on both of them. He had been questioning everything from his survival, to his wounds, to what lay ahead. Difficult as it was to press on, she knew the importance of letting Greg cope with his grief in whatever way he could. There was little she could do to help, so she focused on keeping herself emotionally stable, weighing the impact of her words and actions on the kids. But now she thought he seemed ready to talk a little. She leaned forward, sliding on the vinyl cushion as he stirred and opened his eyes.

"You know, if God brings you to it, He'll bring you through it," she said to Greg.

"He will, I know that now." He was pensive, thinking about devil and the light. "God is at work, for sure, and I'm the one being saved."

Life on Ward 57 seemed smoother after that. Greg had a certain grace about him. He had been through Hell—his own and the devil's—and emerged free of hate, free of encumbrance. If the person who had laid the bomb that took his legs stood before him, Greg knew he would lay down his own weapon in forgiveness. The waypoints were becoming clearer. He would recover his body as well as his soul.

. . .

Mike Corcoran, the tall, blond, pale brogue-talking prosthetist, walked into his room on Ward 57 and held out his hand. "I'm a physical therapist here at the hospital. We're going to get you walking." Greg shook it, tentatively, with his good arm, his only fully deployable appendage. He eyed the Irishman skeptically, then glanced at Paul Pasquina, who had also stepped into his room.

Corcoran was no stranger to challenge. He and his partner, Mark McVicker, had co-founded a prosthetics company called Medical Center Orthotics and Prosthetics. He was passionate about getting wounded military personnel back on their feet. His company, MCOP, was contracted with Walter Reed, giving Corcoran access to the hundreds of patients this war was creating. Each case presented different challenges. He and the therapists at Walter Reed were pushing the prosthetics industry to create new products and use them creatively. Mike knew many of the wounded were former athletes. And he relished working with them. Mike had been a standout athlete himself. Born in Ireland, he immigrated to the U.S. and became a competitive kayak slalom racer. He participated in the 1992 and 1996 Olympics. He was driven to be the best at whatever he took on. Mike Corcoran and Greg Gadson were either perfectly matched or would challenge one another to the death.

"Walking? Is this some sort of *joke*?" Greg looked sideways at Kim, who slid back into her vinyl dent, talking with the kids on the phone. She abruptly hung up. Mike looked at Dr. Pasquina, whom he'd hijacked in the elevator moments before. The therapist nodded slightly. This was not Mike's first chilly reception. While he had been looking forward to meeting his new patient, he knew he might be in for a battle. Not every potential client rolled out the red carpet. Some would rather pull the floor out from under him. His patients, by and large, had been leading fast lives, protecting their teammates as well as their country. Most had gone from sixty to zero, in less than a minute, far away from their loved ones. And landed here, in this sterile box, presented with a whole new set of circumstances and a whole lot less body armor. Icy receptions were to be expected.

The lieutenant colonel was giving him that "WTF" look right now. He could see it was not fear. Gadson had been through far too much to be afraid. It was more like bewilderment. Mike could appreciate that. He looked at Kim.

"We met back, uh, while your husband was in surgery one morning?" Kim's face went from confused to slightly panicked. She was drawing a blank and hated to be rude. The brogue seemed familiar.

"Oh!" Kim recalled. "Yes, I'm so sorry, right, it's just that there are so many people."

Mike reassured her. "So much going on, I know."

She explained to Greg. "He came by while Gajewski was operating—trying to save your right leg."

"You know I decided to have the leg taken off. It seemed like it was going to hold me back," Greg told Mike.

"We really discussed everything—it was absolutely Greg's decision," added Pasquina.

"I heard that about you," Mike said to Gadson.

"What's that?"

"You don't like to waste time."

"Well, you got that right," Greg said, his gaze, once again, resting at the foot of the bed.

"We won't then. We'll get started," Mike said to everyone. Mike and Paul left the room.

Kim looked hopefully at Greg. She knew already the decision to take off that right leg had been a positive move. Despite the emotional trauma, she could see his overall health was better. The fevers had already dramatically reduced. He was gaining strength. She thought he had come through the worst of the grieving, but at the moment was looking uncertain, like he might be headed into an emotional backslide. She wanted to keep the positive momentum going, but did not want to push too hard.

"They're really on your side, Greg, you can tell they're all over this. I think they're even kind of excited to work with you."

Greg sighed and looked down. His arm and hand were still pretty messed up from the radial nerve damage. It would take another surgery to possibly release the nerve. He could not even roll himself over at the moment. Even the thought of being vertical was dizzying. But then again, at one time, the thought of getting pummeled by 300-pound linemen on a football field seemed equally insurmountable. Then, his coaches had provided the waypoints. Maybe this Corcoran guy could do the same. He looked at his wife, always the sweet sedative, always the adjuster. When he was going 100 miles per hour, she would hold steady at 10, somehow driving from the back seat. She would help to steady him along the journey.

"Fuck it," he blurted.

"What?" Kim startled. Greg rarely cursed.

"*Fuck it.*"

His nose creased heavily between his eyes, his lips thinned.

"Greg..."

"I'm *doing* this."

"You're doing..."

"This. This whole thing. The damned wheelchair, the fake legs, the whole thing, Kim. I wanted to quit. I really did. But that wasn't me. I can't. Damn. I can't even quit right!" He half-laughed. "It's going to be hard. It's going to take a lot from you and the kids. But what else do we have? What else can we do?"

"Of course, you can't quit" she said, with a stab of relief. "You're you."

. . .

Back at his desk, Mike Corcoran leaned over the paperwork he had started on LTC Gadson.

"Double AK," he wrote. Double, "Above the Knee" amputee. It used to be a prosthetist would see one, maybe two double AKs in a career. The wars in Iraq and Afghanistan had changed all that. Over the last few years, he had probably treated 40 to 50 amputees, seeing them through rehabilitation, all the hardware adjustments, socket changes, and alignments it took to keep them moving forward.

There were, thankfully, more single AKs than double. Those cases were easier. One functional leg made all the difference in recovery. Having a "good" leg gave the patient something to lean on that was familiar and trustworthy. If he or she lost control of or even confidence in the awkward prosthetic leg, the patient could bounce for a bit on the real one. Double AKs do not have anywhere to go but where gravity leads them.

The easiest to work with—from a physical perspective—were the BKs or "Below the Knee" amputees. And if a patient was a single BK, well, that was a comparative piece of cake. Some single BKs, he would often say, just "stubbed their toe" in combat because compared to what a double AK had to go through those guys barely needed a band aid. "Too easy," some of his single BK patients would say.

On the other end of the spectrum, he had seen patients missing both legs, one of them all the way to the hip—just absolutely nothing remaining to catch any leverage. And once an injury goes that high, internal abdominal organs begin to shift around and it can get to be a pretty slippery situation.

Mike flipped through Gadson's medical file. The lieutenant colonel had gone through a lot of blood downrange. The docs had managed to sew him together well enough to see him through transport without incident. Belligerent, if not slightly violent coming off sedatives, which was common for trauma patients. But that had mostly passed.

Paul had filled Mike in on Gadson's less recent history. Football player. West Point. Strong. Mission-oriented. Beloved by his soldiers. Married nearly twenty years, kids in their teens. *Mature*. His quick decision on removing that second leg was gutsy and probably smart. Mission-oriented, alright. Mike felt privileged, excited even, to be handed such a perfect candidate for what he had in mind. Being something of an orthopedic entrepreneur, he believed in pushing his patients and technologies to their limits. Some patients reached that limit quickly. But he had a sense that Gadson could be pushed—would want to be pushed. And he already liked the guy, despite his snippy reception. Mike was developing a new bag of tricks, and Gadson just might be the guy to play with them.

He had other challenge-friendly patients who might like to engage in his wizardry. Josh Bleill was also a double AK. He was younger, less mature than Gadson. At first Corcoran was not sure about Bleill, who had been moody and inconsistent. He was a Marine—a lance corporal who had joined the military because he wanted to serve his country, and he came from a family of Marines. Bleill was only in Iraq for two weeks when his Humvee was hit by an IED. Two of his comrades died in the explosion. In addition to losing both legs immediately, his pelvis was fractured. So was his jaw. His good friend Tim Lang, who was also in the vehicle, lost part of a leg. Josh and Tim had made the flight from Landstuhl to Andrews Air Force Base together, then were hall-mates in Walter Reed's Ward 57. Despite Lang's support, Bleill had been morose and reticent at first. But his tenacity built along with this strength, his character emboldened by his accomplishments, and he emerged as a star in the MATC. Bleill learned to handle interviews with media at Walter Reed with the same easy air he had with his fellow Marines. He was a great example of "can-do" and the hospital loved putting him out there.

Gadson would be the newcomer, Mike thought. Where age might have been a medical factor against him, Mike figured the wiser warrior in him would make it even. He and Josh might be well-matched for the kind of competition that pushed each man to heal.

CHAPTER TWELVE

*"Dark days, you have to let them have that day. And the next day
might not be so great either. It's a long process."*
—Bob Bahr, Physical Therapist, WRAMC

The hum of hard rubber rolling on linoleum was nearly constant outside
Greg's room on Ward 57. Everything in the hospital, it seemed, moved on a
wheeled cart. He waited for the sound to fade, but instead it grew louder,
until it burst through his door, skimming each side of the doorframe with
oversized wheels. Bob Bahr, his new physical therapist, was hanging on
the handles, cornering the contraption toward his bed. It was a cart, all
right. A cart for his butt. Greg stared, feeling the first tingle of this new
love-hate relationship. The chair would mean freedom, from this bed, this
room, this ward and maybe even from this hospital. But he may be tied to
the chair itself, dependent on it, possibly for the rest of his life. Steel, a little
black leather, and a cushion—nothing he would ever really cozy up to. For
some reason he thought about his high school ride—the 1973 Camaro Rally
Sport. Must be the chrome. Once again, he would be a lowrider.

"Now it's going to be a little awkward getting in at first," said Bob, radi-
ating a perfunctory calm. Bob had been through this a bunch of times. He
had no doubt he could get Greg to his feet and he was pretty sure he would
do it without too much drama. Greg almost laughed. "A *little* awkward,"
he challenged.

"You'll need to do some scooching, probably. It won't be as hard as it looks," said Bob with such a matter-of-fact attitude it was almost flippant. Greg was not sure, as a lieutenant colonel in the U.S. Army, that he had ever been ordered to *scooch*.

But Bob's casual attitude lowered the hurdle of intimidation. As it had helped when days earlier Bob first made him lift his head from the pillow, then sit up in the bed for a single minute, then later, for an hour. On those first visits, Bob "cheated" by raising the back of the bed to help him lean forward. It was not long before he could sit on the edge of the bed with no support at all. Small steps physically. Giant leaps emotionally. But this. Greg had known subconsciously this was coming. Still it seemed a capitulation into a new existence, a new state of being.

Staring down at the sterile cushion, getting his butt from the bed to the chair seemed about as likely as doing an aerial backflip. Actually, he thought the backflip might occur instantaneously—a collateral backflip.

"Have you ever gotten in a kayak?" Bob did not wait for an answer. "It's like that. What you need to do is slide your rear end to the edge of the bed and get sort of parallel with the seat. I've got the chair. And the brakes are on. It won't move."

Greg did as he was told. He had to trust the chair.

"Okay, now grab the left arm of the chair with your left arm. Lean out. Hold steady. Now slide toward it." It was an exercise in strength as well as trust. He landed slightly sideways, but solidly, in the chair. Just a little bit of "scooching" around and he was seated. Properly, he guessed. The stumps of his legs stuck out several inches over the edge.

"Is that comfortable enough?' Bob asked. "We have other cushions and we can make some adjustments."

"I'm okay," Greg said, taking in the sensation of being seated in something that felt mostly like a chair. Last time he had been seated, he was shotgun in a Humvee, looking out into a dark semi-urban desert. He blinked back the memory. *No looking back.*

He stared straight ahead as Bob pushed him down the ultraviolet white hallway. The walls blurred in his peripheral vision, the doorways zipping by like little portals into parallel universes. He was light-headed with this first sensation of being ambulatory. They turned into a small room used for low-level orthopedic rehabilitation. After the ordeal of climbing onto a therapy bench, Bob instructed him to lie on his back.

"Okay," the therapist said. "Let's do some sit-ups. Be careful of your neck, come up gently."

Gadson locked his hands behind his neck. That felt familiar.

"Sit-ups. I can do those," he figured out loud. Before the attack he could do a lot of them. What could be different? Sit-ups did not require legs.

Turned out, lying down and hoisting your shoulders anywhere higher than your belly button is considerably tougher when you have lost your anchors. His abdominal muscles clenched, then melted like washed up jellyfish.

"Three," Bob said. He had been gingerly holding Greg's stubs down on the mattress. Now he was scribbling on his chart. "Not bad."

"You're *kidding*. Three? I could do three sit-ups as a *toddler*! Look, I'm *sweating*." Greg was exasperated. How could he have lost so much of his core strength in such short time?

"It'll come back. Really. Try not to get frustrated. I have guys who can't even do one at first. You're an athlete—it'll come back," he said, still scribbling. Bob spoke like an old hand. It was not the sort of hopeful promises Greg sometimes heard from visitors or even a nurse. There was a certainty to his voice that gave Greg confidence. Greg figured Bob had worked on tougher cases and had seen them out the door, standing. It did not seem to occur to Bob that, given the proper amount of time and guidance, failure would have an opportunity.

Sit-ups were one thing, but the day-to-day matters Greg used to take for granted were now exhausting. Probably the most off-putting was the toilet. He found himself procrastinating for as long as his bladder and other parts would tolerate. It was not the exertion itself—the getting there and holding onto the rails. It was the emotional toll of something that had to be done several times a day, was not necessarily under his control and was so darned cumbersome. Add to that a daily diet of narcotics and hospital food and the process became much more central to his existence than he could ever have imagined. It was also something he was required to manage, before he would be permitted to leave Ward 57. Potty breaks, brushing his teeth and shaving were among the obstacles on his path toward the exit. And he had to do it all with only the use of his left arm.

Once in a while he felt himself slip back, emotionally. When the grueling physical nature of dragging himself toward his wheelchair or even *in* his wheelchair got to be too much, all he could see was the side of that mountain, that gravel road, his stumps dragging on the jagged rocks. *Maybe this is just going to be too hard.* But most times, the "fuck it" would come back. The "fuck it" and his faith. There were never going to be any answers to the torturous "why"s of the situation. Only his faith in God could bridge the gap between self-pity and success.

His faith seemed to strengthen along with his body. The days of making his way down the hallway to that small physical therapy room turned into weeks. Bob had been right. His core was getting stronger. He could do more sit-ups. And, despite the problems with his right arm and hand, he could roll the wheels of his own chair. He graduated to the bigger workout room, the occupational therapy area, where other wounded soldiers and Marines were getting their sweat on. Some were encouraging to watch. It seemed like they gained balance and speed daily. Others looked worn and hopeless. Kim was most often with him in the OT room. The kids sometimes hung out, making it feel more like a family effort. He was proud of the young adult Gabby was becoming, sometimes spending her morning helping him with his exercises before wandering the floor talking with other soldiers. She was poised, he thought, thanks to Kim's influence. Gabby would easily engage other patients, telling them about her dad's injuries and comparing his to others. One day she saw a wounded soldier playing pool in the recreation area and he listened as she just talked to him about the game. He seemed thankful to talk to someone new, about something else.

Jaelen noticed other patients, too, and their families—the unmistakable demand of the injuries—the constant caretaking and disruption. The weight of obligation crushed some families literally into pieces, spouses abandoning their partners who'd been mangled in war. Jaelen knew he was capable of making some pretty bad decisions of his own—misbehaving at school, bullying his sister. But his perch at Walter Reed was providing perspective. His sister was becoming less of a verbal punching bag and more his friend. His mom, an incredible role model of stoic strength. And his *dad* . . . it was still all so very raw . . . to have been so angry when he deployed and now, equally afraid of *not* having time with him. Sometimes his feelings of gratitude overwhelmed him. His family wasn't sagging under this weight. They were thriving.

Six weeks after Greg's second amputation, he wheeled himself into Walter Reed's prosthetics laboratory. His stumps had healed enough from the surgery that he could now tolerate being fitted for his first prosthetics, called "stubbies." Stubbies have no knee joint and they are short, keeping the patient close to the ground, decreasing the distance of inevitable falls. In the lab, he lay on a padded table while a tech made casts of each thigh, putting on a big, rubberized, condom-looking thing first, then wrapping each stump with pasty gauze. The goop had an industrial institutional smell and when he wiped some off his thigh it felt like oatmeal. Once it set a bit, the tech pulled off the cast and went to work filing rough edges and sanding the outside into a smoother finish. This would be the socket of the leg, where Greg's stumps would slide into his man-made extensions—where humanity would meet technology, like a finger on a trigger. It was interesting to see how much one leg's shape differed from the other. Had they always lacked perfect symmetry? The tech also took all sorts of measurements and entered them into a computer program.

. . .

"Am I confused, or are the feet on backwards?" Greg watched as Mike Corcoran leaned the stubbies against the wall of an ortho room, near where he had done those first sit-ups.

"You're not confused. The feet are attached facing behind you, so you don't fall backwards," he explained. "Your hip flexors are very tight from being seated or laying down for so long. You'll have a tendency to lean back on your heels."

"And what's to keep me from falling forward?"

"You." Mike held up two canes that looked a little like ski poles.

"Now if we've all done things right, these should slip on fairly comfortably," he said, holding up the carbon socket end of the prosthetics that the lab had fashioned from the casts.

"They seem short. You said I'd wind up being the same height I used to be," Greg said, frowning.

"You will. These are your starter legs. You're going to fall. So, we want to keep your center of gravity as close to the ground as possible while you learn to balance," Mike explained, while Greg pondered *falling*.

Mike wrestled the rubbery liner onto the end of Greg's stump, like he was putting a sock on a person with feet. Then he rolled the edges of the sleeve up Greg's thigh, almost like a garter. Or a condom, Greg supposed. Next came the socket of the actual prosthetic, which was attached to the metal rod of lower leg. Mike eased it over the sleeve until it stopped, marrying the dense stiffness to Greg's flesh.

A socket is a natural or artificial hollow into which something fits or in which something revolves. The original French meaning of the word socket is "plowshare"—the head of a spear, or the main cutting blade of a plow. A plowshare functions to cut the top layer of soil. It is the starting tool, the one that gives birth to more labor, the tool that allows a farmer to do his work, to make his way, his living—to provide for his family and possibly a community or even a country.

Greg looked down where the ends of the rods were capped with the goofy little duck feet. They looked like they were made for a child. They did not look like they could support an adult male.

"Are you sure these legs are mine?" Greg asked Mike. "I think these belong to the short dude down the hall."

Once assembled, Mike pulled Greg to his feet. His backwards feet. It was not as hard to balance as he thought. The backwards feet forced him to stand straight, leaning on canes. Mike waited while Greg reunited his mind with this lost sensation of standing. His lower back tightened. He worked to engage his abdominal muscles, all at once understanding the importance of all those core workouts.

"Ready to try a step?" Mike asked. "Just see if you can slide a leg forward."

Greg pushed one hip forward—grinding the metal and plastic across the floor. It sounded like Legos scraping linoleum. Then he slid the other. He paused and took in a deep breath. It was a step. Not a big one or a graceful one, but it was a step. The first he had taken since he stepped into the Humvee in Iraq. He figured face-planting into the floor tiles would have a better outcome than being propelled through the air by lethal explosives. Still, the exertion of lifting each stump enough to drag the webbed foot across the floor was tremendous. The gray of his Army T-shirt turned dark with moisture. But for the first time in nearly two months, he was vertical.

Daily workouts were most often held in a medium sized ortho room equipped with various cushioned tables and parallel bars. There were no windows. Florescent lights hummed overhead. The room was often crowded with mostly soldiers and Marines slowly, and sometimes pain-fully, pushing themselves through grueling exercises. Some were missing an arm or a leg. Others wore eye patches. Still others seemed to be pretty much in one piece from what could be seen from the outside.

If Greg was supposed to "bond" with the stubbies in the coming weeks, the relationship was not sticking. He did learn to put them on, then waddle across the floor. Mike soon turned the flat little feet forward, so he finally had toes. It was more of a morale booster than it was a sign of actual prog-ress. But he still felt like a dwarf, a character from Oz. Looking *up* into the medicine cabinet mirror gave him a new perspective on his nostrils but he was not sure this was useful. He was used to seeing the world from about 6 feet up. On the stubbies he could easily walk below his wife's outstretched arm, could lean into her armpit. Next, he imagined, his voice would gain octaves and his testicles would shrink.

The sensation most difficult to contend with was that when he walked or shuffled there was no part of his body that ever actually made physical contact with the floor. His peg legs did, but he could not feel it. He could hear them scrape the floor. He knew there was contact because his stump pressed into the socket, but his feet no longer had actual soles. Or souls. He liked the pun. Despite the diminutive length, the stubbies made him feel like he was on stilts. They seemed about as reliable as a spare tire. And he was not a person who was used to relying on anything that was not himself or part of his team. And these were not him. Nor were they teammates. The only way to lose them was to graduate to the next level of leg. So, despite his mild disdain, he worked hard. When he could out-walk the length of the OT room he would turn down the hallway, bobbing along a little further each time.

At first Bob walked behind him holding onto a large brown leather harness, which wrapped around his middle. It stabilized him slightly, but maybe more importantly when he started to tumble at least Bob was able to break his fall. After a while he could walk the whole hall without falling. But there was little he could do without sweating. Each time he put on the legs it was a workout. And then there were the drills on the parallel bars and with a walker. Sometimes Bob put a wobbly cushion, sort of like a Bosu exercise ball, in his wheelchair, which forced him to work his core muscles. Almost everything was designed to strengthen his core, so he could better propel his hips and thighs.

Falling sucked. Despite Bob's ability to anticipate a potential face plant, it seemed as if once he lost his balance and gravity took over there was no recovering. He felt like he fell in two stages. First he would start to lean precariously to one side or the other. Determined to catch himself, he would shift his hips the opposite way and lift his head, trying to throw his weight in the other direction. Sometimes he could stop the fall. Sometimes Bob could. Most of the time, he clattered down, stick-legs splayed awkwardly beneath him. If he had been a regular run-of-the-mill 42-year-old lieutenant colonel, getting up after a fall would be difficult enough. But the sticks slid around sloppily at the end of his stubs, which still seemed other-worldly. And he was essentially one-armed. So, realigning his head with his torso and hips with the plastic duck feet flat on the ground below him was next to impossible.

One day Greg was sitting on a table in the occupational therapy room, waiting for his daily workout when Mike sat down beside him, obviously frustrated.

"What's up?" Greg asked. It was not often that Mike seemed surly.

"That patient I've been working with today, kid's afraid of falling. Can't get anywhere with him 'cuz he won't move. He's got the physical ability. It's all mental, you know?"

"Yeah, I guess . . . " Greg trailed off as Mike went back to work on his literally petrified patient. Greg looked down at the flecked marble floor and all of its hardness, slowly realizing his own hesitancy. Truth was, he was frightened of falling too.

"Fear prevents progress," he overheard Mike telling the young amputee. Greg knew as much intellectually, but it took a minute to internalize the concept. His experience on the football field had taught him about the failures of hesitation. He also knew that soldiers on the battlefield who showed signs of fear were more likely to get hurt. They paused. They blinked. As a commander he worked with those soldiers, trying to get them to let go of their fear. Apparently, he needed to do the same with himself. His fear of falling was less about physical pain than it was about emotional distress. There was the getting up thing, but there was also the embarrassment. He had been a soldier for more than a decade. Public displays of imbalance were unacceptably undignified. It was humbling to ask for help, which he often needed to get back up, which only compounded the stress. It was all just another cumbersome thing. But he needed to jettison that fear. Train as you fight. Do not treat it like a rehearsal. It is always the real thing. As he always told his unit, reactions in battle all go back to training.

. . .

Greg passed the weeks watching other soldiers in the therapy center struggle at first, then move ahead. Mike Corcoran, his prosthetist, had been right. He and Josh Bleill developed a friendly competition on the track. Another double AK patient, Andrew Kinard, had also suffered a hip disarticulation, and had more rehab to do than Greg. He was a Marine—and a U.S. Naval Academy graduate, making the rivalry even more real. Working as a group made the long days of OT more bearable. It was good for Greg to have a team again, ragtag as it seemed. "The Land of the Misfit Toys" provided the camaraderie he was missing from his unit. *Pride. Poise. Team.* The football mantra was coming back to him. He did feel a lot of pride in his posse at Walter Reed. Doctors, therapists and all the staff there were deeply dedicated to their mission. And he could not forget the pride he was slowly reclaiming in himself, had in himself for all he had accomplished so far. Poise? Well, in the traditional sense of the word, that needed some work. But euphemistically, he was poised. He was ready. The team part was building. In addition to the love and support he had from Kim and the kids, there was Chuck front and center along with the entire West Point football family, which included Pasquina, right here at Walter Reed. Add to those, professionals like Mike Corcoran and Bob Bahr and he had a formidable lineup.

Greg was by now getting around pretty well on the stubbies, though he still held them in some contempt. It was not like he could throw them on and go get a cup of coffee. He did his PT in them, then went back to the chair. His stamina was growing but it still only took a lap up and down the OT wing to wear him out. And now there was this growing discomfort inside the sockets. He had heard about phantom pain—the sort of aching or stabbing pain the brain or spinal column sometimes generates in the wake of an amputation. But this seemed different. He put off telling anyone about it because he just did not want anything to be wrong. Any sort of problem might delay his progress—his final departure from Ward 57. But gradually the poking sensation grew worse—enough that it was wearing down his stamina.

"I think there's something in here," he said, handing a socket to Mike after what felt like his umpteenth physical therapy session. "It's pinching my stub." Mike ran his hand inside the lining.

"I don't feel anything," he said, checking the other one, just in case. "What does it feel like?"

"Sharp. Like there's a tack or a nail stuck in there."

Mike was afraid of this. It happened to most amputees.

"Well, what we'll do is take you down for a bone scan. I don't think it's the socket. You may be getting a little bone growth. We call it HO: heterotopic ossification."

"You mean my leg bone is growing back?"

"Not exactly. There is bone growing but it's a random protrusion—an abnormal growth—not unusual to see in an amputee."

"What do you—go in there and file it down or something?"

"Well, I hope not. Let's see what's there." Instances of HO seemed to Mike to be more and more common. It usually developed within six months of an amputation on the combat guys. Mike figured it was the body's response to the explosion—a protective mechanism. The docs would routinely radiate the residual limbs after they were amputated, but it did not seem to stop the irregular growth, which usually occurred in the area where the wound VAC—that suction device that had filled with blood and sent Greg to the operating room—had been attached.

It turned out that Greg had about an 8-inch long strip of HO which was growing from his femur in such a way that it was hard to get the socket liners to seal properly. The stubs of his legs were also shrinking, which is typical in the first few months following surgery. Between the HO and the natural reduction and reshaping of both legs, Greg underwent four or five socket changes. In the end the protrusion actually helped him out a little. It gave him the ability to nearly stand on his residual limbs. He could not get far on them, but it gave him the occasional lift he needed to get from the floor into his chair or some other elevation. Mike was also able to create custom liners, which saw Greg through to the next level of prosthetic advancement: C-Legs.

C-Legs, or computerized legs, had hydraulic knees, controlled by a microprocessor which reacted to a person's gait. Bendable knees would make walking more normal, closer to the "before." The legs were what therapists called "intuitive," but Greg saw them as another intimidating, uphill step—literally—toward the door. He never thought a knee joint would be such a carrot and at the same time an impending threat. But it was time to get rid of the trainers.

The Humvee that carried Lt. Col. Greg Gadson on the night he was wounded in 2007. The vehicle was targeted by an IED, or improvised explosive device, as the lieutenant colonel and his crew were returning from a memorial service for two soldiers who'd been killed just days earlier, also by an IED.

Photo by Brad Lee Bandy.

Greg Gadson wears his Army football uniform during his sophomore year. One of the physicians working on Gadson in a Baghdad hospital recognized him from their football days. "I used to scrimmage against him at West Point," recalled Dr. Al Beekley. "Guy could put a hurt on me."

Photo courtesy of USMA.

Greg Gadson wears number 98 at the far right. Gadson played outside linebacker for the U.S. Military Academy at West Point. Will Huff, #78, front row, would play an important role later on when he escorted Gadson on flight from Baghdad to Landstuhll, Germany. Behind Gadson stands Chuck Schretzman, back row. *Photo: USMA.*

Army teammates Chuck Schretzman and Greg Gadson. Gadson was a regular first-string player his sophomore year, with Schretzman right behind him. Though the two were competing for the same position, they became friends and pushed each other on and off the field. *Photo: USMA.*

Greg Gadson and his wife Kim, at the Saint Barbara's Ball in Fort Sill, Oklahoma. Kim Thomas had caught Gadson's eye, and he sought her help as an Arabic language tutor. The relationsip go off to a shaky start when during a study meeting he said, "I like you" in Arabic, and she fled the room.

Photo courtesy of Greg and Kim Gadson

When flying by helicopter from Bagram Air Force Base to Forward Operating Base Salerno, Gadson was struck by the contrast of the gunsight against the mountain scenery, and quickly took this photo.

"Gun, Afghanistan"
Photo courtesy of Gregory D. Gadson.

Lt. Col. Greg Gadson sits with an unidentified Iraqi girl he'd befriended during a visit to a local shop just weeks before he was wounded in an IED attack.

Photographer unknown, courtesy of Greg Gadson

Lt. Col. Greg Gadson with 1st Sgt. Fredrick Johnson, who was the acting sergeant major on the night of the IED attack that wounded Gadson. This photo was taken at Fort Riley as they were assembling their unit. Johnson would wind up saving Greg's life by administering mouth-to-mouth resuscitation, at the site of the blast. Johnson and Pvt. First Class Eric Brown (not pictured) received the Bronze Star for their heroic actions that night.

Photographer unknown, courtesy of Greg Gadson

Greg Gadson attends a June 2009 practice at the new training facility for the New York Giants in East Rutherford, N.J. Gadson became linked to the team's success following his motivational speech right before the team's first victory of the 2007 season.

Photo by Evan Pinkus, owned exclusively by and reproduced with the permission of New York Football Giants, Inc.

Gadson and New York Giants quarterback Eli Manning have a chat in 2009 in the new Giants indoor training facility. Manning earned the first of his two Super Bowl MVP awards in 2008 in an upset victory over the New England Patriots, spoiling their bid for an undefeated season.

Photo by Evan Pinkus, owned exclusively by and reproduced with the permission of New York Football Giants, Inc.

Gadson talks with Giants linebacker Antonio Pierce, who played an important role in the Giants 2007 season, particularly with a defensive play in the NFC Championship game against the Green Bay Packers.

Photo by Evan Pinkus, owned exclusively by and reproduced with the permission of New York Football Giants, Inc.

Giants Coach Tom Coughlin and Greg Gadson embrace in the team locker room following a victory against the Green Bay Packers in November 2012. Coughlin had asked Gadson to be honorary co-captain in the game against the Packers for the 2007 NFC Championship.

Photo by Evan Pinkus, owned exclusively by and reproduced with the permission of New York Football Giants, Inc.

Gadson and Mike (Sully) Sullivan on the sidelines. A Giants coach and former teammate of Gadson's at West Point, it was Sullivan who came up with the idea of asking Greg to speak to the Giants. "I just want you to tell them your story," he'd said.

Photo by Evan Pinkus, owned exclusively by and reproduced with the permission of New York Football Giants, Inc.

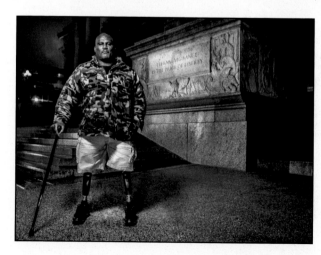

Gadson stands outside the National Archives building, in Washington, D.C., for a photograph promoting Össur Prosthetics. Following the loss of his legs to an IED explosion in Iraq, Gadson first learned how to use C-Legs, and then assisted Össur as a "human guinea pig" in the development of a more advanced robotic set of prosthetics called Power Knees.

Photo courtesy of Össur.

Greg Gadson and Brooklyn Decker go over the script for "Battleship," on location at the Center for the Intrepid at Brooke Army Medical Center, Fort Sam Houston, San Antonio, Texas. In the 2012 Peter Berg film, Gadson plays an Army officer, Mick Canales, and Decker plays his physical therapist.

Photo courtesy of Gregory D. Gadson.

Preproduction photo of Greg Gadson in the role of Mick Canales in the movie "Battleship". The object in front of him will later be digitally replaced with an alien spaceship.

Photo courtesy of Gregory D. Gadson.

Greg Gadson talks with Rihanna on location in Hawaii for the filming of "Battleship." Gadson plays an Army officer, while Rihanna portrays a Navy specialist, in the 2012 movie.

Photo courtesy of Gregory D. Gadson.

Greg Gadson and Terese Schlachter, after a bike ride on the Baltimore and Annapolis Trail in Maryland, part of their monthly fitness routine.

Photo courtesy of Gregory D. Gadson.

. . .

Bob and Mike started him out on C-Legs using a walker. If he moved his stump forward, they explained, a system of hydraulics would kick in. The knee would bend, and help execute the step, almost like a real leg. Once he put that foot on the ground the leg would straighten, simulating a step, putting him into position for the next step, which then brought about the matter of the other leg, which Greg would have to lift and push forward while balancing on the straightened leg. Then the microprocessor and hydraulics would prevail, taking him another step forward. He had watched others learn to use them in the OT room. There was definitely a rhythm to it. After sliding into his new sleek sockets, he stood, leaning hard on the walker, concentrating on this confusing cadence.

Move the right stump forward. Know that the knee is bending. Feel the impact of the foot, not your own, make contact with the floor. Trust it to bear weight. Straighten the leg. Now the left. Herky. Jerky.

It seemed an odd combination of effort, followed by a slight loss of control. One step. Then two. Then another. His breathing quickened and grew deeper. He felt the dampness on his forehead. He bobbed around a bit, then leaned heavily again into the walker. The bright yellow running shoes Kim had picked up from the Red Cross and stuck onto the smooth metal pod-feet seemed like theatrical props. Slowly, he shifted his weight back onto his feet, lifted the walker and moved it forward. It came down heavily. Then another step. Despite moving slowly, it was exhilarating to have the sensation of walking again, even if he still felt disconnected from the ground. He felt less like a duckling. Still, he had to keep his focus. He took a few more steps, then looked behind him. He had not traveled very far but he needed a break.

"Worn out?" Bob asked. There was something in his voice that made Greg wonder if he was giving up too easily. Kim sat on one of the OT benches, watching. Mike was preoccupied, tinkering with the C-Leg settings which were housed in a hard-plastic case, separate from the legs themselves. He wanted to be sure they were set properly, giving Greg the correct amount of support without throwing him over.

"I can do a little more," Greg said. Mike moved out of the way as Greg pushed the walker and took a few more steps. It was a like a new football drill—he just had to get the hang of it. He step-jolted slowly to the bench where Kim was sitting. He shuffled in a half circle, bent at the waist, aimed his behind, and fell backwards into a seated position. Kim braced him to keep him from rolling off the back of the bench.

"I need to practice that, too—the sitting down!" They both laughed. She handed him a towel.

"You might want to wipe down a bit," she suggested gently. He looked down to see his sweat-soaked shirt.

"Boy, it's time to hit the shower," he said, thinking what he really needed was a rest. Bathing still amounted to another chore. If only he could bend that arm, all of this would be easier.

He left the walker behind, quickly moving on to crutches, then canes. He moved less like an elderly impaired person and more like, well, a young one. At least he could maneuver into tighter corners with a little more agility. And the C-Legs took a little less exertion to operate than the stubbies, since they did a bit of the work for him. Still, he worked up a sweat just getting them on and making a quick trip down the hall. Standing still was the most difficult. Holding himself upright without the forward motion of the legs was like some sort of cruel amputee yoga. If someone stopped him to strike up a conversation, he would burst into a sweat. Still, simply being vertical, once again eye-to-eye with the rest of the world, put him lightly in touch with his former self—the self who had stood before a battalion of soldiers and led them into war.

"Kim, did I tell you?—I got an email—my unit is coming back to Fort Riley in April," he said one afternoon, as he slid the machinery off his stumps.

"That's great. Maybe you can go see them."

"I think I will." He twisted toward the other side of the room. "Hey Mike, do you think I can be, you know, *functional* on these C-Legs by April?"

"Oh sure, easily," Mike hollered. "Why?"

"I need a goal," Greg announced. "I'm gonna be there waiting when my unit deploys back from Iraq to Fort Riley. And I'm going to be *standing*."

CHAPTER THIRTEEN

"Greg was a great mentor to so many newly injured service members. He doesn't give himself enough credit for that."
—Cheryl Jensen, Founder, Vail Veterans

Cheryl Jensen was an athlete, a hiker, long-distance runner and general outdoors enthusiast, but mostly a snow skier. She lived in the outdoors enthusiast's mecca of Vail, Colorado. and in the early 2000s had started a program called "Sharing Warmth Around the Globe." The philanthropy collected ski suits, slightly used by the safety patrol or the local well-heeled, to be distributed to people in need who lived in cold places all over the world. She had traveled to Washington, D.C., to gather support for her efforts and in a meeting at the Pentagon learned of the catastrophic injuries America's armed service members were suffering in the wars. Naturally, the former adaptive ski instructor had an idea—why not bring wounded service members to Vail to ski? Just a few months later she met Army Captain Dave Rozelle, who had lost his foot to an anti-tank mine in Iraq. After that he went mountain climbing, ran the New York Marathon and became the first amputee to return on active duty to his combat unit in Iraq. Rozelle was Cheryl's kind of athlete. Cheryl was Rozelle's kind of philanthropist.

That encounter quickly grew into a mind-bending lifesaver. The following winter, the two of them offered a reprieve for seven soldiers, in various states of recovery, from Walter Reed, and took them on an adaptive ski weekend in Vail. "Operation Escape" went off beautifully. Cheryl and Dave were thrilled and perhaps even a little smug in their tremendously good deed. They provided instruction, guidance and adaptive equipment for a group of wounded vets to ski for one weekend. They had no intention of a repeat performance, until one new mono-skier, a double amputee named Heath Calhoun, changed their minds.

"I don't know why you did this for us," Heath told Cheryl after his first days on the slopes, "but you changed my life." Calhoun went on to a successful skiing career in the Paralympics. Cheryl went on to create Vail Veterans, a program which annually hosts veterans hurt or traumatized in combat, and their families, for a five-star adaptive ski weekend. She added an annual summer program where wounded vets whitewater raft, ski, ride a horse, fish or take part in a number of other activities which would not normally be friendly to a person missing an arm or a leg. Cheryl and her growing band of volunteers made it happen for hundreds.

By 2007, Cheryl was spending most of her days fundraising, making deals, arranging and organizing. It all suited her. But the best part of her Vail Veterans program was watching the change in her charges. They arrived subdued, slow and uncertain. By the time they left, just a few days later, they were a boisterous flock, teasing, wheeling and backslapping. Those who brought families grew from individuals coping with a catastrophic event to a unit, bound by adversity. She took the most pleasure observing each family member as they determined their new role—how they would snap into the puzzle of their new lives. It was tricky for them, trying to figure out what was expected, feeling for that evanescent line between being helpful and being patronizing.

Rozelle's story was becoming modern lore echoing through the hallways at Walter Reed, which made it that much easier for him to recruit disabled skiers. Harvey Naranjo was the adaptive sports program manager at the hospital. He was the one who planted the ski seed in Greg's skeptical mind. Every so often Harvey would add a little fertilizer.

"You liked skiing before you were wounded, right?" Harvey coerced.

"Yeah, but at the moment, I might be rolling rather than shushing," Greg countered.

"Just call. Have a chat with Cheryl. You'll love her."

Greg looked at some photos Harvey left in the MATC. There were men and women with burns, amputations, brain injuries—all sorts of life-altering wounds—screaming down snowy mountainsides, casting fishing lines and generally having the time of their lives. He ran a mental check of those things he had been told would qualify him for leave: He was off intravenous drugs. Everything he took now went down his gullet—needle free. He was able to use the bathroom by himself. And he could, albeit gracelessly, after a quick lesson from one of his rehabilitation mates, Andrew Kinard, get in and out of the family van. And he knew Harvey would not put him in a position to injure his person or his pride. So he called. Cheryl picked up the phone. Once again, Greg felt that all-too-frequent uncertainty.

"Uh, hello, my name's Greg Gadson and I'm calling from Walter Reed. I'm a patient. I lost both my legs just a few months ago . . ." He waited for her to protest.

"Are you interested in skiing?" Cheryl asked.

"Uh, no, I want to take my son fishing." Greg had not even realized that was what he wanted most until it came out of his mouth. He wanted some dad time. Real dad time.

"There's room in our summer program for another family," Cheryl chirped. "How many?"

"Four—are you sure I'm . . . ?"

"Done." Cheryl said. They hung up with a plan to talk again soon.

Greg looked at the brochure again. He would not only have to get in the van, he would have to board an airplane. How would that happen? He pictured himself going head over steel heel into a fishing boat. Still, he figured, other families were doing it. If this Cheryl Jensen person was in the business of taking folks with fewer limbs than most into the wilds for a few days of communing with nature, he was in. It just might be a much-needed salve for the whole family.

. . .

Cheryl mingled with all of the families as they arrived in Colorado for the 2007 summer camp. But she was especially looking forward to meeting the Gadsons. She watched as everyone spent a few days grinding about the privileged streets of Vail, shopping and enjoying the "crunchy" restaurants and bars. Then Cheryl and her band of volunteers gathered up wheels, canes, crutches, their owners and those people traveling with their owners, and headed to the cabins. Greg and Kim would stay at the Yarmony Creek Lodge. The kids would camp outside.

The Gadsons were something less than a well-oiled machine that August. First, there were the simple mechanics and logistics. Airport security was not insurmountable. It was just different. There were ramps to discover, elevators to search out. The wheelchair-unfriendly terrain at the camp presented challenges, as did the occasional narrow doorway. One way or the other Gadson was usually able to come up with some sort of work-around. And so they tumble-bumbled forward.

While other families seemed to jostle into one another in their efforts to be helpful or to define territory, Cheryl noticed the Gadson clan operated with a certain comfortable confidence. They had been culture-shocked, for sure, just like all families who sustain critical injuries. But they all seemed to fall into their new caretaking roles efficiently.

Cheryl watched as the family knitted together their plans. Greg had lost a lot physically. He was thin but still carried his own emotional weight. He was still the patriarch first, the colonel next. The other Marines and soldiers felt it, too. Even from his wheelchair he commanded respect. Greg and Cheryl quickly became friends.

Greg chatted amicably with his fellow travelers—some he knew from the MATC at Walter Reed. The kids looked through schedules of activities, like fishing and horseback riding. While they were getting better at managing day-to-day life with their dad, they no doubt wondered just how much he could join in more active recreation. He did not say much, but their dad was wondering that, too.

Aside from fishing with Jaelen, the outing Greg was most fired up about was horseback riding. The notion of him balancing his new body atop moving, willful livestock drew a small crease in Kim's forehead. But the kids' excitement seemed to win her over.

His trail riding adventure was preceded by that of a man named Tim Johannsen, an Army sergeant who lost one leg above the knee, one below, when the Humvee he was driving hit a pressure plate. He had come to the camp with one request—that he be able to trail ride with his wife. So, the wranglers at the ranch crafted a special saddle which kept Tim in place riding sidesaddle. The Johannsen saddle became the go-to way to get amputees on horseback.

Greg, Kim, Gabby and Jaelen arrived at the corral and began sizing up the horses. They were magnificent, smooth, cool and vibrant. Greg breathed in the farm smells, the manure, the hay, and rejoiced in its utter lack of sterility. This was far from anything he had ever experienced. He gazed in wonderment at the elegant, muscled animal one of the ranch hands was walking towards him. Greg could not wait to feel that power, to manage and control it, with his own physicality.

But there was a problem.

"I don't want to ride like that," he said, pointing to the sidesaddle—the one that had been made for Johannsen.

"That's the way the saddle is made," the ranch hand answered. "See, your legs'll fit right in here . . . "

"But it's not—that's how girls ride, right? I want to ride like a man."

The ranchers looked puzzled. How would he stay on without being able to use stirrups? What if he slid sideways and hit his head?

"I'll be fine. Just get me up there," Greg said convincingly, while the rancher unbuckled and slid the sidesaddle off the horse, which seemed to be eyeing his next passenger skeptically.

"You want to get on that horse on a regular saddle, sir, that's what we'll do, but I want you to hold on tight to this," the wrangler said, grabbing the horn of the replacement seat. "You go slidin' off there it's a long way down. And Jesse here doesn't have a lot of sense. She's likely to put a hoof right in your head."

"That's my thickest part," Greg joked, glancing at Kim, who was busy making sure the kids were being helped onto their horses.

Once again, "poise" had to be dropped from the equation. While the wrangler cupped his hands, holding his right stump, Greg threw his left around the other side of the horse. Slipperier than he thought. Squeezing his inner thighs tightly, though, he was able to sit upright. The rancher was right. It was a long way down. Greg looked forward, then around the corral, relishing his height. He patted Jesse's neck, stroking her luxurious mane. She kicked her back leg slightly, rocking him backwards, but he quickly recovered, thankful once again for the rigor his physical therapists had applied to his workouts.

After a quick bit of instruction, the four of them fell in line behind their guide. The trail was wooded and cool. Walls of forest replaced the hospital's concrete hallways and sounds of hooves scraping mud and rocks replaced the whir of wheeling medicine carts and beeping monitors. Jokes and laughter mixed in with the sounds of the forest. The horse swayed easily beneath him, Greg gradually sliding into her rhythm, her strength and nobility surging through his core, tightening and releasing with each step. There were no robotics, no canes or wheels. One day on the trail was worth a hundred at a fancy rehab center. For the first time since the explosion, he felt free, in command, the potency he had thought lost surged through his body. Greg glanced around, observing his wife—the way the sun was catching her hair—the fresh air's erasure of the creases that had often lined her face over the past months. Gabby and Jaelen giggled and played with their horses, in surreal disbelief that all of this was happening. They were just a normal family, enjoying a beautiful day in the heart of Colorado's ranch country. Greg's throat tightened for a moment. For once, it was not anxiety catching up with him. It was a deep dose of *grateful*.

There was more for which to be thankful.

There was that fishing trip—fly-fishing on the Colorado River. Even though Greg had to cast left-handed from the drift boat, he and Jaelen landed a bunch of trout.

"Jaelen, I bet you didn't think we'd be doing *this* any time soon," Greg said to his son as the preteen pulled in a shiny, flipping fish.

"I wasn't sure, Dad, I'll admit it," Jaelen answered. He didn't say it, but as Jaelen watched his father battle back from near-death—so quickly—and with such vigor, he was proud. It was a lesson in hard work and perseverance.

Greg had not been sure either, but in that moment he sensed he would not be missing out on as much parenting as he had thought. If he could do this, he thought, there was not much his more challenging child would be able to get away with.

They went rafting. The rapids were not enough to throw the boat around but they were turbulent enough to make it fun.

Every time Greg anticipated an impossible task, the Vail Veterans volunteers had already figured out the possible. Greg was blown away by what with their help and accommodation he was able to do. And see. The scenery was stunning. He missed his camera a little.

The Gadsons hung around the camp, getting to know other veterans and chatting with local folks. There were other guests there, including some business groups. There was a Stetson hat giveaway. Greg figured it would be a good way to commemorate his first legless horseback ride, so he got in line. As he was watching others be fitted, he heard a familiar drawl behind him—someone from "before"—way before. Even before the real Army. But not before West Point. He wheeled over to the man he finally recognized.

"Are you Bill Curry?" he asked the man.

"Yes, I am," the man answered, a little puzzled.

"Greg Gadson." They shook hands.

"You were the coach at Alabama when I played for Army. We met up at a bowl game."

"I remember that game!" Curry said. "The Sun Bowl. What position?"

"Outside linebacker. I was small for that job. I always had to line up against someone bigger. I only weighed about 185 pounds! I wore the number 98."

"You know, I remember you," Curry said. "We couldn't block you."

Greg laughed. "Well, we lost by one point anyway. You know what? That was the last football game I ever played."

Curry looked sadly at him, at his stumps.

"No, no it was my last game because I graduated. I graduated, got married, then my first assignment was in Fort Sill. This," he gestured toward his thighs. "This happened in Iraq."

They talked for a long time about the war but mostly about football.

"It's funny," Greg offered, "in football or in war you can't really ever think about getting hurt. It'll stop you. It will paralyze you both in battle and on the field. You just got to go out and play or fight and figure you're trained. You'll come out okay." Curry nodded and thought a moment.

"You know you should talk to people," Curry said.

"What do you mean, talk?"

"Well," Curry explained, "I get the feeling you have something to say to the world. About fighting, not just on a battlefield or a football field, but in life."

"Huh. Well. I never thought of that. But I'll keep it in mind, Coach."

CHAPTER FOURTEEN

"The entire building, constructed between the world wars,
often smells like greasy carry-out. Signs of neglect are
everywhere: mouse droppings, belly-up cockroaches,
stained carpets, cheap mattresses."
—Excerpt from "The Other Walter Reed," by Dana Priest and
Anne Hull, *The Washington Post*

The opening of the new Military Advanced Training Center (or the MATC) at Walter Reed Army Medical Center coincided exactly, to the day, with the one-year anniversary of the original *Washington Post* scandal series. And it is on this day that I step into the story.

WRAMC had continued to fight a public relations battle with the media—mostly the *Post*—and it was about to pull out the heavy artillery. For months, the newspaper had been relentless with follow-up stories. The local television stations and networks had joined in on the floggings. The harder the hospital public relations team tried to show the media how it was dealing with the problems, the more difficult it seemed some reporters became. If they described one area of improvement, surely the DOD beat reporters would find something else to criticize. Problem was, they were at least partly right. While the media tended to focus on a small number of extreme cases, there was no excuse for letting even one soldier receive substandard care.

The new MATC had been under construction since before the scandal broke, but the timing of the September opening could not have been better from a PR perspective. If patients were going to benefit from the new training center, which was connected to the main hospital by a sky tunnel, the PR folks wanted to be sure they performed a proper ribbon cutting for the media. It was the perfect public comeback to the lickings they had been taking in the press.

I had spent a portion of the day before arguing with the guy who ran the assignment desk at The Pentagon Channel[4] about attending the media tour. I had only been working at TPC as a producer for about a month, but I was pretty sure it was important for the channel to be represented. The desk guy, Master Sergeant George Maurer, immediately ridiculed me for thinking anyone at Walter Reed would answer questions about the scandal or their treatment of wounded personnel.

"George, the scandal is *why* they're *doing* this. It's their comeback. We need to go."

"You know what they're going to do there?" Maurer condescended. "They're going to pat you on the head and say, 'that's a nice little girl,' and send you on your way."

This may have been why I often envisioned MSG Maurer with a chunk of raw meat around his neck, sitting in the cheetah cage at the Washington Zoo. I tried to smile pleasantly but I probably looked more confused.

"No, George, I think they *want* us to show up and ask relevant questions. They're staging this for the media. It'll be a good opportunity to get inside Walter Reed and get some good video."

Begrudgingly, he relented. I had no idea how this would change my life.

---

4 The Pentagon Channel was started in 2004 and offered programming about Department of Defense, military news and stories about United States military personnel. The channel was rebranded DoD News Channel in 2014 and curtailed operations in April 2015.

. . .

In the days before the opening it seemed to Greg that the public affairs folks at Walter Reed were hovering, casually observing Greg's progress as he lumbered through the hospital. He knew the unveiling was critical to repairing the hospital's reputation—but he was not sure of his role in that. Greg kept the hospital PIOs, or public information officers, in his peripheral vision as he executed his laps around the outdated OT room. His latest therapeutic trick was to catch a round rubber ball in his hands while walking with his canes. He felt a little like a seal at Sea World.

Greg watched the flacks watch him back. Occasionally he would miss the ball and it would ricochet off his hinges or canes, then bounce away. Not quite ready for prime time, he thought.

The state-of-the-art facility would be filled with cutting-edge digital therapy equipment and highly trained staff. But the flacks needed people to showcase along with the place, patients with positive attitudes to take the stage, to demonstrate all the new gear, dazzling and engaging various reporters. Colonel Gadson, because of his maturity, rank and general willingness to push on with things, was showing considerable promise. Only days before the opening, Greg and Bob were asked to be spokesmodels on the new track.

As the MATC debut loomed, Greg was still finding the C-Legs challenging. For the event, he and Bob would be staged on a large indoor track which wound the circumference of the second floor. In the ceiling above the contoured floor was a groove from which hung a pulley system and a harness. The patient—Greg—would be strapped into the harness, then could walk the track while wearing prosthetics, assured that in a fall, gravity would be defied by the harness. Rather than land in a disheveled pile on the floor, he would wind up suspended in air. Greg was not sure which was worse. He was not looking forward to carrying off some sort of midair trapeze mishap while cameras were rolling. In the meantime, uptight executives tried to look at ease while therapists and other patients rehearsed facts about the new machinery and technology. He did his best to ignore clipboard-clenching pleasantries and focus on getting one fake foot in front of the other.

On the morning of the media opening I arrived at the hospital, along with videographer Steve Greisiger, and we assembled for a press conference featuring the new hospital administration. NARMC (North Atlantic Regional Medical Command) Eric Schoomaker and Colonel Patricia Horoho, commander, let us know what to expect inside the facility and welcomed us to a tour. They answered many questions about how patient care had been improved over the past year, and what was being done to ensure no patient would ever again be lost in their system. Then we were permitted to wander through the various rooms asking questions of what the military called "Subject Matter Experts," or SMEs, about the various new techniques and supporting gear. At just about every turn there was a recovering wounded Marine or soldier, demonstrating some sort of recovery training. Marco Robledo was a National Guardsman and a double amputee. He had lost an arm and a leg, both on the same side. Steve and I stood alongside the track, watching him work up a sweat in the harness, but manage the new contraption quite well. He chatted with reporters as they called out questions and snapped photos. Steve got plenty of video of Marco who, after a few laps, stopped and was helped out of the harness. Fascinated, I watched intently, as the next soldier, a skinny, thin-lipped Black man, was strapped in.

The man did not seem nervous to get in the harness; but he also did not seem crazy about all the cameras. A physical therapist helped assemble the two-inch-wide straps which came up between the man's legs then around his thighs while thicker, more cushioned holsters wrapped his shoulders. Everything clipped via a carabiner to a lanyard, which ran to a pulley, connected to the groove in the ceiling. Essentially, he was harnessed to a metal rope attached at one end to his back and at the other end to the ceiling. He was wearing two computerized legs and had a cane in each hand.

"Now, just like you've been practicing, Greg, but remember, instead of me holding you by the waist, this line has you. You really *can't* fall," said a man who I would later learn was Bob Bahr. Greg did not look at Bob but nodded, sternly zeroed in on the mission. His face steeled, as he took one mechanical step forward, then another. The whir of the metal wheel rolling in its slot overhead was drowned out by the swish of cameras assembling beside him. It took only a moment for Greg to work up a sweat.

Steve and I stayed in position as the Greg-and-Bob team step-clomped by us. The patient seemed to really have it together, despite his missing lower limbs. *There was some sort of story here.* I wanted to talk to them, but being new to this whole military thing I had no idea how to address either of them. He was not in uniform, not that I would have been able to interpret the hardware anyway.

"How's that working for you?" I called out awkwardly, holding a microphone as close to his already perspiring face as I could get.

"Uh—good, good," Greg answered. "It'll take some getting used to, but I can tell already it's going to be better than the old system, where someone just held on to you."

He did not offer any more of an answer because he was busy trying to stay vertical. Sweat was seeping through the back of his shirt. He had made it around the first couple of turns okay. Back on the straightaway, he started to pick up speed. That is when, apparently, one of his prosthetic feet did not get the message. He teetered, his head and torso getting ahead of the foot that was stuck on the track behind him. He tried to pick it up but he was already falling forward. Pushing off with his cane in front of him helped for a moment, but the stick went sideways. His head swerved toward the gray floor. I sucked in my breath and held it there. He looked like a marionette, his various parts, biological and procured, jumbling up then flailing outward. It took several moments before he completely surrendered to gravity. For a second, I thought he was going to do a header, but most of him never touched the ground. He just hung there, suspended halfway through a swan dive. It was awkward, to say the least. I felt my hand cover my mouth. Cameras whirred and flashed.

Bob yanked at the clip on Greg's back, swinging his top half back up. Greg tried to get his legs back under him, but he could not quite pull it off. Bob wound up standing next to him so Greg could push off his shoulders to get himself righted. It was a bit of a scene.

"Can you walk some more?" Bob asked.

Greg looked behind him.

"Up to you, Greg," a woman who had been following him said, quietly. She did not seem a fan of the paparazzi either. "Do whatever you feel like."

Greg straightened out his shirt and shorts and started walking again. He got about another half a lap in when he began losing his balance again. This time he could not get his cane out in front fast enough and he found his upper half almost upside down, both legs dragging behind him.

Hangman.

More clicks and flashes.

It was a pretty spectacular landing. I looked over to see if Steve had been rolling on the fall. He was. And there was something about this Greg guy. I could not put my finger on it, but I knew we would want him in our coverage. He peered out the corner of his eye from his nearly upside-down position.

"You gonna use that in your story?"

I bent over and cocked my head, so I could see his face.

"Yep," I answered. He drew in his breath and let out some combination of a sigh and a chortle. A schnortle.

I schnortled back.

"All right. All right," he said, resigned to his newfound inverted fame. He struggled to gain his composure while Bob played Geppetto. Back on his feet, he looked straight at me.

"Okay, well thanks a lot. Millions of people get to see me fall down," he grimaced.

"They will also see you get up," I said, unsure of my own footing.

Then he smiled. It was like a lighthouse beam in a Lake Erie fog.

"I guess," he said, and turned to get back to the business of clomping, then stopped.

"Hey, what's your name?" he asked me.

"Terese. What's yours?"

"Greg." He left out the "Lieutenant Colonel" part. Truth was, at the time, I would not have known an LTC from the janitor. I had worked in many newsrooms across the country, winding up most recently at NBC's Washington bureau. But because of the stringent credentialing situation at the Pentagon, I had rarely been in the building. Still, I knew a good story when I fell over one. The opening of this facility, of course, was a positive piece for the Pentagon, which was my current employer. And the man I had just met, it seemed, would make a great "character"—someone through whom I could tell today's story. Steve continued around the room, shooting various exercises and people. I stayed at the track, waiting for the team to come around again. But they didn't. I watched through the glass wall as Greg, in a wheelchair now and surrounded by his tiny entourage, pushed himself down the hall. I realized only as they disappeared around the corner toward the main hospital that I had not gotten Greg's full name.

There were lots of other people and things to see in the MATC. The facility itself was connected to the main hospital by a glass skywalk. Glass walls allowed real daylight, a relief from the hospital's neon innards. Modified stair-steppers and stationary bikes lined one side of the track. Therapy benches and beds crowded the middle.

I wandered down the hall into a darkened room where there was another demonstration underway. A properly shorn, muscled Marine was strapped into a harness, much like the one Greg was using, but instead he stood, using prosthetic legs, on a platform.

"Ready, Reid?" a therapist called from behind a podium of buttons.

"Go!" Reid answered.

Only then did I realize that the middle of the platform was actually a treadmill. Then the entire platform started to swivel, like an amusement park ride. The Marine at first struggled to walk but caught on quickly. Just when he seemed to get into a rhythm, the therapist hit another button and a screen lit up in front of him. First it showed a forest scene, with bumpy paths and darting squirrels. Next it changed to a choppy boating scene, complete with toothy sharks. The panoramic views called for more precise footwork. Reid tripped, and wobbled. I clenched my jaw. With the help of the harness, he quickly regained his gait.

"There's even a city scene," the attached SME offered. "Guys who are stressed, you know, have post-traumatic stress, can test their tolerance for an urban setting—the loud noises, traffic and stuff."

I nodded. He continued, "It's supposed to be New York or somewhere I think. An Elvis impersonator even walks by."

"Well, that'd stress *me*," I answered. "What's this thing called?"

"It's a CAREN, stands for um, Computer Assisted Rehabilitation Environment."

As the hours passed I became so enamored with the machinery, the people and mostly the patients, I almost forgot to take notes. The positive side, the real work of recovery of wounded military at the time was only beginning to seep into mainstream news coverage. It was surprising and sad to me to see so many, but at the same time, it was mind-bogglingly inspirational to hang around with them.

Down the hall from the CAREN was a gymnasium-like high-ceilinged room where a single-leg amputee was walking a straight line, alone in the middle. Another therapist in a corner behind another bunch of buttons and a screen, was calling out instructions.

"Ok, Marcus, come back toward the wall now!" Marcus turned.

Several people, including myself, stared in intervals, first at Marcus, then at the screen, then back to the shirtless Marine, then the screen again. The Marine had electrodes stuck all over his body. I nudged my way behind the gathering to see that the electrodes showed up on the screen as points of light. As the Marine walked, the lights moved on the screen with him. It reminded me of the "Lite-Brite" colored bulb game I had played as a kid. When the constellation of Marcus stopped moving, I looked overhead, finally noticing dozens of small cameras on the ceiling, all pointed at him.

"What's this for?" I asked one of the SMEs.

"It's a gait lab."

"Gait, like walking?"

"Yes. It enables us to record a very detailed picture—a video, really—of how the patient, in this case, the gunny Sergeant, is walking."

"Okay. Why?"

"Sometimes it's hard to eyeball if the prosthetic is fit perfectly—properly aligned—or is somehow affecting a patient's gait. We don't want them to be further injured by favoring one leg or the other. This shows us if there are any problems."

I watched the lights move around some more. The Gunny seemed in no danger of wearing out. He was tall, muscled, good looking and capable. I barely noticed he was missing a limb.

Then, I noticed that I had barely noticed. I learned a lot in that moment.

My cell phone was ringing. Good ol' George was probably wondering what was taking so long for me to get kicked out. I stepped into the hallway and tried to answer but the hospital corridors were less than cell-friendly.

I jogged a little further, then mashed my head up against a window, hoping to get a signal. I looked super cool.

The call dropped.

"Hey, you calling me?" A man's voice echoed from an office I'd blurred past.

I turned toward the door. "I wasn't calling. I was answering, or . . ."

"Yeah, the signal isn't so good in here," said the voice, which had grown a head and was sticking out the door of an office. "I'm Ross Culquhoun. I run this outfit here." I tried not to gape at the tall, fit, silver-haired blue-eyed gentleman as we stepped inside the room, which was actually a shooting gallery.

"It's all run on Bluetooth technology," he said, gesturing at the targets projected on the wall. "We've got guys who injure their hands or arms. I teach them to shoot again using their prosthetics. Want to try it?"

"Oh, thanks, no, I'd rather watch one of the patients," I said, looking around for Steve, so we could get some video. Besides, I was not keen on looking like a klutz in front of Mr. Handsome-muscly-guy-who-also-cares-about-our-nation's-wounded.

I watched as a few of the guys propped on their elbows or knelt over mounted weapons and took their shots. One wore a prosthetic hand that actually had a gun mount attached. Different animals and marks appeared on the screen. Ross called out instructions, then: "Fire!" Then more instruction. "Fire!" He gave them their scores. Everyone seemed to be having a good time.

"I'm a little surprised that someone injured in combat would still want to shoot a gun," I said to Ross, quietly, so patients would not hear me.

"Actually, they love it. Even if they can't go back into their military jobs, they still want to shoot. I take them on hunting trips. We have such a blast! It's so good for 'em. A bunch of us are going deer huntin' in a few weeks."

"You're taking patients?"

"Yep. I've got . . ." He looked down at his desk, " . . . six guys signed up."

"You go out in the woods?"

"Where else would we hunt for deer?"

"With wheelchairs and everything?"

"Yep. Just push them on through, tree roots, whatever," he laughed. I could tell he was a strong guy, physically. "We'll be out at Quantico. You could come along if you wanted to do a story."

A *great story*.

He handed me a business card.

"Just gimme a call if you wanna go."

Deer hunting. Who would have thought? I put the card in my wallet. That was a keeper. I walked back into the track room. One of the hospital PR staff was standing there looking helpful. By that time, I must have looked confused.

"My name's Pat Cassamatis. What can I help with?"

"The gentleman who was on the track earlier—he said his name was Greg."

"That's Lieutenant Colonel Greg Gadson." She smiled, proud and mom-like. "He's one of my favorites," she confided. "He's just always ready—amazing spirit."

"Yeah, I caught that," I said, jotting down the title. "He seemed really cool."

"*Really* cool," said Pat. "I think you'll be seeing more of him."

• • •

The next day Greg's and Marco's faces were everywhere—even *The Washington Post* begrudgingly did a decent story about the MATC. Just three paragraphs in, however, Steve Vogel, the writer, mentioned the scandal. Still, the event was deemed a success, with positive spins and comments from various soldiers splayed across newspapers and televisions throughout D.C. and some national outlets.

It was not long before Greg became one of the key in-house spokesmen for the hospital, sort of a firsthand SME. Any time there was a celebrity visit or other media event involving the war-wounded population, Greg found himself there answering questions for a curious and concerned media gaggle. He became more and more comfortable in front of the camera, even as he sometimes bobbed and weaved a bit on his legs. From his perspective, most of the staff were dedicated and helpful and he felt to some small degree back in the role of protector, even if it was just of his hospital's reputation. *Pride, poise and team.* He was beginning to feel a part of the Army again.

Only a week or so after the MATC opening, the actor Robert Duvall came on a tour. Media were invited along, so there I was following "The Preacher" around the hospital. His entourage included his wife, Argentinian actor and director Luciana Pedraza, and Alan Geoffrion, the writer of Duvall's latest made-for-television series "Broken Trail." As Duvall moved hesitantly about the occupational therapy wing, stopping to chat with patients here and there, he seemed uncomfortable. He was slight, his thin arms hanging off his body awkwardly, searching for somewhere to go. This was not his typical audience, I guessed. And maybe he understood that on this stage he was no longer the star. Duvall's wife, however, a tiny, beautiful South American woman, dressed in a snugly fitting blue suit, chatted amicably with patients.

"I wasn't expecting this," Geoffrion, the writer, said quietly to me, when I pulled him off to the side of the action to ask a few questions. "I didn't know there were so many." His eyes brimmed with tears.

It was a busy time in the OT area. Just about every piece of equipment was in use. A young soldier who had lost a leg was working out on the parallel bars as his wife cheered him on.

"Hey Mr. Duvall! 'Gone in Sixty Seconds'! Ha! That was great," he yelled out to the actor. "Did you do all those stunts yourself?"

"Sure I did, sure I did," Duvall yelled back, then laughed and handed the soldier's wife a signed photo promoting the upcoming Western, glad to have something to do.

"That was smokin', Mr. Duvall!" called out another soldier.

I split off from the pack. In a wheelchair toward the center of the room was a Marine, probably about 20 years old. He had a scar that ran from under his chin on the left side, through his lip and ended near his right eye. He wore a black T-shirt with white letters that read, "U.S. Marine. Some Assembly Required." I laughed. So did he.

"Did you meet Mr. Duvall?" I asked him.

"Nice of him to come visit. I love that 'napalm' line from that movie 'Apocalypse Now,'" he answered.

Only then did I notice Greg sitting on a bed along the far wall of the room. Duvall and his wife had stopped to chat with him. And sitting quietly next to him was the same woman I had seen walking behind Greg at the MATC opening. Greg was doing all of the talking. He sounded strong, commanding the conversation always away from himself, back to the actor and Hollywood. He asked Duvall about his current project, trying to make him feel more at ease.

"Hey, you look familiar," Greg caught me watching. "Terese, right?" I could not believe he remembered my name. It was not like he had nothing else to think about. I walked over, wondering how many times in my life I would be invited into a conversation with a really famous actor and a legless Army LTC.

"This is my wife, Kim."

He handed me a small camera and I snapped a picture of the Duvalls with the Gadsons. After the Hollywood crowd wandered off, I watched as Kim pulled the wheelchair up to the side of the bed, and Greg slid his posterior close to it, then with one smooth, brilliantly choreographed move, he was in the chair and she was behind it.

"Ready?" she asked, grasping the handles for their quick getaway.

"Yep!" he said, waving goodbye to me. Then he turned his head toward the exit. "Let's roll," he said to Kim.

"Let's roll," she repeated.

I scribbled in my notes: *Lt. Colonel Gadson—still the warrior,—out front—door kicker, calls the shots. Kim—quiet—background caregiver—new role, smooth transition. Team.*

CHAPTER FIFTEEN

*"To see this guy who was so strong, this great football player and
soldier, the condition he was in, broke my heart."*
—Mike Sullivan, New York Giants Coach and
former West Point teammate

Mike Sullivan pulled his truck into the dark, damp, overcrowded WRAMC parking garage. Dim yellowish lights guided him vaguely through the rows of SUVs and cars, the smaller vehicles tucking up into their spaces, teasing with opportunity. He had left his New Jersey office early in the morning, taking advantage of a slower chunk of the football offseason. There would be just a few weeks before the rookies showed up at Giants Stadium and he needed to take advantage of the downtime. Back home, his young daughters were involved in all sorts of summer activities and June was when he packed in more of that precious father-daughter time. But this was an important trip.

It had been some time since he had seen Greg Gadson. They had kept in touch loosely since they'd graduated from West Point. Greg had been a three-year starter and had lettered all four years. To Sully, who played only as a fill-in for the Black Knights, Greg was a star. The year they won the Commander-in-Chief's trophy they were unstoppable as a team. Number 98 was a big part of that, Sully thought, because of the way he played and the way he led. Greg Gadson drew people in. He gave them credit. He made players who barely got on the field feel like the team could not do it without them. Gadson was a gifted player and friend.

Sully had completed his 5-year military commitment following school as an infantry officer, and got out while Gadson pursued an Army career track. They did not see each other again until a decade later, at a West Point alumni golf tournament. By then, Sully was back at West Point, working as an assistant coach under Coach Bob Sutton. Greg was moving up in rank quickly but was excited to hear all about West Point football and Sully's work. After that Sully kept an eye on the alumni newsletters and would hear from other teammates from time to time how Greg was advancing, finally getting his own command. It made sense. Gadson was a natural leader. Mike had been proud to hear his old football friend was headed to Afghanistan, and relieved to know when he had made it back from that deployment unscathed.

It was the phone call Sully had received from Greg the previous winter, though, that really touched him. Sully was working for the New York Giants by then, having been hired by Coach Tom Coughlin to work on the team's passing game.

The phone call came out of the blue that January. It was Lieutenant Colonel Greg Gadson, calling to say hello, and that he would be deploying to Iraq in a month or so.

"I just wanted to tell you, Sully, how proud I am of you that you're working in the NFL. It's tough and you've made it and I just wanted to let you know I'm inspired by you," Gadson said. Gadson's words had set Sully back in his chair. Here was a man who was devoting his life to keeping this country safe, getting ready to head off to a war zone, calling *him* to say he was proud. He was sure Gadson had many other things to do as he prepared to leave Fort Riley. Both of them had teams in training. Sully said he would keep Greg and his family in his prayers.

Then in May, Sully had seen the email from Schretzman. Sully had been getting ready for a Giants' staff meeting. Pretty routine—they had them every morning on what became known as Tom Coughlin time: 8:00 really meant 7:45. Tardiness was not tolerated. It took Sully several moments to gather himself after reading the note about number "98" in the online journal. At the time, according to the note, doctors were not sure Greg was going to make it. Sully felt like someone had kicked him in the gut. Rattled and scattered, he was the last coach into the meeting that morning. All he could do was get through the day and wait to hear more.

Later, it was an email from teammate Will Huff, who had traveled on the medevac flights with Gadson, that filled him with relief but was horribly unsettling at the same time. Gadson was alive and recovering but had lost both of his legs. All the communications, mostly from Schretzman, were asking folks to sit tight, that Greg's condition was still fragile and he was not up to visitors. He could only imagine what Kim and the kids were going through. So, Sully had prayed harder than ever.

The big prayer, the one asking God to keep Gadson alive, had been answered, Sully thought. But at the moment, he chuckled, what he really needed was some good parking karma. Finally, he slipped into a newly abandoned spot and headed to the main entrance. Free to roam the halls, he searched for Greg's room number. He noticed a woman leaning on crutches in the hallway, near what looked like a physical therapy area. She was wearing a T-shirt and looked to be about 20 years old. Army, he presumed. He could not tell what rank. She swung forward from behind a low bookcase. She was missing a leg.

It struck him then, like an illegal tackle near the goal line. This is what had been happening. This was the war. The violence, the sacrifice, the ruination was far away from the Meadowlands, from the cheering crowds, the players' drama, the days he never saw the sun. Thousands of miles away, there were kids, the same age he had been when he left West Point, who were fighting for America and winding up here, grounded, in braces and casts and bewilderment. His old friend, his teammate Greg Gadson, was bringing the war home to him. Sully was unsettled and grateful at the same time.

Sully saw the room number and stepped in, tentatively.

"Hey, Greg," he said.

"Is that Sully?" Greg called out, at first not seeming to recognize his old teammate.

Physically, he could see that Gadson was broken. The man who had strode toward him on the golf course, gripping his hand 'til it almost hurt, seemed shrunken now in his bed. The voice that had so confidently called him the previous spring was subdued. Still, the man's soul was almost palpable. Sully could feel his self-assured spirit, his confidence, his mighty presence, as sure as he could see his physical nature had been sapped. Gadson had taken a beating, but it seemed it had not even occurred to him that anything was different. Gadson seemed to Sully to be the same in spirit as he was on the football field so many years ago.

The number 98 Giants uniform jersey hung in Sullivan's hand. Tears welled up.

"Sully, how are you?" Gadson beamed, "How's the team?"

Criminy. There it was again. Like this was about *him.*

Gadson's face was thin, but he still flashed a broad smile. Mike pulled up a chair and handed Gadson the Giants jersey.

Sully talked with his old teammate about his military unit and his future. Gadson was reassuring, Sully thought, trying to put others' fears aside. Greg pointed out the healing nature of having Kim and the kids nearby. And he said Chuck Schretzman and his wife Stacy were constantly in touch, as were many other former teammates. Sullivan could detect no self-pity, no pauses for dramatic effect. Sully was awestruck. He knew about his players throwing an incomplete pass or fumbling the ball. And that could make for a bad day—a really bad day. This man had lost his legs and he was still in the game. Smiling, even. Mike Sullivan found it preposterous.

Greg turned sideways on the bed, sitting up so the two men could talk, face to face. Their conversation easily closed the gap between graduation and the present. After a few hours, Sully got ready to head home. There was still a three-hour drive back to New Jersey.

"Is there anything I can do for you, Greg?" Sully asked.

"You know, Sully, they say I'm going to be up and around and able to get in and out of here, unsupervised, soon—just with Kim and the kids. By the time the Giants play the Redskins, we could probably go. Do you think you could get tickets for us?"

"Of course! Done. I'll call you with details. It's our third game this season, so it'll be fairly soon," Sully said, eyes grazing Greg's scarred stumps.

"It's a date then," Greg said, seemingly oblivious to Sully's concern. "This will really be a thrill for Jaelen, Sully, thank you."

"It's going to be a make-or-break season," Sully said. He headed back into the hallway. *It would be for all of them.*

CHAPTER SIXTEEN

"As long as you stand beside each other, you'll be victorious."
—Lieutenant Colonel Greg Gadson, September 23, 2007

At the Meadowlands, the start of the New York Giants' 2007 season was gloomier than fog and rain on the New Jersey Turnpike. The Dallas Cowboys and the Green Bay Packers had left them 0-2. Star running back Tiki Barber had just retired, leaving a gaping vacancy in the lineup. Eli Manning, the starting quarterback, had played well early in 2006, but a lackluster performance by the first overall draft pick through the second half of that season had been disappointing, especially to team President and co-owner John Mara. Even more disenchanting was the 8-8 record that Head Coach Tom Coughlin had handed Mara the previous December. Coughlin's so-called no-nonsense approach to coaching had made him also unpopular with some of the bigger player personalities, like Barber and receiver Plaxico Burress. Coughlin's firing was an acceptable convention to those who considered themselves "in-the-know" that winter. But by January of 2007, *The New York Times* reported a phone call of reckoning between Mara and Coughlin had put them both on the same page, and Mara, confident Coughlin had a plan to turn things around, had recommitted to Coughlin.

Mike Sullivan hoped for the sake of the team and his own career that Mara was right. Two out-of-the-gate losses were making for a lot of tension on the field and, worse, in the locker room. Rumors and mumblings made for a depressing atmosphere, pushing each player even further into his own funk. The team was dragging, physically and emotionally. Sully knew how bad season starts could take a slow skid downward, forever spiraling south. The next game would be against the Redskins at FedEx Field just five miles outside Washington, D.C. Another loss would surely put the entire season and many destinies back in jeopardy. He was convinced the team had the talent, the ability to create an awesome season for itself, if they would only get out of their own way. It was purely psychological, he felt. They needed to be inspired. They needed a spiritual jump start.

In a rare moment of calm, Sully sat in his office, surveying the roster, watching the Jersey sun set over the Meadowlands. His mind wandered back to the last time *he'd* felt inspired.

"Hey Sully, how's the team?" The question, and the familiar voice asking it, kept poking at Mike's subconscious. For a moment he was back at Walter Reed Army Medical Center, standing in Greg Gadson's room. Despite Gadson's injuries, his old friend's spirit had lifted *him* in that moment. Gadson had been handed his own early season losses and was battling back. If the players were feeling as if the deck was stacked against them this season, maybe a word with his former teammate would do them some good. Sully was pretty sure if they could see Greg, talk to him, hear his story, they just might *get it*.

• • •

Greg, Kim and the kids had luckily been able to move off the Walter Reed campus into accessible base housing at Fort Belvoir in Fairfax County, Virginia. It seemed a little rushed, but they needed to establish a residence in a place where they felt comfortable sending their kids to school, and where Kim might eventually teach. Kim made the long drives with Greg to his many physical therapy sessions and other appointments at Walter Reed. He was home one Monday morning when his cell phone rang. Greg recognized Mike Sullivan's number.

"Sully!" Greg shouted into the phone.

"Hey Greg—how are you doing?" Sully sounded tentative.

"Good! I've been watching—you really had some bad breaks in the last two . . ."

"Yeah, we're struggling again," Sully understated. "I'd love for you to come, though, on Sunday. I'm holding four tickets."

"Four, that's great! Thanks, Sully!" Greg was thrilled, not only to see the Giants play, but at the idea of another family outing. Jaelen was especially going to love this.

"So," Sully hesitated, "I wanted to ask you a favor."

"Sure, Sully, what is it . . ." . . . *that I could do for you in my condition?* Greg finished the sentence in his head.

"I want you to talk to the team."

"To the Giants? About *what?*" he asked. He looked down at his stubs.

"I just want you to tell them your story," Sully said. "I haven't talked to Coach Coughlin about this yet. I wanted to check with you first."

Greg went silent for a minute. He had not counted on being anyone's spiritual role model, especially for a whole team of people, especially one that played in the NFL. He was barely holding himself together, some days.

"Do you really think it would help them? I mean—my level of play—I didn't . . ."

"Yes, it would help. Yes," Sully was convinced. "Look, these guys have the ability. They just aren't playing *together*. I think they could learn a lot from you and—" he paused, "what you've been through."

Greg could not imagine what he would say to them, but he remembered his conversation with Bill Curry, the coach he had run into in Vail—the guy who suggested he might "talk" to people.

"I'll do it, Sully, yeah, of course. When?" The confidence in his own voice surprised him.

"Let me check with the coach and I'll call you back," Sully said.

Greg ended the call with Sully, pondering this really weird turn of events. He was a college player. Former college player. Former college player with no legs. What the hell was he going to say to a room full of professionals?

Coach Coughlin called Greg at 7:00 that Friday morning. The conversation was brief. They agreed that Greg would address the players Saturday night before their team dinner. Greg hung up the phone thinking two things: Tom Coughlin must put a lot of trust in Sully. And the head coach had not given him much to go on. He was not sure exactly what he was supposed to say. He sure could not talk about football. Their sports careers had gone much further than his own. He figured he would think of something. By Saturday afternoon when he, Kim and the kids got in the van, he still did not know what he would talk about. He held a 3 x 5 index card in one hand, a pen in the other. The trip took about an hour. He never wrote anything down.

• • •

Sully greeted them as they arrived at the hotel where the players were staying in Washington. Greg was in his wheelchair, Jaelen pushing behind. Greg seemed calm, Sully thought, much calmer than he was feeling, himself. With so much at stake in this game, he was really going out on a limb with this plan. Adding to the pressure was the fact that Coughlin had not warmed to the idea immediately. Coach was the one who always did the talking. He never invited guests. And Coach was fairly set in his ways. But Sully guessed the few minutes Coughlin and Greg had spent on the phone Friday were enough to convince him.

Greg was looking better than he had in June, Sully thought. The hollows of his cheeks were filling in and he looked less tired. Gadson was making a quick comeback.

"Are you all set?" Sully asked.

"Yep, all ready," Greg said looking straight ahead. Sully watched Greg's right stub jitter up and down, belying his calm expression. What if he had misjudged the situation? The guy had been blown out of a Humvee in the desert less than five months ago—maybe it was too soon. These were young, multimillionaire athletes. They were not having a great season and they were pretty caught up in their own circumstance. How would he bring his story home to this team? Sully just hoped they were open to the message.

"Okay, Coach will say a few words, then I'll introduce you," Sully said to Greg, calming himself. "We didn't tell the players you were coming. You're a surprise guest."

Coach Coughlin and the team had already assembled when the Gadsons and Sully walked through the rear double wood-paneled doors of the dimly lit gray-blue conference room, into the rough sea of square-suited shoulders. A few heads turned, revealing diamond-studded ears, jaded eyes. There was a slight murmur. Greg looked at Kim, who gave him a nearly imperceptible nod. Jaelen and Gabby took to the edges of their seats, nearly disappearing inside the oversized audience. Jaelen marveled at their gargantuan profiles, perceptively sensing the chill of opposing personas.

Sully introduced Greg to Coughlin, who seemed to make a note of Greg's golf shirt and shorts. To the coach's side were dozens of men wearing suits worth thousands. Some of their shoes cost as much as a car. They wore dreadlocks, tattoos and thick gold rings. Coughlin said a few words to them, then stoically handed the floor over to Sully.

"I've brought a friend of mine along tonight," Sully began. "And I'd like him to say a few words to you guys. His name is Greg Gadson. Lieutenant Colonel Greg Gadson. He played for West Point, then made an impressive career in the Army. Last spring, he was injured by an explosive device in Iraq. He lost both of his legs. I think now is a good time for you all to hear his story."

Greg wheeled himself to the front of the room, which was small for, well, Giants. There was no clapping. Only the rustle of large men shifting in their seats. He looked out into his audience, each seated man still dwarfing him in his chair. He remembered how it often looked on the football field, as he lined up against players whose shoulders spread twice the width of his own. Still, he knew he could hit harder than the other guy, move faster. The other thing he knew was—while he did not necessarily know the psychology of this team, he knew the psychology of *a* team. So that is where he started.

"Thanks, Sully and Giants team members, for inviting me here. It's, uh, a real privilege to come here to D.C. to talk to you—your team." He glanced down at the index card he was still holding in his hand. It stared blankly back. No one made a sound.

Linebacker and special teams player Chase Blackburn was in the front row. He looked at the thick, purplish scars which ran along the end of Greg's stumps. His arm was bandaged. Whatever had happened to this guy, he thought, it had not been too long ago.

"Like Sully just said, I was an outside linebacker for Army. When you play for Army— it's different from playing for other colleges. You wouldn't spend much time worrying about going pro—because you're going in the Army."

He heard a few chuckles.

"My unit and I deployed from Fort Riley to Baghdad last February. When you have a command—meaning I was in charge of a couple of hundred soldiers over there—you have a security team, and I was with them, on our way back from a memorial service for two guys who'd paid the ultimate price . . . " He stopped, as he always did when remembering the fallen. "And that's when our vehicle struck an IED. So, one minute, I'm driving along a paved road in Iraq, thinking about my job, my mission, what I'm going to have for dinner and the next minute, I'm at Walter Reed and—and nearly half my body is gone." He looked around the room, immediately recognizing Giants defensive end Michael Strahan, who seemed fixated. Strahan was considered to be the best defensive end in the NFL. He had spent his entire career with the Giants.

Strahan was not sure how this was all going to tie together, but he was pretty sure this was going to be good. He felt this year, especially, he was among great football players. But it did not feel like a team. It was too loose. Each player was well-intentioned, but he was not sure everyone was on the same page. Strahan's father had been military. He immediately respected the strength and resolve of this man and his message.

"*That's* how fast your life can change," Greg plowed forward, feeling his words press the air. "In an instant, everything as you now know it could be over. You could have a career-ending injury and lose your job. Then what happens to your family? It's over in a second."

No one spoke. They did not even look at each other. Every Giant stared straight ahead at Gadson.

"That's why you need to use *every* opportunity you have." He glanced at Sully. *I am here now, in this moment. I'm living testimony to my own words.*

"That's how you need to play tomorrow. It's easy to get caught up in other things—the media, the attention. But none of that matters. The only thing that matters is what's in this room: your teammates. You can do nothing without the guy next to you. *Nothing.* On May 7, I would have died without the guy next to me. By the time they found me—I'd been thrown a ways from the vehicle—I was barely breathing and I'd lost a lot of blood. First Sergeant Fredrick Johnson started breathing his own *breath* into me. You know, Johnson is this big fast-talking southern guy—you can barely understand him when he speaks but he is a great man. He saved my life. Because he knew what to do in the heat of battle. He knew that in that moment nothing mattered but his teammate. Johnson and another guy, Eric Brown. Brown was just a kid. Private First Class Brown was our unit's medic. He wasn't even trained to be a medic. He was trained to handle chemicals, to hand out gas masks. But our unit needed a medic and he was an EMT back home, so he stepped up. He trained. They all trained. And that night they knew instinctively what to do. I'm alive because of their training and their teamwork. Private Brown put tourniquets on my legs—slowed the bleeding—then I guess it took a few of them to get me in the truck and to a medical facility. It was dark. And it was dangerous. There was another man injured, who they also had to look after. They had to secure the perimeter, to make sure nothing else happened. They had to control that chaos. And they had to save my life. And that's what they did. They confronted all that adversity with teamwork. They came together. And they were successful."

"Bam!" Strahan thought. There's the challenge. How could this team not take this guy seriously? This was exactly what this team needed, and this was precisely the right time, he thought.

Greg paused again.

"This team is in the heat of battle. You have trained. You have learned. Now you know what you have to do. It's that simple."

Blackburn knew about the war. His brother-in-law had been in Iraq. He had heard about the fear being trained out of them. They were so confident in their ability to complete the mission, they were literally fearless. He understood what needed to happen to this team, if they were to complete their own mission.

"That group of soldiers, out there in the desert, started out having no idea what they were capable of," Greg continued. "They didn't know if they could survive the heat, or an enemy attack, or some crazy disease. They didn't know how to fight in an urban desert. But they learned. They became each other's lifelines. In the end they saved my life, and formed that important chain, forged those bonds that got them through that night. And they all made it back to base, back to safety. That was their victory."

Sully watched as each player absorbed the words. It was not your traditional pregame rally. Some nodded. One or two even choked up a little. They were getting it, definitely. Greg was proof that any adversity could be overcome, that egos could be turned inside out. A powerful message might be turned into a powerful game. Sully was more proud of his friend than ever. Plus, he noted, he had had a darned good idea, himself.

"See this?" Greg held up his battalion coin. "It says on the back, 'Can Do.' That's it. That's all you have to think about."

Greg stopped talking. The room went silent. Then there was a clap. Then another. Every player rose from his seat, smashing huge hands together, the sound echoing through the room like firecrackers.

Mic drop, Jaelen thought.

Coach Coughlin normally would have retaken the podium. He would have told some sort of parable or delivered inspirational messages. But tonight was unprecedented. He knew there was simply nothing left to say. He dismissed the team for their pregame devotions then invited Greg to join the team in chapel for prayers and afterward for dinner.

In the dining room Coughlin looked around for Gadson. He had presented a tremendously important message about lack of self, and immersion in team. And just when he thought he could not be any more impressed, he caught an image that set him back for a moment. There was Gadson chatting it up with his hardest nut to crack. He would not call Plaxico Burress impossible, but he was hard to handle. And he had sure handled some tough ones. Burress was an all "I" guy. Not the sort who would warm naturally to an "outsider." The coach may have wondered if the lieutenant colonel would next offer up two fish to feed thousands.

• • •

On Sunday, Kim, Greg, Jaelen and Gabby were headed for their down-in-front seats at FedExField, but were stopped by Sully.

"Good afternoon everyone!" Sully hugged each of them like he was welcoming new family members. "Why don't you all come with me—we'd love for you to be our guests on the field for the pregame."

Greg could not have sat more upright if General Odierno had issued an order.

"Yes, of course!" Greg said, side-glancing at Kim and the kids, who were a little bewildered by the invitation. Greg jerked forward to feel the fanny pack he had attached under the front of his wheelchair seat, to be sure he had his camera. He had purchased a small digital SLR he could easily manipulate with one hand. *He was going to be back on the sidelines with the Giants—like he was part of the team!*

They all spun around to follow Sully, who was moving quickly toward the stadium's underbelly. They emerged near the turf, Sully helping to push the chair over the rough terrain, stopping at the sideline, a short distance from where the coaches would be gathering. The team was already working out, stretching and doing drills, and the whole family could see every determined grimace, each bead of nervous sweat.

Greg looked up at the few clouds dotting the September sky. The temperature was nearly 80 degrees and he was thankful for the slight breeze wafting the lure of hot dogs and popcorn across the stadium. An old, familiar feeling—was it contentment?—crept into his chest. What a treat, for him and for the rest of his family. He only hoped some of his words had sunk in with the team. When he had rolled into the meeting room the night before, he had felt a disjointedness, almost a chill. By the time he left, there was a thawing. He only hoped there was enough heat to get them back on track today.

After the warm-ups, Greg and Jaelen remained on the sideline, but Kim and Gabby settled into their seats. Kim breathed in the approaching autumn, feeling the power of progress as her husband evolved further and further from the despair of only a couple of months ago. She hoped he was far enough away from the emotional trauma now—distanced enough to make a lesson of it for others, for this team. Interesting how God had so quickly given Greg a purpose, a channel for all he had learned so far.

The Gadsons had long been a football family always supporting Army. They did not really have a unified NFL favorite. Gabby had been something of a New England Patriots fan and luckily for her the Giants' red, blue and silver colors were similar, so it was an easy switch from a 13-year-old girl's fashion standpoint. Jaelen was in awe of the whole emerging situation, and easily latched on to his Dad's new mentees. They watched the pageantry as both teams filled the field, excited and hopeful.

The start of the game was disappointing. The team seemed disorganized and unfocused. Their defense, unstable in the first two games of the season, was completely falling apart. Offensively they were clumsy. Plaxico Burress dropped the ball three times. Greg's disbelief was tempered only by his disappointment. Still, he held out hope. He had no idea if his words had meant anything to the team, but he felt Sully was right. They had the talent. He said a quiet prayer that they just hold it together. *Together*. But by halftime the Giants were down 14-3. The Washington Redskins seemed ripe for a victory. He thought about his old team, how, when victory might have seemed uncertain, Coach Kish would work Greg and Chuck into a single force, turning their love for the game into raw power.

He wondered what sort of emotional fuel Coach Coughlin was feeding the team, what words could empower them to play the game he knew they had in them. He hoped it would be a different group of men who stampeded back onto the field after halftime.

The first three plays of the third quarter were solid milk toast. But by the fourth quarter, the Giants began to serve the Redskins notice. Greg glanced down the bench, trying to read dozens of fixed eyes. There was something new, he could smell it like freshly shorn turf. Three touchdown drives later he was sure of it. The Giants had found their harmony. It was a newly enlightened Burress, who had been suffering from an ankle injury, who snatched five receptions. The Giants tied it up 17-17.

Now the Redskins offense could barely get on the field. Burress caught fire. With 5 minutes and 40 seconds left in the game, Eli Manning took aim and Burress took notice, catching the pass, and blazed across 33 yards to the end zone, scoring the winning touchdown. The Giants defense made a dramatic goal-line stand, holding the Redskins off until the clock ran down. The Giants had their first win of the season.

Burress raced across the field, ceremoniously slamming the football into Greg's lap. Up in their seats, the two other Gadsons shook their bench with celebration. Jaelen went home with Plaxico's signed jersey. Gabby went home to a lot of ribbing from friends at her new school about her sudden Giants obsession. Greg and Kim went home feeling like just maybe they had been a part of something. Mike Sullivan went home sure of it.

. . .

Mike Sullivan had not been the only coach who saw in Greg the ability to lead. Coach Tim Kish was one of the West Point brothers who'd made his way through the halls of Walter Reed, checking in on his former linebacker as he recovered. By then, Kish was an assistant coach at the University of Arizona. He kept in touch with dozens of his players as he progressed in his career from team to team. But the West Point alums made up the majority of his former player network. When he'd first seen Greg at Walter Reed, Greg had made a point of not wanting to be around the other wounded service members. Kish was agonized to see one of his best sidelined to such a dark space.

Figuring it might be a salve for both Greg and his own team, he invited Greg out West to speak to his players.

Greg felt at home in Tucson—back with his athletic peers in the NCAA. And Kish had become more like a brother to him than a coach over the years, especially since his injuries. His message to the Wildcats on that warm November day did not change much from what he had told the Giants. As he spoke of the Wildcats' potential for opportunity, he could not help but reflect on his own.

"The Lord has given you this chance," Greg said, to another riveted audience of players. "Not everyone gets a chance like this, to play the game at this level. You are gifted. You have to take advantage of that gift, you have an obligation to make the most of that gift every single day." This audience was younger, less jaded, more hopeful. They had their sights set on the big time—careers in the NFL. "And it's not just that way on the field," he advised. "It's that way in life. The glass is always half full. Respect the game. But respect your life, too."

Kish listened, observing his players as Greg spoke about the concept of team.

"You might think you can shoulder all the burden yourself, that making that point or that play will make you a hero. But playing for *yourself* will cost you your career. No individual wins the game. I know because my team, my military *team*, saved my life. And if they hadn't played as a team, trained as a team and fought as a team, I wouldn't be standing here in front of you today."

Gadson and Schretzman had been Kish's "bookends," on either end of the line during their junior year. Both linemen displayed a work ethic he had not seen in other players. They were the toughest, most passionate teammates he had ever seen in his career. Schretzman was a hard-nosed Philly kid. Greg was tough too, but the game was his intellectual fulcrum. Kish loved being around the two of them.

Kish was a powerful influence. In addition to the "punch board drill" there was the constant refrain, "low man wins." Kish would create a low ceiling of rope, stretched across the practice field and players would have to conduct drills beneath it, keeping their knees bent, essentially in a squat. Then there were Schretzman's favorite "kick-out drills," where blockers would plow into them head-on and try to knock them out of bounds. It was as close to physical combat as the players got, many of them taking a beating that made Saturday matchups seem like a tepid game of tag.

(When I got to meet the coach, some years after Greg's visit with the Wildcats, Kish recalled the camaraderie between Greg and Chuck on the field at West Point, even as they had vied for the same position. Coach told me he especially relished the banter as Chuck sat on the sideline with some injury or other, while Greg took their hits on the field.

"When you're a coach, you're a . . ." Kish sucked in his breath, ". . . a dad." He laughed, a little tenuous about claiming such an important role in the lives of men he had come to admire so deeply. "So, they're my sons. When the attack in Iraq happened, like any parent, my heart sank. I just wanted Greg to know I loved him and if there was anything I could do, I would. My role, at the time, I think was to keep him connected to the athletic arena, the football arena. I knew that meant a lot to him. Having him talk to my team was a great way to help him reconnect. And it helped the team.")

After Greg wrapped up his talk to the players at Arizona Stadium, the family headed home for the evening with Kish. As they settled in for the night, Greg felt the familiar edges of darkness creeping in, dimming the light he had so recently discovered. Now, he fought it, thinking he should be feeling pretty good, here with his old coach, having just delivered a speech to a group of young players. Maybe he had done some good. But he could not shake the shroud that seemed to be enveloping him, making it hard to concentrate, difficult to make conversation. Coach wheeled him into the guest bedroom of his home, helping him get ready for what would be a short night's sleep before the next day's game. Maybe the college players had been too close, too familiar, a universe nearly parallel to what he had lost. Greg stared at his stumps, feeling the grief rising up through his lungs.

"Greg, I'm here. What is it?" Coach asked, uneasy with Greg's silence.

"Coach," Greg said, breathing heavily through sudden tears, "Could you have ever imagined pushing me around in a wheelchair? Having to help me get ready for bed?" He slid from his chair onto the floor, looking up at Kish, who sat down on the bed, near his former player, his "son."

"How could this have happened?" Greg asked, wildly. "This is . . . it's for the rest of my life!" He sobbed openly, out of control. Coach gave him a few minutes to feel his despair, to scrape the bottom of his sorrow.

"Greg," Coach started, gently. "You're one of the toughest guys I know. You played, you beat dozens of linemen who were bigger and stronger. You kept me in awe—you and Schretzman both, with your never-say-die attitude. You never quit. You didn't quit then. You won't now. I'm here. Everyone is here to help. You're going to find your way. From what I saw you do tonight, you're well on your way. Those kids love your story. You inspired them. You could have heard fairy dust hit the floor, it was so quiet in there. That's your path. That's *your obligation* now."

Greg was calming now, feeling his way forward. "You think?"

"Once a leader, always a leader, Greg. You're really not that much different now."

Greg sighed. "Coach, I was strong. I was a mentor to hundreds of military guys, tough guys, who had a mission. Now I can't even get into bed without . . ."

"You're still a mentor, Greg. You're coping. You're struggling with your own demons but you're still a role model. You just don't have a specific unit anymore. Your team is everywhere."

Greg turned the coach's words over in his mind. Was it possible to still lead, to set an example, even if he had to do it from a chair, or even wobbling around on something like legs?

"Get some rest," Coach advised. For a minute, they were both back at Michie Stadium, Kish running the team through that crazy board drill. "Tomorrow, you gotta punch."

"I think I gotta punch for the rest of my life, Coach."

CHAPTER SEVENTEEN

"I am glad to see you and take you as a friend.
For one who knows how to show and accept kindness
will be a better friend than any possession."
—from Sophocles' *Philoctetes*

Back between the pasty white walls on Ward 57, physical therapy and other doctors' visits became more routine. Greg would spin down the hall to the occupational therapy wing and go through his daily exercises with Bob Bahr or with Kyla Dunleavy, a young woman who had recently joined the Walter Reed occupational therapy team. Then he and Mike Corcoran would work with the C-Legs. He was able to put them on and stand up by himself. Walking was still a challenge. It really took a lot out of him. And Mike was already talking about trying out yet another, more advanced set of prosthetics, called "Power Knees," developed by Össur, an Icelandic company.

Routinely, Greg enjoyed visits from West Point teammates. Sully checked in frequently, sending messages from various players, which left him bemused. Was Sully just being nice? He could not believe he had really had that much of an impact on this group of literal and figurative Giants.

While Greg's military career was on hold, his old teammate Chuck was gaining experience and working toward promotion. While Greg was with the Vail Veterans in Colorado, the Army had moved Chuck out of Canada and back to the states, into his own mentoring position at the University of Dayton. As a professor of military science, he now managed the ROTC program there, where he was responsible for the training and education of 120 cadets. Stacy's hometown of Troy was nearby. And he was not so far away from Walter Reed anymore. Just for fun, Greg decided to throw Chuck a curveball.

"Hey, Professor!" Greg chided over the phone, "Wanna go skiing?"

"Yeah, sure," Chuck snorted. "When we leaving?"

"December 3."

"Wha ... can you ski? What are you talking about?" Chuck was a pretty avid skier. But he had two legs, which seemed to him paramount to the task.

"This organization, Disabled Sports USA, takes amputees skiing," said Greg, arriving at his decision as he spoke. "I'm going."

"Snow skiing, like on slopes, like mountains?"

"Yeaaaup. In Colorado."

Chuck tried to envision how a person with no feet would keep themselves attached to the skis. "I just started this job, man, I can't leave ... "

"Tell them you have to help out your brother, your teammate!" Greg said, knowing a ski trip was more than his friend could resist. And probably more than he expected they would ever share again.

"What about Kim?"

"No. She's got other things going on, and she needs to stay with the kids. C'mon. I need to bust out of this place. Let's go."

Kim was wisely absorbing the caretaking counsel she had gotten at Walter Reed. She needed some time to herself. A long weekend without the intense triple time she had been doing for a few months would refresh her, give her time for her own workouts, time to visit with some friends, maybe even get a haircut.

"Lemme see what I can work out, man," said Chuck.

"Okay, you're in, then."

"Greg, I . . ."

Click.

He waves his magic wand, and as usual, I make it happen, Chuck thought. And then it occurred to him, he had not used the word "usual" in a long time.

• • •

Since my first verbal wrestling match with George on The Pentagon Channel desk, I had been carving out a beat of sorts covering wounded military personnel. Now, I managed to persuade News Director Gene Brink to send me and my cameraman Steve to Breckenridge to cover the Disabled Sports USA ski weekend. Our travels had gone smoothly until we arrived at the base of the ski slope. I had arranged a snowmobile lift up to where we could better see skiers in action. But the snowmobiler failed to surface, making both of us nervous about the outcome of our story. Executive Director of Disabled Sports Kirk Bauer was on his cell, working to find us a way up. The gray sky matched the color of the falling snow, which was being whipped around by a steady breeze. Despite the unpleasant conditions, dozens of skiers popped around the horizon like pinballs. From somewhere midmountain, I saw a man seemingly squatting on skis, zooming toward us. Next to him was a tall Nordic-looking guy in a bright red jacket. They both shushed to a stop next to us.

"Hey, Terese!" the squatting guy called out from behind snow-caked goggles. It took me a minute to realize it was Greg, beaming at me from his perch on a modified snow ski. "Have you ever met my friend Chuck?"

Chuck and I shook thickly gloved hands. I had heard Greg talk about Chuck a bunch of times by now, but this was our first face-to-face. I had pictured someone, something else, but I was not sure what. Chuck was broad-shouldered, tall, and a very closely shaved blond with blue eyes. He reminded me of Buzz Lightyear from the movie "Toy Story."

"Hey, did you see us come down? I'm already on the blue slopes!" Blue is the second-highest degree of difficulty.

"He's back in action, man," agreed Chuck, grinning, sliding away, out of the spotlight. "This place, this trip, it's all so amazing, what this group is doing for wounded guys. We're having a blast!"

"How fast do you think we're going?" asked Greg. "Like, forty?"

"Mmmm, I'd say probably thirty."

"I'm going faster," Greg challenged his friend.

"No way, no way, man," Chuck laughed.

The skis had evened their competition.

"What's that thing you're on?" I asked Greg. He was sitting in a chair, attached to a single ski by a metal brace and what looked like a giant spring.

"I guess you call it a mono-ski," Greg answered. "I just kinda sit in here. It's pretty comfortable. It's got, like, suspension." He gestured with one of his shortened ski poles. Greg's smile lit up the mountain like a stadium light during a night game.

"Let's get a few more runs in, then break for lunch." He agreed to do an on-camera interview with me later in the afternoon up on the heated porch of the lodge. The two of them headed off to the lift. Meanwhile, Kirk had found us a way up the mountain. With our gear secured to the snowmobile, we headed toward the peak.

Steve and I positioned our gear so we could shoot video of skiers coming down the hill without being pummeled. An older, African American man skied up.

"I'm Billy Demby. I'm with Disabled Sports. Can I help you guys with anything?"

I didn't know Billy Demby, but I liked him right away. And he had a lot of information about the organization, which was helpful for our story. He talked with us on-camera, about how Disabled Sports had been providing an outlet for physically challenged people for a couple of decades. And he talked about the Vietnam War, which I always find fascinating. As we wrapped up, the small light on top of the camera caught a glint of metal at Billy's ankles. It was only then I realized he had prosthetic legs.

"You were injured, yourself?"

"The truck I was in took fire. It was a Vietnamese RPG. Took both my legs right below my knees and plunged me into a world of pain. Emotional pain. Did all the drinkin', druggin' I could, until I met some other wounded people who were up and out doin' things. I started with wheelchair basketball, and, well, here I am." He grinned.

Billy Demby would stick in my mind for a long time. I often thought about what he had overcome and the graceful way he handled himself and so many others who stood to slide down the same path. Standing on the side of that mountain, wind slicing at my cheeks and crisping the inside of my nose, I felt—maybe for the first time in my life—*lucky*.

Demby skied smoothly away and our snowmobile transport returned. Steve and I clomped into the lodge to warm up and de-ice the gear. It was a large outdoorsy room, with lots of glass, so you could watch the skiers. I looked around for a fireplace. That's when I saw Chuck and Greg sitting at a small table, away from the crowd. I went to the bar and grabbed two beers.

"Hey, gentlemen!" I called, jauntily approaching the table, sure they would be happy to see my liquid offerings. Neither of them looked up. I stepped closer, then stopped short, the drinks suspended in midair over the table. Greg and Chuck were bent over Greg's phone. Thick streams of tears poured from the corners of Greg's eyes. I stood frozen. There was no way out. But I was not sure I could stay, either.

"I can leave you guys." I stammered.

"No, sit down, Terese. We could use that beer," said Chuck. Greg looked down, then pushed his shoulders back and took a deep breath. He did not wipe the tears, though. He wore them like shiny metallic ribbons.

"I was just showing this to Chuck," Greg said, holding up a picture on his phone. It took me a second to recognize the mangled Humvee. "That's what I was riding in when I got hurt." His voice was gravelly.

"Oh my God," I murmured, "I'm sorry." I instinctively leaned over and hugged Greg. Like *that* was going to solve anything.

He turned back to the photo. "See those holes in the door? That's from shrapnel."

"Jesus," I heard myself utter.

"Those doors are like, four inches thick. So." He took a deep breath. "No wonder I'm sittin' here like this." He said it matter-of-factly, like the explosion had been some sort of science experiment testing the durability of flesh vs. armor, and they had both failed.

"Hey," said Chuck, lightening things up, "Terese, why don't I get *you* a beer?"

"No, thanks, I'm working. But I'll have one with you tonight," I promised. And later, I did. It was "casino night" at the lodge. We played cards and poker games with dozens of other skiers and Chuck bought me that beer, which I nursed all evening. I did not live that down for a long time. My beer grew warmer as I watched different scenes unfolding around the room. There was lots of noise, egging on to higher bets, jeering at the wins and losses—and the occasional dark, humorous jab that can only come from one wounded person to another. It was a scene to which I would always be only a respectful witness, never a member of the club.

It would take a while before my less than graceful refreshment delivery morphed into my own takeaway. It came to me months later, as I watched Socrates' "Philoctetes" performed by "Theater of War," a project which performs readings of ancient Greek plays as a means toward healing, for staff at Walter Reed. As the story goes, Philoctetes is banished to an island because he has a very painful and foul-smelling wound. But he has a weapon, a bow, which could help win the Trojan war. A plan is concocted where the young Neoptolemus is sent to the island to steal the bow from Philoctetes but he does not take it. Instead he stays with Philoctetes through his pain and stench and helps him to heal. They both return to much glory back in Greece, but that is beside the point. The point is that Neoptolemus stays. He is not embarrassed or upset or otherwise squeamish. He sits down and delivers the beer. My experience was a nanosecond of what caretakers of the sick and wounded must feel: the excruciating endurance of another's physical and emotional pain.

In my interview with Greg at the lodge, he talked about freedom—not the constitutional kind that he and Chuck defend, but the kind that lets a person career down a hill at outlandish speeds, barely in control, and reach the bottom, not with a crash but with a flourish. He had gotten a taste of it on top of the horse in Vail some weeks prior. Now he was completely liberated, the wind freezing his tears as he rocketed down the side of a majestic, jagged mountain, letting him go, letting him let go. Therapy that could not be had inside the pallid walls at Walter Reed. He loved the medical staff and therapists at the hospital, but exhilaration and independence like this did not come on a track and did not have hinges. And he said, until that moment, he had not imagined he would ever be skiing again.

In the coming weeks there were more trips. The Wounded Warrior Project evolved and became popular and well-funded. While Kim had what they called "right of first refusal," and Jaelen sometimes missed school to go along, Chuck often side-kicked the adventures. They fished in Alaska. They skied again, in Vail. Chuck loved going. They both did. They developed a sort of travel rhythm, one that other wounded men and women saw and wanted to emulate. They got a schtick going—calling out "Cooomming throooooough!!!" in airports and hotel lobbies, and occasionally getting so out of hand Chuck wound up dumping Greg out of the chair. They would laugh hysterically. Their humorous banter, their teamwork, reminded them both of what was still the same. Even in their most slapstick moments, they could be leaders. Chuck saw that the two of them, together, were giving others hope.

At the end of that Breckenridge weekend, Greg, Chuck and I said good-bye. It seemed inevitable that we would all meet up again, but we did not know where or how. None of us could have foreseen how their story would invert, how the role of Neoptolemus would turn from one to the other and how a decade later I would still be a witness.

CHAPTER EIGHTEEN

"Gadson said when he went in for surgery, if we won at Dallas he'd be at the playoffs. It was motivation to win— to get him back on the sidelines again."
—Chase Blackburn, Linebacker, New York Giants

Some were calling it the Miracle at the Meadowlands. Beginning with the Redskins game, the New York Giants had nearly whiplashed themselves with a turnaround season. Sully knew it was, at least in part, the words of Greg Gadson that had flipped their odds. The week after the Redskins game the Giants easily handled Chuck's Eagles 16-3. Then followed nearly weekly victories. The New York Jets, Atlanta Falcons, San Francisco 49ers, Miami Dolphins, Detroit Lions, Chicago Bears and the Buffalo Bills all fell to the team that had nearly gone bust in September. Their only four losses, following their so-called morph, were to the Dallas Cowboys, the Minnesota Vikings, the New England Patriots and the Redskins, who had taken revenge in a second matchup.

Now the Giants, unbelievably, were headed to the playoffs, where they would meet the Tampa Bay Buccaneers on Tampa's home turf in a Wild Card Game. Greg was skeptical when Sully mentioned that players had been asking about him through the season. He had only met them once, and as individuals he had only spoken to a few. Clearly, as Greg had seen in some of those televised victories, they were bonding with their mission— kicking ass as a team. But he did not think he had much to do with it. Still, when Sully called to ask him to surprise the team in Tampa, Greg was happy to make what he figured would be for them a cursory appearance.

Away trips were always more taxing on players than home games. So, when the bus, teeming with sweaty athletes, pulled up to their lavish Tampa hotel, players were looking forward to a little downtime. They began filing off the stuffy bus into the thinner Florida-in-January air.

"Colonel Gadson!" one player yelled, when he saw Greg waiting in the lobby.

"Hey, Gadson's here!" Word passed down the lineup. Soon they were nudging each other forward.

"We almost didn't recognize you standing up!" one player said as he swaggered past the reception desk. Greg shook each hand offered, as he stood in the humidity on his new Power Knees. He had decided to wear them as a show of strength, in honor of his team. But he was soaked in sweat, reminded of the temperature in Iraq as he balanced, making sure he greeted each player individually. More than handshakes, there were hugs. Huge smiles, surprised shouts and engulfing embraces. Greg laughed and braced himself on his canes, struggling to stay upright. *Maybe Sully wasn't kidding.*

Earlier in the day he had met up with Coach Coughlin at Raymond James Stadium, a place famous for the pirate ship replica near the end zone. As Greg had pushed his metal appendages forward across the concrete floor something caught on his shoe, sending him chin-first toward the concrete. The team security guard, Mike Murphy, took a made-for-TV dive, catching Gadson before he splayed himself. Now, as his feet teetered on the concrete, he silently thanked the Lord for giving him the strength to stay standing for more than 60 heartfelt greetings. Any doubts he had about the effects of his words back in September were subdued. Greg could see it. The way they carried themselves, the way they moved together—not bumping each other but as a gentle but powerful swell, shoulder to shoulder, peacefully. There was a joyful serenity about them now, which enveloped him. Not a quiet serenity. They were loud as hell. But an internal peace and confidence—a sublayer to their exterior cajoling. All the time he spent battling gravity was worth the reveal—to see what they had become. And their own deepening admiration of him was touching.

All the standing had worn Greg out so he decided to use the wheelchair for game day. So, when Coughlin and Sully made it clear they wanted him to ride on the team bus to "Ray Jay Stadium," the chair created a small hitch. Greg sat outside the bus, chatting with charged-up players as they boarded. It took a minute for them to realize the problem—he could not board.

"Colonel, do you need some help getting on?" It was Dave Diehl, a starting left tackle. At 6 feet 5 inches, and 315 pounds, he towered over Greg in his chair.

"I gotta be honest, Dave, I've not tried to board a bus since . . . "

"No problem, Colonel!" Diehl smiled widely. He had a brown scruff on his chin and cheeks and a tattoo on his left arm. A few other players had gathered around.

Diehl knelt down in front of Greg, who suddenly felt large arms and hands of other players wrap around his chest. For a minute he was airborne, then sliding onto Diehl's shoulders. Diehl easily stood, elevating Greg about 9 feet into the air.

"It's a great view from up here!" Greg laughed, as Diehl walked, carrying the team's lucky charm toward the bus, ducking deeply to clear the top of the door, then crouching as Greg slid into a seat near the front.

As Diehl stood back up, he saw Greg studying the tattoo.

"It's the Croatian coat of arms. My mom's Croatian." Diehl held out his arm so Greg could look more closely.

"Staima!" Greg said, in Serbo-Croatian.

Diehl grinned in recognition of the informal greeting. "How do you know . . . ?"

"I was deployed to Bosnia as part of the U.N. peacekeeping force. Chief of operations," he paused, focusing again on the ink.

"And what's that word written underneath the coat of arms?

"Neunistiv, " Greg answered. "It means 'indestructible.'"

· · ·

The Tampa Bay Buccaneers had blamed some of their away losses on the shock of cold weather. But at home, they had no excuses, and at first it seemed they would not need any. Again, for the Giants it was a tough first quarter, ending in a 7-0 Bucs lead. In the second quarter, the Giants rallied with two touchdowns, going into halftime 14-7. In the third quarter, Corey Webster recovered a fumble, leading to a Giants field goal. Then Webster intercepted a pass in the end zone. Finally, in the fourth quarter, Giants Quarterback Eli Manning threw a touchdown pass to Amani Toomer, wrapping up with a final score of 24-14. It was Manning's first playoff win and Coughlin's first with the Giants. The Giants would move ahead to play Dallas, a team that had handed them a 31-20 loss earlier in the season.

Greg joined the team for a post-game celebration and unending piles of well-earned nourishment.

"You coming to Dallas?" Plaxico Burress asked. The two were forging a friendship, based partly on their common roots—Burress was from Norfolk, Virginia, near Greg's hometown of Chesapeake—but mostly on kindred spirits.

"No, sorry, man. I've got two surgeries scheduled for Tuesday."

"Two? What for?"

The heterotopic ossification that had bothered him a while back had gotten worse. He was going to have to go back to the hospital where they would slice open the end of his stub and carve out that pokey bone. And they were going to try to put a better bend back in his arm, which had actually functionally recovered from the radial nerve damage but apparently still needed attention.

"My arm," he bent the arm in question as far as it would go. "And my residual leg on the one side. So, I can't make it, but I'll be watching."

"Sorry man, good luck," Burress offered. "I feel ya. Came off an ankle injury earlier this year, but, jeez."

Both men were a little disappointed. The team was getting slightly superstitious. Could they win without him there? He was more than a good luck charm. He was becoming one of them.

. . .

The dim lights in the bottom floor lobby of Walter Reed Army Medical Center were probably supposed to be soothing but it seemed to Greg more like he was underground, submerged with a population equally unwilling to be there. It felt like purgatory where all he could see were the pained faces of the eternally waiting. Elbow to elbow misery. He and Kim wheeled their way through the crowd, all too familiar with the plight of the masses. And here they were, re-entering the vortex.

Compared to what he had already been through the surgeries were minor. A small incision would be made near his elbow so doctors could surgically release his arm. And another larger incision would be made at the end of his left stub. It should not have felt like such a big deal. But it did.

He flipped on the bathroom fan in his hospital room. It might as well have been the blades of a helicopter spinning him back into his chair. It roared at him relentlessly, reminding him he was far from home and despite the distance he had come was also far from finished. Once again, an empty bed threatened to hold him captive. The smells and the noises sent him back to the blurry days of the intensive care unit and Ward 57, with all of its ins and outs, visitors, doctors and therapists. He missed Bleill. He missed Andrew. He missed his kids and his unit. He even missed his new normal. And now, just for a moment, he missed the old normal—the one where the only impediment to getting out of bed was sleep. The only thing stopping him from a Greg-and-Chuck roadshow was his job. Or kids sports. There had been nothing stopping him from much else. He had had everything. He had not taken it for granted. But he had not expected it to end, either.

He flipped the fan off. Damned thing.

A nurse wheeled him to pre-op. He reluctantly leaned forward into what felt like the past. His vitals were checked, measurements taken, his left residual stub marked to prevent confusion in the OR. They asked his name. And his rank. And his name again. He hated those questions. They made him feel like he was being interrogated, like a POW—like the enemy.

After his surgery, part of his new rehab was to sit in bed with his arm in a continuous motion contraption that moved it back and forth. At first, it seemed the surgical plan had come together. The arm was released. The PT part would be critical. His stub was bandaged and sore. Like before. No steel cages but the similarity of the gauze and tape were disturbing. At his bedside was a hand pump, primed to administer painkilling meds with just a little pressure from his thumb. But he resisted. He did not want to get hooked again, then feel as awful as he had coming off it the last time. It was more the frustration than the pain, anyway. And that made him even more frustrated. He often thought about how lucky he was that he had Kim and the kids, who were weathering everything amazingly well. Other guys did not have families. Some wives left their wounded husbands. Usually, thinking about his good fortune buoyed him. This was just a setback, he told himself. It happens in life. He told himself to lumber forward. But he was without both of his teams—the one he had left in Iraq and the other, now in Dallas. The edges of that old dark place began to fold up over his soul, dragging it down until he was nearly splayed out again.

By Thursday he was restless, still stuck in the bed. He picked up the corded hospital phone and dialed Sully's number, knowing chances of him picking up were slim. With Dallas looming, it had to be a crazy week at the Meadowlands. Greg felt his heart thump an extra beat as he listened to the voice mail greeting, assimilating his thoughts. The tone was his cue:

"Hey, Sully, it's Greg. I just wanted to let you and the team know how much I'm thinking of you this week. And I want to thank you for letting me be a part of the Giants. It's a tough time for me, I'm—in some ways, I feel like I'm starting over, and I won't lie—it's painful. I'm sorta struggling, here. But what's getting me through is you all and knowing I'm part of something bigger. How can I talk to you about facing adversity, then not fight back myself? Anyway, thank you for everything. And I'll be watching Sunday."

Greg hung up the phone, hoping he had not sounded like a teenage girl without a prom date. He grabbed the remote off the nightstand and flipped on the television. Some sports cable channel would probably be previewing the game.

. . .

The team meeting in Texas before the Cowboys game had the happy intensity of an overdone summer wedding. The atmosphere was electric, powerful, edgy. They were a team that had come from the bottom, the very edge of complete failure, all the way to the playoffs. The Cowboys were formidable. Dallas was favored to win.

Coach Coughlin went to the front of the room, standing before a white screen. He spoke for a moment, then flicked on a computer, flashing Power Point text over their heads.

". . . I just wanted to let you and the team know how much I'm thinking of you this week . . ."

The room got quiet as Coughlin read the message Greg had left for Sully out loud, his voice catching. When he finished he could hear the eerie calm.

"Can you imagine?" he asked them. "After all Colonel Gadson's been through and now, having such a setback—and he's thinking about us. He's deriving his strength, his endurance, from *us*." There was a low murmur of agreement and some head shaking. The emptiness was palpable. They could either let it swallow them or fill it with their own resilience.

. . .

Facing a team like Dallas, which had already beaten the Giants once in that season, carried a bit of psychological baggage. Still, history provides lessons. The previous game, and the loss, had given Coughlin and the players an opportunity to study the competition up close. They decided they needed their defense to focus on disrupting the Cowboys' passing game. Dallas seemed to use a lot of long plays. And much of their scoring was due to their competition's mistakes.

The two powerful teams took to the field and went body blow for body blow, neither making much progress. But neither was wearing out, either. Twice, passes from Manning to Toomer wound up safely received in the end zone. Dallas's great hope, Tony Romo, completed a touchdown pass to Terrell Owens during the second quarter, followed by a 1-yard run by Marion Barber. At half time the Giants and the Cowboys were tied at 14.

. . .

Greg had mentioned the upcoming surgery, so I had made a plan to hang around D.C. after work one Sunday evening instead of driving back home to Annapolis. I wanted to visit in the evening, when it would be clear that I was not on duty. After letting the PR folks know I would be roaming the halls for personal reasons, I checked in at the visitor's station and looked for his room.

"Terese!" Greg called, as I peeked my head in the door.

Of course, the Dallas game was on the television. Schretzman was lounging in a chair alongside Greg's arm-moving machinery.

"I'd get you a beer, but . . . " Chuck teased, remembering how slowly I nursed mine in Colorado. He found another chair so I could sit with them and listen as they made manly football-watching noises. I studied Greg's bandaged stump.

"It doesn't hurt too much," Greg said gruffly. "They got all the HO off, they said, so as soon as it heals I can get back to the coal mine. But for now, I'm stuck in da bed again."

I grinned dumbly. I knew what heterotopic ossification was from doing so many stories. But there was no sense in so much of this. He did not seem to want pity, so I did not offer it. He seemed down, or a little off. I did not know at the time how much these surgeries had set him back emotionally.

"What are they doing with your arm?" I gestured toward the metal plate, rocking back and forth.

"I don't really know what this does, it just keeps it moving. Continuous passive motion. I have to keep it on here for hours at a time."

"Seems uncomfortable."

"It is," he admitted. I was glad Chuck was there. He told me he had to leave the next morning. He had come in from Ohio to help see Greg through the surgeries but needed to get back to his cadets. I watched, once again an outsider, as they focused on every nuance of the game.

On the screen, the Giants were rallying in the third quarter. After scoring a 34-yard field goal, Dallas began making its own mistakes. And the Giants lit up. Manning pushed down the field, and Brandon Jacobs scored from the 1-yard line.

"Touchdown, Giants!" Chuck yelled. Greg jiggled his thigh nervously. He wondered if Sully had heard his message. *Maybe he shouldn't have . . .*

"Think they can win without you?" I asked.

"They'll be all right," he said, confidently. "Besides, I'm right here!"

And just then, a pass from Romo into the end zone was intercepted by the Giants' R.W. McQuarters. The Giants walked away with a 21-17 victory, a date with the Green Bay Packers in Wisconsin, and a shot at the Super Bowl.

CHAPTER NINETEEN

"Struggle is okay. It means you're living."
—Colonel Gregory Gadson (Ret.)

Greg's bandaged stump was sore to lean on, but limping around the track in the MATC was better than sitting in bed, staring out the window at January's dismal wrath. The docs had cleared him to walk indoors. His arm was regaining some function, though his hand was still messed up. The feeling had never quite come back to his third finger and pinky, attributable to some new collateral damage to his ulnar nerve.

A few months earlier Mike Corcoran had pegged him for a small experiment.

"I think what we'll do, Greg," he had said, back in October, "is we'll try these, one at a time."

He held up a prosthetic leg. It was thicker than the C-Leg, sturdier looking, bulky even. "It's a Power Knee."

"Al-righht . . ." Greg's voice raised with skepticism.

"It fits a lot like the one you have on, but it's able to sense your movements and actually help you walk."

"Sounds bionic."

"It is, actually. We'll try one at a time. There's a sensor that we'll put on your other leg, the C-Leg. It can measure the load—how much weight you're putting on that leg, the position of the leg and how fast you're walking. Then there's this other piece called the APM. It's a transmitter.

You wear it on the C-Leg ankle."

"Okaaaaaay." This play was getting complicated. But very interesting.

"The transmitter uses Bluetooth technology to tell the Power Knee what to do. That's how the Power Knee reacts to the C-Leg." Mike's enthusiasm drowned out Greg's dubious sigh.

"I think you're going to like it, Greg. It's incredible technology. You'll still use your hamstrings and quads to move them, but the knee will take some of the work out of walking."

A few other patients and therapists stopped their workouts to watch as Mike handed Greg the new leg. For this crowd it was like the unveiling of the latest Ferrari. This was the first Power Knee any of them had seen. Össur was pioneering cutting-edge prosthetics in response to the needs of the world's war wounded. Its relationship with Walter Reed, Mike Corcoran and Paul Pasquina was deepening as it worked to meet patients' needs. The company's reach would eventually wrap around its newest test pilot.

"It's heavier than my other leg."

"It is," answered Mike, "it's a little over 10 pounds. It's also more expensive. You'd pay $20,000 for the C-Leg. Add another $100,000 for the Power Knee."

"For that money, it should shoot me to the moon!"

"It's all new technology, Greg. The company designed the knee for single-leg amputees. The sensors are supposed to be on the functional leg."

"I'm a little short on those," Greg joked. The group grinned at his self-deprecating humor.

"Right, so I figured, why wouldn't it react to a C-Leg?"

"This is an *experiment*," Greg observed.

"I can't think of a better guinea pig. You and Josh Bleill. He's going to try it too."

"Is he?" His competitive spirit was stirring.

"Yes." Mike lowered his voice. "Keep this quiet. I'm hoping to get you both on *two* Power Knees."

"So, the sensors will play off each other?"

"Yeah. I can calibrate everything to work together." He gestured toward a big blue case, sitting alongside the track. Inside were bunches of sleek buttons, knobs and screens.

"Why keep it quiet?"

"Some folks around here think it's dangerous to use two at a time. They're afraid you won't be able to control both legs at once and they'll throw you like an angry bull."

"Didn't you tell me a while back, you and Bob, that I'd better get over the fear of falling?"

"Yes, because you might! But I think it's worth a try," Mike said.

"Roger that."

Greg needed to get stronger on the C-Legs before he attempted any sort of transition. But he did not want to disappoint Mike, who was putting his reputation on the line with this Power Knee thing. The only way to get stronger was to work harder. He stood up, grabbed his canes and began working his way around the track. Breathing heavily, sweating, he managed a few laps before he finally sat down to rest. He worked out like that for a couple of days. Then it was time for a change.

• • •

"You ready for this today?" Mike had been calibrating the leg, trying different settings, making sure it performed well.

"Today's as good as any," Greg wheeled himself closer to the computer and the appendage.

"We'll try your right leg first," Mike said, helping Greg take off one of the C-Legs. The prosthetist shimmied a new liner up his right stump, pulling the suction ring tight at the top. Then he pulled the power leg over the liner, working for a few minutes on the fit. He expertly placed the sensors on the C-Leg.

"I look like C3PO from Star Wars," Greg said, laughing a little.

"Remember this is what it reacts to. When this moves," Mike pointed at the sensor, "this starts moving." He bent the Power Knee at the joint. "It'll take some getting used to, so use your canes."

As expected, a small crowd began to assemble. The surgeon, Dr. Donald Gajewski, Dr. Paul Pasquina, physical therapists Bob Bahr and Kyla Dunleavy and now Kim had formed a curious group. Gajewski and Pasquina were in on the experiment and stood fixated on their latest trial. If it worked, this technology would open doors for hundreds of other patients.

Bob and Mike stood on either side of him as he pushed himself up, putting weight on both legs.

"Step first with the left, the C-Leg. We have you," Mike instructed.

Greg lifted his C-Leg up and stepped forward. Obediently, the right leg bent at the knee and angled for its first step. He engaged his quad reflexively.

"Just go with it. Let it do some of the work."

Greg leaned heavily on the canes. The leg had to earn his trust. He took another step. The Power Knee jumped forward, sending Greg into a wobble.

"Steady, there," Gajewski said softly.

Greg looked up and saw everyone staring. "Do I look that bad?"

"You look great!" called Kyla.

"MAHvelous!" said Bob.

Greg worked his way around the track a few times, gaining more confidence and ability with each step. Mike was giddy. "That's great, excellent! It comes naturally to you!"

"He's catching on quickly," Pasquina said, thinking again about their days at West Point. Then, nodding at Mike, "We'll be moving forward in no time."

"Let's not wear him out," Mike said, "Greg, are you ready to call it a day?"

"Yah, I'm getting pretty tired. Let's put our new toy away. We can work with it more tomorrow." He did not want to seem too proud, but he was thrilled that he had made their experiment work. He was taking to this new guinea pig role.

Every day that fall he would spend a few hours with the bionic knee, working mostly on his balance. Sometimes his mind would wander, and the motion of the leg would surprise him for just a half-second, enough to make him wobble. Soon he could strap it on himself and hit the track with little fanfare. He tried moving it faster, seeing if the sensor could keep up. Then he tried moving backwards. It was awkward, but he could do it. Next, he worked his way around corners, which required a sharper turn than the gradual turn of the track. Feeling pretty confident, he gazed out the glass windows facing a little-used road and a grassy area. What would it feel like to go for a walk *outside*? His eyes came to rest on the glass door. Could he get out unnoticed? Would it matter? One thing prosthetic legs are not is stealthy. He pressed on the metal bar and leaned into the door lightly.

For the first time he stepped outside, alone in the autumn sun. His feet tentatively skimmed the asphalt and he stopped, holding the C-Leg still so he could absorb this moment, alone on the edge of the season's first chill. He took another few steps before realizing the driveway had a slight slope to it. The forward momentum of gravity made going downhill a little tricky. He realized then how terrain, an unpredictable factor, would always play a role in his ability to function on the legs. A literal learning curve. He wished he had something to lean on, where he could stop and rest without the risk of falling on concrete or brick or gravel. And that is when it first came to him. A broad, sturdy dog would come in handy. He had seen other patients using Labrador retrievers, or longer haired goldens, for support. A well-trained dog would give him something or someone to lean on if he started to fall. A dog might even help him get up, since he was still mostly one-armed. Greg made his way back through the glass door, and into the MATC, hoping he would get away with another little walkabout later. A few weeks later Mike added the second Power Knee to the mix, making Greg the first double amputee to use them bilaterally, a big accomplishment for the rehab duo, and a huge win for Össur.

Back in the MATC after his revision surgery, he wanted to level up— regain his stamina. He worked with the C-Legs, then the Power Knees again, each day pushing himself harder. One afternoon his left stub began to sting at the tip. He wanted to get in a few more laps, so he ignored the pain and kept clomping around the track. But a couple of laps later, the stinging sharpened alarmingly. The end of his stump, soaking with sweat, was slipping inside the liner. Something was wrong. His heart palpitated, his breathing got heavier. This was no time for another setback. He could not afford it. It was not fair. *Please, Lord, no.* Mike was on the other side of the track, talking with another patient.

"Mike, I think I have a problem here!" he called across the room. Greg sat down on one of the workout benches and started pulling at the leg.

"It's really sweating and it hurts!" He yanked off the liner, revealing a bloody, sweaty, gooey mess.

"Whoa!" he yelped.

"Looks like you tore it open," said Mike.

"Tore it open? Looks like a hemorrhage!" The red blood on the white liner made for a murderous-looking scene.

"Aw, your stitches just came open, that's all. You're working a little too hard. We'll get you fixed up. Better get in the chair."

One of the other therapists was already on the phone with Ortho. Greg looked down at his oozing limb. He hoped this did not mean another surgery. God help him if it were that. All he wanted was to get better, to put on those crazy bionic legs and clomp off into the sunset. He plopped, defeated, into his wheelchair, watching the grey tile disappear under his seat, one by one, until they reached his room. He had been hoping he was not long for the hospital. He wanted to get back home to Fort Belvoir. Instead, he was sliding down the rocky mountain slope.

Mike seemed almost cheerful, grabbing some disinfectant wash and cleaning up the wound. Hadn't he seen that mess? It looked like it would be weeks before he would be on his legs again.

"Greg, it's not at all as bad as it looks. It happens. Really. Surface stuff. It'll be better in no time. Promise. It's like you skinned it. Heals fast."

Greg wanted to believe him. But the sight of Paul Pasquina seemed to confirm his worst fears.

"You just trying to stay here a while, now?" the doctor asked.

"I was trying to get out!" Greg answered. "I tore it all up!"

Pasquina bent over to look directly at the bottom of the stub.

"Nah, it's okay—just a little too much wear and tear. I don't think it even needs to be re-sewn. Just stay off it a couple of days and ease back into the therapy. Not so much all at once. Maybe some ice. Does it hurt?"

"A little."

"Not throbbing?"

"No, not throbbing."

"You're good."

"Really?"

"Yah, you're fine. It looked a lot worse than it was. Just take it easy. You'll be out of here soon."

"How soon?"

"Maybe a week."

"Another week?" Paul might as well have said light-year.

"We'll see how it goes in a few days. I have to get back to my office. We'll talk some more later."

"Okay, Paul. Thanks." Pasquina was so damned unflappable, he thought. "See you after a while."

He settled back into his chair, where he figured he'd be stuck for a few days. He sighed. He hated to complain or even to get grumpy.

Kim and the kids stopped by. Jaelen was fascinated by his dad's bloody wound, but Gabby would not look.

"Still hurt?" Kim asked.

"Not really. It's just frustrating."

She looked at him sympathetically. "It's hard for you to take it easy, but—"

"I know."

"You'll get out of here soon enough. And we'll get on with our lives."

"Right. You're right. I know," he agreed. He looked out the window. "Hey, now that we have our own place, what do you think about getting a dog? Have you seen the dogs working with the guys in the MATC?"

"They are cool. Let's think about it," Kim said, then herded the kids to take them out to dinner. A dog would be another thing to take care of, but it might also give her husband more independence. The kids, of course, would love it.

The 1970s-looking hospital banana phone on the nightstand rang around 7:30 that night. Tom Coughlin's reserved tone sat Greg straight up in the bed. He could not imagine why the Giants coach would be calling him—he had to be near out of his mind getting ready for playoffs.

"Coach! How are you?"

"I'm good, good, the question is, how are you?" Coach sounded stern, fatherly.

The pain and anxiety of the day slipped like protective pads off his shoulders.

"Not too bad, Coach. Had a little injury today as I was training. The therapists here have me working with these high-tech Bluetooth prosthetics."

"Are you back on your, uh, feet?"

"Just for short periods. I worked out for too long today, opened up the wound from the surgery, so now I have to take it a little easy."

"You're pretty driven, but there's such a thing as over-training," observed the coach. "Listen, I'm calling to ask you a favor."

"I'll do what I can."

"I'd like you to come to Green Bay this weekend. I'd like you to sit with the team as our honorary co-captain."

"Really? Did you say co-captain?" He wanted to be sure he had heard right. *Honorary co-captain of the New York Giants? Did coach know he had only played college ball?*

Coach cleared his throat.

"Of course, Coach, I'd be honored! I'm not sure I'll be allowed out of here by then." Greg remembered Pasquina's parting words. He had said a week. That was not soon enough.

"You know what, Coach? Never mind that. I'll *break* out! Are you kidding me?" His mind was racing. *How would he pull this off? Kim could drive, he would just walk out the front lobby . . .*

Coughlin laughed. "Don't push anything. We want you in good condition."

"I'll be there, Coach Coughlin. I will. I'll find a way."

"Okay, the team will be thrilled. I shared your message with them—the one you left Sully's my phone before the Dallas game. I think it really had an impact."

"Really?"

"Greg, the players understand you're going through a lot. They can't imagine that you're thinking of them while you're laid up and having a hard time."

"I'm really flattered they're thinking of *me*. What do you need me to do?"

"Just show up. You'll be on the field. Like the last time. But now you have a position. You have a title."

"Coach, you said co-captain—who's the other honorary captain?"

"Harry Carson."

"Giants Hall of Famer Harry Carson!" Greg echoed. Carson, in Greg's mind, was a Mount Rushmore figure in the NFL's history of linebackers.

"Whoa. Wow. Right! Great! I'll see you soon, then." *This weekend!*

It was Wednesday. He would need to be on an airplane in two days. He picked the banana phone back up.

"Paul?"

Pasquina assumed the call was about the freshly opened wound.

"Paul, you have to get me out of here!"

"What do you mean? What's wrong?"

"Coach Coughlin just called me. He wants me at the game this weekend in Green Bay. He asked me to be honorary co-captain!"

"Wow." *This guy.* Pasquina shook his head.

"Paul, I have to . . . I need to travel Friday."

"Ohhhh, no. You just split the thing open. A minute ago, you thought you were bleeding to death!"

"I know!" Greg laughed. "But I'm *fine* now!"

"Maybe there's something wrong with your head."

"Maybe. Just get me out of here by Friday morning."

"I'll see what I can do," the former quarterback said, realizing that stopping the new Greg Gadson might be even more difficult than stopping the old one.

CHAPTER TWENTY

"I would have taken any of them with me to Iraq.
That's how much of a team we had become."
—Colonel Gregory D. Gadson, (Ret.)

"Greg, really you should go inside. You can watch from the booth," Sully coaxed, tentatively placing a hand on Greg's wheelchair that was parked just behind the visiting team's white sideline at Lambeau Field. At the 3:33 p.m. kickoff, the temperature was -1 degree Fahrenheit. The windchill was -23. It was nearing the end of the first quarter. The Giants had managed to put three on the board while Green Bay remained scoreless.

"No, Sully, I'm good," Greg answered. "I'm staying." He tugged his hat down and looked at Jaelen.

"Do you want to go up to the box?" he asked his son. Jaelen shook his head adamantly, but eyeing the heaters the Giants staff had rolled out behind the sideline.

"If you go under one of those, you'll never come out," Greg warned. "And you'll miss all the action. You need to suck it up." His son understood "once-in-a-lifetime opportunity," even if his lifetime was only 13 years. He shoved his mind over the matter.

For a minute, Greg's mind shot back to those moments after his last amputation, when he was not sure he would be able to be the dad he had wanted to be, doing all those father-son things a dad dreams about. And here they were on the sidelines of an NFL playoff game. Jaelen had just a moment ago walked with him to the center of the field in front of 72,000 people for the coin toss. The Giants lost the toss but Jaelen had gotten to shake the hand of Green Bay Quarterback Brett Favre, which was way better than a fishing trip.

The temperature rose by 2 degrees, but the wind chill dropped another degree. The players' broad bodies were completely covered, their hands only exposed while the ball was in play. Coach Coughlin's face grew redder every minute. His ears, already purple during pregame warm-ups, were now covered by a blue Gumby-like hood.

Lawrence Tynes duplicated his efforts and put another three points on the board in the second quarter, but Favre completed a pass to tight end Donald Driver, who was wide open because the Giants' Corey Weber had slipped on the frozen turf. Driver ran for 90 yards for a Green Bay touchdown—the first one of the game. Then a 36-yard field goal put the Packers ahead 10-6 going into halftime.

Halftime in the locker room is often an opportunity to cool down, but at Lambeau Field that day everyone was looking for a little heat. Jaelen basked in what felt like a tropical island, his dad's warning coming to mind. Coughlin talked about everything the players were doing right, but added that they needed more than field goals to get out of there with a victory.

"You look like a popsicle, Greg," Sully joked gently, when they went back on the field. He was truly worried about his friend's prolonged exposure to such harsh conditions, especially being fresh from the arm and stump surgeries.

"Do I?" Greg laughed. "I feel okay, really, I have these hand warmers."

"Yeah, if you change your mind . . ."

Coughlin's face was now plum-red and the unknowing recipient of many texts from concerned family and friends. He looked on, once again admiring Gadson. *One tough son-of-a gun*, he thought.

Greg watched the players come back onto the field, seemingly oblivious to the piercing wind. He scrunched himself down in his chair. *At least I don't have to worry about keeping my feet warm.* His lips curled up at the edges.

Out on the tundra, running back Brandon Jacobs' short jump into the end zone put the Giants ahead, but Favre and Donald Lee then came back with another TD for the Packers. New York's Ahmad Bradshaw then scored a 4-yard touchdown, putting the Giants ahead again. A 37-yard field goal by the Packer's Mason Crosby—and two missed field goals by Tynes—sent the decision into overtime.

By now, everyone had quit asking Greg to go inside. The heart-racing tension of the 20-20 tied-up contest for a trip to the Super Bowl was keeping everyone warm enough.

A little more than two minutes into the overtime period, Giants corner-back Corey Webster got his shot at redemption, intercepting a pass to Driver and returning it for 9 yards. But Webster did not stop at the whistle. He jogged straight off the field, right over to Greg, embracing him, then thudding the intercepted football into his lap. Greg whooped as the slap of leather stung his thighs. Still, the game was not over. Tynes next took his turn to redeem himself, kicking a 47-yard field goal, the longest by a visiting team at Lambeau, and by some accounts the longest successful sub-zero temperature kick in the history of the NFL. The Giants, by a three-point lead, would be making the trip to the Super Bowl.

Chaos erupted on the sideline and spilled onto the field. Strahan hugged Manning off his feet while Coughlin was swarmed by the other coaches. "We're going to the Super Bowl!!" they each screamed into network television cameras. Madness leap-frogged into the locker room. Greg and Jaelen rolled along with them in amazement as helmets and pads crashed together. Shoulder-crushing hugs and walloping back slaps came from every direction. Greg held the ball in his bare hands, oblivious to the iciness of the pigskin. Then he handed it to Jaelen, who hugged it with both arms.

"You coming to Phoenix?" a few players called out. Other heads turned, waiting for his response.

"If I can bring my family," Greg answered, uncertain of what was next. There were glints of those missing waypoints again, though now diffused, by the mayhem in the locker room. The New York Giants were headed for the Super Bowl, and he was going with them. He believed they would win.

. . .

In the winter of 2007-2008, just having come off a pretty long run covering mostly politics at NBC News and MSNBC, I was oblivious to the New York Giants. I was generally oblivious to the entire NFL and had just begun to learn about the military. To me the Pentagon had been just another concrete building to be avoided, somewhere near Washington, D.C. When I first started working at what was then known as The Pentagon Channel, I had a lot to learn about the military. After meeting Greg, I found that niche at Walter Reed covering the recovering. I was sitting at my desk in our Alexandria, Virginia, offices that January, when my phone lit up with a familiar number.

"I wanted to let you know something, to give you a *tip*!" It was Chuck, who I was just getting to know from my brief adventures with the traveling duo.

"What's that? A tip on beer drinking?" I joked.

"You know about this thing Greg's doing with the New York Giants?" At the time, I had no idea. Chuck filled me in.

"I think it'd make a good piece for the channel," he pointed out, unnecessarily.

"On it!" I sang, joyful at the prospect of a really good story.

I pitched the story to our desk but was edged out of traveling to Phoenix myself to cover it. Always looking to keep a uniformed face on things, they chose instead one of my military colleagues to interview Greg and cover the game as well as Greg's contributions. I got it but was disappointed in their decision. Still, I learned what I could about the New York Giants.

The last time the Giants had made it to the Super Bowl was in 2001, but they were denied the title by the Baltimore Ravens. The last time the Giants won the championship was in 1991.

Historically, the Giants were a team that could be fueled by emotion. In 2005, the deaths of two Giants patriarchs had propelled them to two unexpected victories. Wellington Mara, co-owner with Bob Tish, had been with the team since the mid-1920s, working as a ball boy when his father founded the team. Beloved by many of the players, he insisted on getting to know each one personally. The 2005 team dedicated the game following Mara's death to the co-owner, costing the Redskins a humiliating 36-0 defeat. Just 20 days later, Giants' Chief Executive Bob Tish passed away at the age of 79. This time, the Philadelphia Eagles took the punishment, 27-17. The Giants finished that season 11-5, but were taken out of the playoffs by the Carolina Panthers. And that was more than I had learned about any other sports team in my entire life.

Back at the Meadowlands, with a week left to prepare, Coughlin leaned back on his first hunch, the one he had had the previous September: this team had physical talent. Now they had proven it. Sunday, they played the game with their minds and their guts. Strahan, a 14-year Giants veteran, talked to the team about getting rid of the distractions. He told them, in the end, without the hype, *it's just another football game.* Players arranged for their families' tickets and travel, staying on task.

Super Bowl XLII would be played in the desert. The University of Phoenix in Glendale was chosen because its stadium was state of the art and February in Arizona is moderate, almost always sunny with the tiniest chill on the edge of the bone-dry air. Good football weather.

The team traveled west on Monday, January 28th, lodging in a somewhat secluded hotel. Burress, still nursing the ongoing ankle problem, unbelievably injured his knee in the hotel shower, further complicating the lineup. The swollen knee kept him off the practice field and rendered him physically unreliable for the game. Burress was replaceable, but his outstanding reception record had helped keep them on the scoreboard at Green Bay. The freak accident cast a weeklong shadow on the roster.

Greg, Kim, Jaelen and Gabby arrived in Phoenix on Friday. For Jaelen, a big perk of traveling with the team was the food. The spread laid out at away-game hotels was huge and always seemed homemade. He was a skinny kid, about 85 pounds, and often, after he'd eaten his fill, Strahan, the team captain, would try to get him to go back for seconds and thirds.

"Eat some more, Jaelen, you need to get bigger," he and linebacker Zak DeOssie would say. And they'd make him huge, delicious milkshakes.

The host city threw out a big welcome to fans. The glowing desert sunshine seemed to increase Greg's confidence, despite the Giants' oft-mentioned "underdog" status and the word that seemed to always precede any mention of their Super Bowl opponent, the New England Patriots and their record: undefeated.

Patriots superstar quarterback Tom Brady had passed for 50 touchdowns that year, an NFL record. His passer rating was just under the NFL record. The man was on fire—seemingly unstoppable, leading his team to a 16-0 blockbuster regular season, then winning playoffs against Jacksonville and San Diego. The 1972 Miami Dolphins were the only undefeated team in NFL history, and it looked like the Patriots were about to join them. There was no sportscast, no publication that gave the Giants the slightest of chances.

Still, it seemed to Coughlin and to Greg there were possibilities for the Giants. They had lost to the Patriots in the final game of the regular season, but only by three points. New England had come back from a 12-point deficit, which was the most they'd had to breach all year. And the Giants were dominating in every playoff game on the road. The Dallas and Green Bay wins were considered upsets.

Greg rode with Coughlin from the hotel to the field for Saturday's final workout at the Arizona Cardinals' field. The team's honorary co-captain sat in his wheelchair near the bench, watching his team play with almost too much intensity. He saw Plaxico Burress run onto the field but turn almost immediately, limping back to the sideline. Greg got the sense they were beginning to believe the hype—the constant drumbeat, pounding out a rhythm of defeat, impossible to ignore. And it was the wrong rhythm. He needed to reach out one last time.

Coach Coughlin was concentrating on the field. Greg approached, prepared to be shot down.

"Hey, Coach, what do you think of me saying a few words tonight, maybe before dinner?"

He would certainly understand if the coach had his own plan—one which Greg was no part of. He was the coach after all, and this was a huge career opportunity for him as well as for the team. Greg figured Coach might need to keep things routine. No left turns.

"Well, Greg . . ." Coughlin cleared his throat and kept staring at the field.

Maybe I've over-stepped. Greg thought.

But that evening, Coughlin made his routine appearance, delivering an upbeat "keys to victory" speech, and a few other messages and quotes. Then he shot an enthusiastic, "You're up!" to the team's honorary co-captain.

Greg wheeled himself, once again, to the front of a hotel conference room without having put a whole lot of thought into exactly what he wanted to say. But he did have a clear message in mind. This team, now on the very brink, needed only to understand its own power and to believe in it. Belief, Greg thought, eliminates all other possibilities.

It had been eight months since he'd been blown up, that much he was sure of. He had been told he'd nearly died. He'd nearly died more than once. But in all the struggle, it never occurred to him that he really *could* have died. He believed Private Brown and First Sergeant Fredrick Johnson would not let it happen. Nor would Dr. Brad Woods, the surgeon in Baghdad. Even as he was rushed back into surgery by Dr. Gajewski, putrid fluid oozing from his collapsing artery, he somehow knew death was never on the table. It was not that he knew he would live. He *believed* he would live.

Tomorrow, there could be nothing on the table but belief. Greg put on his soldier face—the look of a commander. This was his unit. They were going into battle.

It was a very different atmosphere on this Super Bowl eve from the one he had wheeled into in September. The men were different. They had grown together, they had learned to watch each other's backs. They were stronger and more focused. There was a mighty cocoon that encapsulated them now. They were no longer individuals. He hoped he had imparted some of that spirit. He knew he had become part of it.

Greg had also evolved. He had worked hard physically, just as they had. And he had seen some dark days over the past several months, just as they had. Like soldiers in trenches, they had fought their greatest enemies together. Players knew him now. They knew his sense of humor and his sense of self. Something close to relief swept the room when he began to speak this time. They saw a man who had for sure been straight up on the edge of death but had grabbed onto life and stuffed it back into his soul. His spirit was not only intact, it was flourishing, nearly pouring out into their consciousness. Gadson was learning how to turn hardship not only into a lesson, but into success.

Chase Blackburn, the special teams member and backup linebacker, leaned back in his chair, enjoying the moment. He knew he would walk away with a plan for tomorrow—something he might not have thought of on his own.

"If I could be anywhere right now," Greg began, "I'd be in Iraq with my unit, because that's where I belong. I know that's not going to happen. But I'm proud and immensely thankful to be here with you all tonight. I've come to know you as a group and some of you as individuals and I can honestly say you have what it takes now to be champions."

Michael Strahan smiled. He was looking at winding up his football career for real now, searching for his own waypoints. He figured the colonel might help smooth his exit.

Greg continued, "I'm going to talk to you about three words I learned in the Army: pride, poise and team. You have *pride*. You are proud members of the New York Giants, an organization with a lot of history and you are one game away. You're *poised* to create an even deeper history of victory tomorrow. You know how you gain poise? You gain poise with practice and training. Poise means you are ready to make that difficult play, catch that impossible pass because you have gone through that motion so many times, you instinctively know what to do. It's automatic. It's rote. In the Army, we couldn't step onto the battlefield knowing what lies ahead without the unwavering confidence that comes with hard core training and repetition, hammering through those drills every day—that's poise. And *team*. You already know about team. I told you in September, there will only be one 2007 New York Giants team and gentlemen, this is it. This is the team that will sustain you for the rest of your lives. This is a team that I'd take back to Iraq with me—every one of you if I could--that's how strongly I believe in you and your commitment, your bond, to each other. I trust you because you trust each other."

A few players looked at each other, cementing that bond in their glances, nodding in slow motion at his words.

"Now there's one more word I'm adding, and that's *belief*. Most importantly, you have to *believe*. Believing is better than knowing. It's that powerful. When I was lying down in the desert, weak, bleeding, unable to call out, wondering when my soldiers would come, even then I *believed* I would live. Dying wasn't an option. And here I am talking to you right now. Because I *believed*. That's what belief will do for you."

Michael Strahan's gap-toothed grin grew wider. He knew some things. But in this thing, he was a believer.

"You have all worked hard this season. You've come together through training. The simple repetition of tasks, of plays, of passes and runs and hits. But you've also come together in spirit, the sort of unbreakable bond that no offensive or defensive line can hold back or break. Tomorrow, it's time to reap the benefits of all that hard work. It's time," he paused, "to *relax*. Rely on what you know. Enjoy it. Let go of the hype. Have a *great* time. And you can't help but win."

Greg knew he had their attention, but he could not be sure they *owned* his words. They were quiet, pensive even, not the lot of restless skeptics he had met a few months ago. Still, it was impossible to know from where he sat at the front of the room if they had embraced the faith, the *belief* that he had in them, that they needed to have in themselves.

CHAPTER TWENTY-ONE

*"Greg instilled in the team a tremendous example of
sacrifice and self-denial for a greater cause."*
—New York Giants Coach Tom Coughlin

"We would not have won without him."
—Michael Strahan, New York Giants Defensive End

The New England Patriots were billed as the greatest football team of all time. The betting public, a week ahead of the game, was predicting an 11-to 12-point spread. The only doubt factor radiated from New England quarterback Tom Brady's much-talked-about on-and-off-again leg injury. Anyone wanting to put money on the game seemed assured at least a little cash back on the heads of the team holding the season's perfect record. Whether it was the allure of the 18-0 or just the mystery and awe brought about by a mythically storied team, Las Vegas casino experts predicted the most bet-upon Super Bowl in its history, exceeding $100 million. On February 3, 2008 *The Boston Globe* was so confident it went to print with a commemorative book, "19-0"—featuring a picture of Brady, and the subtitle, "The Historic Championship Season of New England's Unbeatable Patriots."

The University of Phoenix Stadium was a unique sports venue because both the floor and the roof are retractable. Normally it is the home team's decision whether to play under the sky or the ceiling, but since in this case the stadium was neutral territory it was up to the NFL. With rain in the forecast, league officials chose to play under cover. While the flooring was retractable it was made of real grass. Kickoff was scheduled for 6:30 pm.

Riding on the shoulders of one of the players onto the bus, Greg squinted a little into the afternoon haze. He floated above the excitement. Just below him a wave of adrenaline was rushing down the aisle of the bus, flowing between the seats like a river in spring. He loved the thrill, the layers of electricity while at the same time he felt calm. A shroud of silent confidence puffed up around him, and as he was drawn in with his teammates it also set him a centimeter apart. He felt a little like the eye of a hurricane—he was still surrounded by fury but only he knew in which direction they would be moving.

Arriving at the domed field, Coughlin still had some work to do before kickoff. The NFL required him to submit an inactive player roster 90 minutes before the start and there still was no decision from medical personnel on Plaxico Burress. They had tried to run Burress on the field earlier in the day, but he could not make the sharp cuts required to dodge opposing players. Team medics pulled out all their tricks, the most magical being good old-fashioned tape. And Coughlin noted, as he watched his once hard-nosed player silently kneel before his locker, there was some prayer involved. Medics finally cleared him to play, just as NFL officials were knocking on the locker room door asking for the roster. All that was left for Coughlin, then, was to deliver the downside of that news to Sinorice Moss, who had practiced well all week in case he needed to step in for Plaxico.

At 4 o'clock straight up the team came screaming out onto the field, like a formation of F-18 fighter jets, all steel and power. Greg wheeled into the draft, sucked along in their vacuum, Jaelen pushing the hard rubber wheels as fast as he could against the shorn turf's friction. It was already getting dark and camera flashes nearly blinded them. Murph and Mike, who'd become something like a security detail, ran along either side of Jaelen, the sheer emotion of the moment seeming to suck them all along with thousands of pounds of muscle, grit and determination. Jaelen, always vigilant about wheelchair hazards, tensed as he witnessed the low-lying threat, but the atmospheric propulsion was too much for his small frame. He called out as the wheelchair banged into a cable. Jaelen nearly tumbled headfirst into the back of the chair while his dad, unable to stop his momentum, flew into the air.

"Jaelen?" Greg yelled as everything blurred into slow motion, the chair, suddenly light and mostly empty, lurched ahead. Jaelen's breath caught in his throat. Then, in what seemed like a superbly coordinated defensive move, Mike and Murph swooped in beneath Greg, catching him just before he face-planted. They calmly set Greg down squarely back in the wide leather seat. They barely stopped running.

"What was that?" Greg called out, wide-eyed, looking to see who had noticed their bungled approach.

"It was one of those cords!" Jaelen pointed to a six-inch thick cable, probably part of the massive television coverage.

Greg looked at the Giants security team. "That was some stunt!" Their recovery was so smooth, not one of the nearly 100 million people watching on television, including of course the Schretzman family in Ohio, had noticed the mishap. Greg and Jaelen burst into giggles. So much for their grand entrance.

The pair made their way to the sideline and tucked in among the players and coaches near the defensive end of the bench. Singer Jordin Sparks belted out the national anthem while players stood and Greg sat tall, their hands on their hearts, as a gigantic flag unfurled across the field.

Coughlin caught a glimpse of Gadson, then watched as Strahan gathered players for a last-minute pitch for victory.

The Giants called tails to win the coin toss, then immediately maneuvered a 10-minute drive, the longest drive in Super Bowl history, before being stopped at the Patriots' 14-yard line, where they successfully kicked a field goal. Being the first on the scoreboard gave the Giants a good boost to their psyche, but New England pushed back hard with a kickoff return to the 44, and three completed Tom Brady passes. An interference penalty on Giants linebacker Antonio Pierce landed the Patriots on the Giants 1-yard line, and from there they went ahead, 7-3. The score locked in. Play after play was thwarted by either team, no one making significant progress. At half time, the Giants were still getting beat by four points. Rockers Tom Petty and the Heartbreakers took over the field, kicking off their 2008 tour to the tune of "American Girl" and "I Won't Back Down." Appropriately, he handed the field back to the players with, "Runnin' Down a Dream."

On the first drive of the second half, New York suffered a 5-yard penalty when Blackburn did not make it to the sidelines before a snap and Patriots Coach Bill Belichick challenged the play. The Giants were called for too many players on the field. Next, Strahan executed one of his trademark sacks, costing New England 6 yards. The score remained 7-3 going into the final quarter.

Greg could not help but think back over his own football career—a series of pinnacles and troughs. In his neighborhood junior league, he was told he was too small. Then in high school there was an unexpected rejection from University of Virginia, and finally, that character-defining moment when he was tossed off the starting team sophomore year at West Point. He had always come back. He had always recovered. Sitting on the sidelines at the University of Phoenix Stadium, he had the same feeling. They would come back. He had never felt more confident. Like he had told them last night, they had trained. They had what it takes. All they needed to do was play.

Strahan glanced at the sideline, as he had done many times this season, catching sight of Gadson. This was a game he was playing—a fearsome, exhausting one, but the lieutenant colonel's battle had been first against death, then for the rest of his life. It was impossible not to be inspired, not to forget every hot pain seething through his body. Exhaustion left him. He would do whatever Greg asked. He became tireless, remembering Greg's final direction: believe.

The first Giants drive of the final quarter was a breathtaking 80 yards, completed with a touchdown pass from Manning to David Tyree. With a little over 11 minutes to play, the Giants now had the lead they had been pushing for, but they needed more. The score was 10-7. For the next several minutes it became an intense passing game, settling for a moment at the Giants' 6-yard line. Corey Webster was blocking New England's Randy Moss, when he slipped, leaving Moss open to receive Brady's touchdown pass. New England went ahead 14-10 with 2:39 left in the game.

Small setback, Greg told himself. There were still three timeouts, and more than two minutes to play—just enough time, if all went as planned, for the Giants to put this away. For a split second he felt his own belief waiver, then caught himself, welcoming the challenge. Greg settled further into what was becoming his new comfort zone: facing adversity. He watched Strahan strutting back and forth, a preacher shouting fire and brimstone to his congregation.

All the work, all the power, all the adrenaline seemed to lodge in Strahan's chest. He centered himself before the charged wall of men lining the field. "Now more than ever we gotta *believe!*" he yelled. "17-14 is the final, okay? 17-14. *Believe!* One touchdown and we are world champions. *Believe* it and it will happen!"

Coughlin saw Strahan practically channeling Gadson, as the colonel himself sat calmly on the sideline. It was the sort of mental and emotional teamwork Coughlin knew could win the game. The sort where each man had forgotten the name on the back of his own jersey and focused instead on the name of the player in front of him. Gadson had inspired each of them to embrace that philosophy. Strahan was his evangelist. The men on the field were his faithful.

With 1:15 left on the clock, Manning found himself in trouble as the Patriots rushed him quickly after the snap. With two Patriots players dragging from his jersey, Manning managed a pass to the middle of the field, caught by Tyree, who barely held onto the ball between his hand and his helmet as he hit the ground. The crowd and the players went insane, then even wilder as the astonishing catch was replayed on the jumbo screens. Not only had the Giants just demonstrated some incredible talent, they'd gained 32 yards and time was melting off the clock. Four plays later Manning, under pressure from at least six players, lofted a pass into the end zone where Plaxico Burress, after faking a slant to dodge Patriots' cornerback Ellis Hobbs, was ready to receive. The Giants took the lead, 17-14, with just 35 seconds left in the game.

Burress. Mind *crushes* matter, Greg thought.

The record-setting Patriots offense still had 29 seconds and 74 yards to go, but the Giants defense did not give up a single yard and got the ball back into the hands of their offense.

Now, with just two seconds remaining, there was mass confusion over the clock. In the end, Manning simply took a knee. The Giants had won the 2008 Super Bowl.

The stadium turned to chaos, everyone rushing onto the field. Hands smacked, helmets bumped, jagged tears streamed from the eyes of men who five months earlier had not thought this team had a chance. Team owners hugged each other, and Coughlin was drenched by the traditional Gatorade shower. As Greg watched the swirl of humanity around him, only then, for the first time in weeks, did he feel the difference of before and after. He looked up as his teammates threw whatever they could into the air, crashing into each other, jumping high and landing hard. Spiritually, he was a part of it. Physically, he was tied to his chair. He was jubilant, feeling the thrill of victory. But for the first time in a while he felt weighted down. For a moment, he felt *disabled.*

He scanned the field, wondering how he would find his family, how he would make it back to the bus when a giant figure loomed in his peripheral vision. Suddenly he was airborne again. "Greg!" Strahan screamed, lifting him straight up into the air. "Thank you! Thank you! Thank you! For all you have done!" Strahan bellowed.

Greg laughed in euphoria as all his doubts dissolved into the desert air. He and Jaelen were whisked along toward the locker room, as much a part of the New York Giants as anyone wearing the uniform. This was his team. He had served as co-captain well. Streams of good wishes, speeches and praise mingled with the showery steam and clunky noise of cement and tile. Champagne showers and exhausted storytelling carried everyone well into the night.

It was not until much later, after he said goodnight to his team and his family that he lay in the hotel bed, unable to shake the pinch of reality. There would be no more games, at least not for a while. His own future was still unclear. The Giants' mark on history was made but he had yet to determine his own path. Greg remembered feeling this way at the end of deployments. There was always such a rush, and some chaos, to get to the end of the mission. Then, it would end. The silence would leave a ringing in his ear, like after a loud party. Or a bomb blast.

His mind flashed back for a moment to that Sun Bowl, his final game, when West Point lost to Alabama by one point. But it was not the disappointment of loss that actually brought him to tears that day. It was the finality of it all. After that game, the team members would disperse, and each football player would take on the mantle of soldier. Each would be assigned and deployed on a new mission, their football objective quickly melting into the record books. He shifted his mind to what he had come away with after that final season as a Black Knight. He had married the best woman in the world. And he had a tightly-knit brotherhood of life-time teammates to help him through the rough spots. He was especially thankful for his brother, Chuck.

Monday morning brought a bit of Monday morning quarterbacking, and by chance Greg ran into Plaxico Burress at the hotel. "What's up, Champ?" Plaxico said.

Greg just smiled. *Champ.* He was still one of them.

By then Greg knew this was a high which would come with a sobering detox. By Tuesday he would be back at Walter Reed, resuming his rehab, wrestling with prosthetic legs and what to make of his Army career. He and Kim would consider the next steps. Things that nine months ago had been obvious were no longer so, and he had a path to clear. And now the clock on his gridiron days—these most recent days of glory—felt spun out. He helped Kim, as much as he could, get the kids and luggage ready to head to the airport, where he would load ahead of everyone and wait. He wondered how many more airplanes he would board, how many more hands he would shake—maybe thousands. Maybe none at all.

The plane taxied over the sparkling tarmac one last time before gunning up toward Washington, D.C. Even victory has an ending, he thought.

CHAPTER TWENTY-TWO

"One of the most important things I did was find someone
who was injured like me and watch their successes."
—Colonel Gregory D. Gadson (Ret.)

Greg rolled himself alongside the gray 2008 Toyota Tundra parked in the lot of the Fairfax, Virginia, dealership where he and Kim had come to take delivery on the new vehicle. Ever since he was a teenager, cars had meant freedom to him, a way to get away, to be independent. He felt that nostalgic excitement again, but with a layer of appreciation he never could have anticipated. This car, this freedom, was deeper, clear like the desert night. It smelled of new steel.

With his left hand he gave himself a big push on the wheel of his chair, so he could run his right-hand fingertips over the flawless finish as he coasted toward the driver's side door. The salesman grinned crookedly as he held it open, clearly uncertain how his client would manage that typically magical moment: seating himself into his pristine dream. Greg breathed in the aroma of new leather, then paused, feeling around in his pack for his sunglasses. Confident he had remembered to bring them along, he moved swiftly—left hand on the inside door handle, right hand on the soft seat—easily hoisting himself into the driver's seat. He leaned forward, running his palm across the top of the dashboard, then over the 5-inch navigation screen, before letting the hollow of his hand cup the gear stick. His gaze cast over the levers and pivot points which allowed the hand controls to function. He fingered the touch points on the wheel which engaged things like the windshield wipers and the phone.

Most of the time, in Iraq, he had been driven around by his security team. Back in the States, he had focused on figuring out how to walk or wheel himself from place to place. He had never thought before May 2007 about not being able to drive, so he'd never anticipated how much he would miss it. And he had not craved the act of driving so much as he had of owning a vehicle—his place not only of carefree transportation, but privacy, speed, and when he felt the need, really loud music. Not that he was not grateful for accessible driver's education at the Veterans Administration where he initially took the wheel. His first moment back in the driver's seat with an instructor strapped in the passenger seat was surreal if not a little sterile. Now, the Tundra, by contrast, would be his new path to something so simple as an occasional drive-thru meal and so gratifying as getting back to the business of being a dad. Driving the kids around to their various activities had been a cumbersome chore he and Kim had shared. Now he could not wait to drop Gabby or Jaelen off at their next practice.

He had been a passenger for the last several months in the family van, ever since the first day he was allowed to leave Walter Reed without medical supervision. He remembered the sun beaming down gloriously on the white concrete of the hospital entrance. He squinted up at the sign, "Home of Warrior Care." *He'd nearly died there. They'd saved his life there.* Still, he could not wait to put that sign in his rearview mirror, permanently. And he meant that with all the affection a near-death experience could muster.

• • •

It had only been a few months since Kim had pulled their Honda Odyssey into the U-shaped driveway. One of her co-workers in Kansas had driven the vehicle all the way to Washington from Fort Riley as a favor.

The ocean blue van had been a welcome sight, but that first time he had not been sure how to get from his wheelchair into the car. It all seemed so awkward, so he had enlisted some instruction from one of his therapy mates, Andrew Kinard.

Kim opened the sliding side door.

"All right," Kinard gestured toward the doors.

"It might not *look* easy but . . ." Kinard paused for effect. "Okay the first time, it's not. But you'll get the hang of it," he laughed.

Andrew had been at Walter Reed for several months by the time Greg arrived. The IED he had tangled with left him even worse off than Greg—in the category where he could not even be fit with prosthetics. He had no real residual leg on one side. His life would be spent mostly in a wheelchair. That meant Greg's pal from rehab knew a lot about how to get around on wheels and was equipped to provide a lesson in leaving.

Greg rolled his chair up to the side of the van, waiting for Andrew's demo.

"Just wheel yourself up as close to the opening as you can," Andrew demonstrated. "I think you'll be able to reach the seat. Once you have a hold on it, it's a matter of pulling yourself up there."

Andrew leaned back, then heaved himself forward into the back seat. It occurred to Greg that no, it did not even *look* easy. Andrew pivoted around on his rear end, one stub flying toward the ceiling to avoid smacking the back of Kim's seat, then popped back out and into his chair.

"Your turn."

Greg had wheeled himself up along the open door. It was a bit of a leap, especially since his right arm was still fairly useless. He did not care. It was his first leap to real freedom, even if for just a little while. He lunged for the seat, paused a moment, then, butt in the air, started pulling himself forward. Unlike Andrew, he had two substantial stubs he could use to do an abbreviated crawl. It was not his most graceful entrance, but he got himself in there. And he was learning that appearances were the least of his concerns.

Once he had been seated squarely in the back seat, the kids, who were watching from the sidewalk, piled in. He tried to think of a different word than surreal. "Out of body" came to mind. Out of half of his body. It had been months since he had seen the back seat of their family car. He studied the upholstery. He'd never noticed the gray-brown color, or the light pattern.

Kim had researched and found a wrestling camp in Annapolis for Jaelen to attend for a week. So, on that day, their first family outing was to drop Jaelen off at the U.S. Naval Academy, which was about an hour's drive away. USNA sits on the Severn River, just shy of the Chesapeake Bay. The view would be a magnificent treat. He was anxious and happy and excited all at the same time.

With everyone strapped in, Jaelen in the front passenger seat and Gabby next to Greg, Kim tentatively hit the gas, lurching the van forward.

"Everything okay back there?" she called.

"Great!" they all yelled at once.

She pulled out of the hospital front entrance onto Georgia Avenue. It was an actual city street. With actual traffic, which seemed to Greg to be moving fast.

"I guess there's just so much to learn," he'd hollered to Kim over the seat. "Everything I used to do is different." He had not said it sadly or even in a resigned way. He just knew he had a lot of work ahead of him. Yes, she nodded. She and the kids would be learning a lot right along with him.

That is when the traffic light at Georgia Avenue and Colesville Road turned red and Kim tapped the brakes. Greg lurched forward, nearly smacking his head on the back of the driver's seat. His rear end screeched toward the edge of the seat.

"Whhhooooooooaaaaa!" he yelled.

"What's going on back there?" Kim had asked, alarmed.

"Dad just slid," Jaelen had pointed out.

"Don't be drivin' like that!! I got no legs! I'm like a Weeble!" He pushed himself back into the padded bench seat.

And for the first time in months, he laughed. Hard. So hard that it spread through the vehicle like cartoon lightning. Kim joined in and then they all busted up. The moment held just the inkling of normal they'd all subconsciously craved.

After that, they tried to take regular family outings. Both kids were attending camps, which gave all four of them places to wander, discover and to gulp fresh, unprocessed air. With each outing, Greg felt his moods lighten. Even though he was completely dependent on Kim to drive, and most often on Gabby to retrieve his chair from the back of the van, set it up, and wheel it to his door, it still felt a bit like a prison break every time they left the Walter Reed campus.

Their family rides to freedom included some team training, and life lessons for all of them. Once, while Kim had been back at Fort Riley collecting some of their belongings that had not made it to Washington, his parents, "Memaw"—as Gabby had called his mother—and his dad, Willie, had come from Chesapeake, Virginia, to help out. They brought their car to the Mologne House, the on-campus apartment where Greg, Kim and the kids were living at the time, and they all had piled into the car to go out to dinner. And when they got to the restaurant, they all piled out—without him! It had taken Gabby only a moment to realize she had completely forgotten her job, but not before Greg did.

"Gabby!" he yelled at her gruffly. "You forgot my chair!" Flustered, she zipped around to the back of the car to grab the heavy, folded metal and leather beast. She fumbled around, making him even more impatient.

"Sorry, Dad," she said quietly.

He saw her cheeks burning, but still, he was frustrated.

"I guess I'm just not used to . . ." she started.

That is when Memaw had stepped in.

"Gregory Dmitri Gadson!" she admonished. The sound of his mother's voice reduced him suddenly and unwillingly to toddler status.

"You need to be more polite to Gabby! She just forgot. A simple mistake. She is always trying to help you. Be nicer!"

Greg's cheeks flushed as he pulled himself—or some other self he did not even recognize—out of the moment.

"I'm sorry, Gabriella. Your grandmother, as usual, is right," he said, vowing to never take his kids' or another person's help, as much as he would rather not need it, for granted. He watched his mom wrap her arm around his daughter and walk into the restaurant, silently reminding himself how lucky he was to have a family willing to put up with him and a mom willing to put her son in his place.

• • •

Now, months later on a car lot, with a few more automobile and people skills under his belt, he was being given another gift. Kim folded the wheelchair and slid it into the roomy cargo bed of the Tundra, then climbed into the passenger seat. Greg started the car, touched the satellite radio screen and blasted Boston's "Don't Look Back" as he settled in for the drive home.

Driving meant not only certain freedoms for him, but for Kim too. Now that they were living in Fort Belvoir, Virginia, in base housing, Kim could go back to teaching at one of the area schools without having to worry about getting Greg to his daily physical therapy appointments at Walter Reed, 40 miles away. There was still the small matter of getting his chair from the back of the pickup onto the ground and under his butt, but there usually was someone around to help. As a less practical matter, driving with Bluetooth technology meant he could easily catch up with friends by simply hitting a button while he drove.

I was the occasional recipient, getting my first blast one afternoon through the phone on my desk, situated deep in the bowels of that dated, oddly stacked building in Alexandria.

"Hey, it's Greg—guess where I am."

"Sounds windy," I answered.

"That's because I'm in a car! I'm driving!"

"Wow. How is that possible?" I envisioned him hitting the gas with one of those big, metal feet, slamming it to 90 mph, then clomping on the brake and throwing himself through the windshield.

"Hand controls!"

He launched into an exuberant explanation of how he could operate everything using buttons on the wheel. At that moment he was yelling at me through what was normally the horn.

"I should come pick you up!"

"Working," I said, sadly. "But soon."

As it happened, he did not pick me up at work, but we did soon meet for what would turn out to be a classic Greg adventure.

The Wounded Warrior Project, which was just gathering steam when I ran into some of them on the Breckenridge ski trip, was operating at full throttle. The organization was now running a school in Orlando, Florida, organizing hunting trips, and hosting various point-to-point bicycling adventures, all for members of the military who had been wounded or were otherwise debilitated. Soldier Ride was a four-day organized event, designed to get veterans and active duty military together to do a little riding. That is how Greg first got on a three-wheeled handcycle in the summer of 2008. This was great news to me, since bicycling is one of my favorite things to do. We planned to meet along the Mount Vernon Trail in D.C. one spring afternoon for a bit of training.

I worried for days about our field trip. While I had been in his car with him, (spending most of the time gripping the door handle, screaming, "slow down!!") and I had seen pictures of him on his handcycle, I could not figure out how I was going to help him get from the driver's seat to the saddle. Even without legs, he was not a small guy. There was no way I could lift him or even bear much of his weight. I knew only that I would be able to get his bike out of the back of his truck. But the 3-foot change in altitude from the truck to the low-riding bike would be another matter.

He was in the river overlook parking area when I pulled up, wearing my tights and jersey, my bike hanging off the rack on my Jeep. I eyed the bed of the Tundra.

"So, I can just pull that out of there and wheel it over to you?"

"Yeah, just open the back and roll it out. It's not too heavy."

With minimal heave-ho-ing, I managed to get the steel frame out, wheels down. I started pushing it toward the opened driver's side door of the truck, but it would not go forward.

"Take the brake off."

"Oh." *Duh.*

"Okay, just face it backwards so the seat is that way." He gestured toward the rear of the truck.

I did, then waited for the next bit of instruction, which I was sure would end with one of us nursing a broken rib.

Instead, Greg twisted 180 degrees then swung himself out, left hand on the car seat, right hand on the door, released and landed, squarely, in the bike saddle. It took about three-tenths of a second.

"Huh," I said, impressed. And relieved.

"Would you mind grabbing my camera bag? It goes under here," he said pointing to a metal rack, situated behind his rear end.

And we were off. The pathway leading to Mt. Vernon, George Washington's historic home, was at times flat and close to the road. Then it would veer into the woods, bending and winding uphill quickly. It was a pretty quick spin but still strenuous. I was impressed that Greg still had enough arm strength to pull himself back into the driver's seat when we crossed the finish. And I managed to get the bike back into the truck.

The next time we rode together we started in Georgetown. The Capitol Crescent trail starts at the end of Water Street, by the Potomac River, crosses over the C&O Canal, under a stone bridge, then curves, with the tiniest uphill grade, toward Bethesda, Maryland. Even a slight hill is tough on a handcycle. Greg pushed north, moving pretty slowly, but cheered on by passersby.

"You got it!!" one yelled.

"Keep going! You look awesome!" yelled another.

"Thank you for your serrrrrviiiiice!!!"

The plastic American flag attached to the rear of his bike snapped around in the wind. We both wore red, white and blue jerseys. About 10 miles in, we turned around. With the grade now in our favor, Greg screamed ahead of me, clearly absorbed in his self-propelled loss of limitation. I worried we would attract unwanted attention from the stroller crowd, but no one seemed to mind the squatty silver torpedo blasting through some of Washington, D.C.'s most high-profile neighborhoods. We clocked about 20 miles, threw our bikes in our cars and went in search of refreshments.

With Greg back in his wheelchair, we wandered through Georgetown's busy walkways, looking for a place we could easily negotiate for lunch. It was the first time I had to think about an entrance being wide enough or whether or not there was a ramp. We settled on a place with an outdoor patio, where we could enter and immediately sit, avoiding an awkward weave between tables. Greg wheeled up to a small table and sat across from me, facing the street while I sat looking toward the rear of the patio. As I reached for my menu, I caught a familiar, wide toothy grin in my peripheral vision. I smiled back.

"Mr. Vice President, you should meet Lieutenant Colonel Greg Gadson,"

I said, sweeping my arm toward Greg like he was a prize on the "Price is Right."

The then-vice President of the United States, Joe Biden, followed my gesture, instinctively recognizing Greg's injuries. It did not surprise me in the least that he, along with his wife, Dr. Jill Biden, got out of their seats and came over to our table to meet Greg. They were incredibly gracious. Greg smiled and chatted as if he met up with the vice president every day.

"Beau, my son, is over there now," Biden said to Greg. Beau Biden was Delaware's attorney general, but also a major in the Delaware National Guard.

"In Iraq? Where?" Greg asked.

"Camp Victory. They're working hard, I'll tell you." Biden continued to smile, putting an upbeat face on his son's service. Beau and his brother, Hunter, had survived a car crash which killed Biden's first wife and daughter in 1972. Watching Beau head off to war was heartbreaking for him.

"I was at Liberty, not too far from there," Greg said.

After some more logistics discussions, which got past me, and some arms-length politics, the Veep turned to me.

"You look familiar," he said. I told him I used to work as a producer for NBC and MSNBC and had often manned the live shot position in the Senate, where he would sometimes appear as a guest on the "Chris Matthews Show."

"So, you've seen a little combat too!" he joked. I chuckled at his acknowledgment of my sometimes hairy profession.

The Bidens went back to their lunches and Greg and I ordered ours, quietly pondering the presence, or lack of, the Secret Service. Where were they?

Only as the Bidens stood up to leave could we feel the shift of a half dozen people, in plain clothes, moving with them. Two other restaurant guests stood, and two men who had been inconspicuously hanging around outside the patio moved in unison.

"There they are," we both said.

Despite the expectations of their escorts, both Bidens stopped by our table to say goodbye, then waved as they headed for their designated black armored vehicle. Greg and I were a little giddy from our chance meeting. No one could have known that several years later, Beau Biden would be taken from the reserves, his family, and I believe the nation, by cancer. Resilience does not guarantee survival. It does, however, sometimes mean you are eventually elected president of the United States.

. . .

Though he enjoyed it, riding a bike was purely recreational. Greg was spending more and more time behind the wheel of his truck, taking in roadside scenes that in the past he might not have even noticed. Occasionally, when he saw a heavily loaded cherry blossom tree, or a spectacular sunset, he pulled over and took a few shots with his new camera. His arm was getting strong enough to hold a DSLR again, and he was taking advantage of it. The trick now was maneuvering the vehicle so he could shoot from the front seat. Being able to yell into the wheel of his car also made keeping in touch with people a little easier, if not more fun. He regularly talked with Chuck, who was still working as a professor of political science—essentially running the ROTC program at the University of Dayton. Greg was thinking graduate school might be his next step. He figured he had all the physical challenge he could handle for now but wanted a little more mental stimulation. Chuck offered his encouragement.

"Hey, I'm all about motivating."

"I think it might be harder than undergrad—harder than West Point," Greg hedged. Academics had been his Achilles' heel.

"Don't take Arabic," Chuck laughed.

"I'm thinking something in public policy or management."

"You running for president?"

"Yeah. The first *legless* African American."

"You'll be in the White House while I'm in the sand."

"Oh, uh oh . . ."

"Yep, Afghanistan. I go in a year," Chuck said.

"Not good. Kinda saw that coming though, right?" Afghanistan was more unpleasant than it was dangerous at the time. Still—a world away.

"Yeah, I've had it too easy. Stace is *not* happy."

"What's the job?"

"Follow up. Documenting lessons learned."

"That'll be, uh, interesting," Greg laughed a little.

Some of the "lessons learned" seemed pretty obvious to them both. And the U.S. was still learning. More than 300 Americans were killed in Afghanistan in 2009. By the end of that year, President Obama would announce a surge of 30,000 troops in an attempt to end the conflict once and for all. Greg knew it was important for Chuck's military career to do some time over there, but he would miss his friend's support. Not likely he could pull Chuck out of the desert for a last-minute dash to the slopes.

Greg kept out of the politics of the war as much as he could. People often asked him what he thought of the wars in Iraq and Afghanistan. As an Army officer, he was in no position to be critical. He understood his role as a soldier. So while professionally he executed the wishes of the commander-in-chief, personally, even in "the before," he thought invading Iraq was a mistake, mostly due to the geopolitical impact. Historically, Iraq worked as a buffer between the U.S. and Iran, which was a Shia state. Americans were taking out Iraq's Sunni minority and instating a Shia government, blurring geopolitical borders between Iraq and Iran. He also believed that, whether or not Iraq had the "Weapons of Mass Destruction" that the George W. Bush administration used as a "smoking gun," it had no reliable delivery system. Greg thought it tantamount to arresting a citizen for owning a gun in the U.S. And long-term, there seemed to be no intention to support the new Iraqi government if it ever were put in place. No plan to underwrite the sacrifices made there. The situation was similar, Greg felt, in Afghanistan. Osama Bin Laden and his followers were behind the 9/11 attacks on the U.S. The Taliban had taken hold there due to that government's inability to control its borders, not due to any particular ill will on the part of President Hamid Karzai or his administration toward the U.S. It seemed to Greg neither war had been thoroughly considered.

Generally, he liked George W. Bush. On the day he traveled with the Giants to the White House for their traditional post-Super Bowl meet and greet, they lined up on the front steps for a group photo and Bush made a few remarks. The president had clearly been having a good time with the players, calling out Eli Manning, asking for wedding advice (his daughter, Jenna, had just gotten engaged and Manning had just married his college sweetheart, Abby McGrew) and pretending to forgive the New York team for beating the Redskins and Cowboys. Greg had been thrilled to just be there, so he was astonished when the president of the United States said his name. After telling a quick version of Greg's Giants story, Bush added, "He has got the Purple Heart and three Bronze Stars and now he's got a Super Bowl ring minted for a true giant." And then the president of the United States, his Commander in Chief, said he was proud to share the stage with Greg. It was humbling beyond belief.

Greg felt he had been a good soldier, despite his disagreement with the reason for the war. He viewed the loss of his legs less and less as a cost and more like a necessary sacrifice. Something he and his family forfeited as part of their commitment to country. That is why an unexpected notice from the Army sent him reeling. Sometime in the midst of his arduous physical therapy and his showcasing himself for Walter Reed, the Army had declared him medically unfit to serve. They were about to force him out.

"How can they say I'm not fit! I've done everything they've asked," he complained to Chuck on the phone, as he tore down an Alexandria side street.

"Yeah, you're wearin' the uniform."

"All over the national media!"

"Blue Steel." Chuck laughed, referencing Ben Stiller's role as a male model in the movie, "Zoolander".

"I'm sucking in my cheeks right now!" Greg chortled.

"So, you gettin' out?" Chuck asked. "Or you gonna fight it?"

"I'm going to try to stay in, I guess. I'm not really ready to leave."

"Hooah!"

"Huh, yeah. Hooah." Assembling the paperwork to prove his worth would create a part-time desk job for a few weeks. While he was ready for most any freedom, he was not ready to cut that particular tether. And when he did, he would do it on his terms. He hit the gas with his thumb. Such was his current unrequited love for the U.S. Army.

. . .

Despite what the official Army had to say, Greg was beginning to feel fit once again as a leader—as a commander. And he felt he had left a few loose ends out there on Route Jackson. The last time his soldiers had seen him, he was apparently being dragged, bleeding, screaming and punching, into the back of a Humvee. He wanted to make good on the promise he made to himself in the MATC, when he was first learning to use his C-Legs: he would *stand* and welcome his unit back from deployment. It was perfect timing then in May 2008, a year after the attack, when he and Kim received an invitation to be special guests at Fort Riley's Molly Pitcher Ball.

The Molly Pitcher Ball is an event honoring and thanking military spouses for their service, in taking care of homes and families through long deployments. Greg was aware of the potential for the event to focus on him, so when it came time to select a keynote speaker, Kim reluctantly agreed to take the spotlight. In her speech, she joked that this was just another "hard night" she would work her way through, as a dedicated military spouse.

Before the celebration though, the 420 soldiers of the 32nd Infantry assembled in the bland chill of the common room at Battalion Headquarters at Fort Riley, Kansas. Greg, keeping the stern expression of a commander, surveyed the assembly. He wondered how he must look to them. The last time they'd seen him, he'd had all his parts. Now their former leader, closer to teetering sideways than they could possibly understand, stood balanced on silver bars and hinges, perspiring slightly with the effort.

Lieutenant Colonel Michael Lawson had officially taken command of the unit in early June of 2007, following the temporary command of Greg's former executive officer, Major Jim MacGregor. MacGregor had stepped in the morning after the explosion. Under Lawson's leadership, the unit Task Force Patriot carried out more than 3,200 patrols, gathering intelligence, clearing areas of enemy forces and raiding anti-Iraqi hideouts and headquarters. In all, the unit detained over 30 high value targets, or known enemy leaders, 14 associates and aided in the capture of two dozen others. It is believed that one young member of the unit, after a 12-hour search, netted one of Iraq's al-Qaida member's most notorious IED makers, a coup for the entire unit.

Many of the soldiers wore a specially created patch as a tribute to their former commander. Brigade Sergeant Major Jim Champagne, who had helped carry Greg into the medical unit at Falcon that night, had No. 98 patches made for members of the unit. The half-moon shaped army-green tab had to be worn under a pocket flap or be otherwise hidden in order to comply with Army uniform protocol. Champagne knew the unit was devastated by the loss of their beloved commander. But he also knew Gadson would not want them to slow down, to pause even for an instant.

"Any time you're having a hard time, any time you're feeling down, you lift up that flap and think of LTC Gadson," Champagne had told them. "He's in worse shape than any of us, and for him, we need to get this job done." It was a stealthy homage to their former commander—a reminder of his leadership and their dedication.

In addition to the captures, the unit completed an impressive number of rebuilding and gentrification projects. It created a census designed to gather vital demographic data about Iraqi residents and it built security barriers in neighborhoods. The unit set up a grant process and awarded $300,000 to local business owners. It created an Iraqi civil service corps, established trash collection points and built $2.2 million of infrastructure projects.

Now, in the somewhat surreal gathering spot at Fort Riley, Greg sized up the gathering. They seemed fit and ready, despite a 15-month deployment.

"I want you to know I'm proud of you," Greg said to the group, looking around for members of his security detail—those who were with him the night of the attack. His eyes came to rest on Eric Brown, the medic who tied the tourniquets around his thighs, stopping the bleeding, saving his life. Brown, sensing Gadson's gaze, squared his shoulders and lifted his head slightly, staring straight ahead as tears glazed his eyes.

Gadson kept talking.

"You all persevered through adversity. Stepped up, under new leadership." Greg glanced at MacGregor, the former XO. "You didn't let my absence affect the mission. You didn't let the enemy distract you. You carried out your many duties and brought everyone home safe."

A few faces tightened. But he meant what he was saying. He was safe. And he was stateside. Two things that might not have been true on this cool day in May had they not carried out their duties so expertly. Losing their leader had no doubt affected them deeply, and he sensed his appearance here was helping them to heal.

He also suspected he was further along than they were emotionally. He lived through the surgeries, the physical therapy, the prosthetic fittings, the horrible sense of loss, the bloody victories, all of it. But they had been isolated from all of that grief, as well as the healing, and were left only with the memory of their battalion commander being carried away in a helicopter with prospects for survival uncertain. Likely they were feeling some pangs of survivor's guilt. Why had each as an individual come back home alive, all limbs attached? He understood. Despite his own injuries, he had a few of the same questions. The 32nd was the only one of the sister battalions to bring everyone home alive. And while they were there, the unit also made significant contributions to the well-being of the Iraqi people.

Greg was incredibly proud of their accomplishments. Over the few days of his visit he was able to connect with a number of his soldiers who hosted barbeques and a few other gatherings where they could relax and tell stories over a few beers. While time felt short, Greg left Fort Riley knowing he not only had met his own goal but had provided a waypoint or two for his soldiers as well. He showed them that they could create their own path forward, no matter the obstacles.

Later, when Greg and I talked about his visit, I asked him if it had brought them all some closure.

"I don't believe in closure," he said. "Closure is about looking backwards, trying to close something out. That's counter-productive." He said he would rather use an event as a launching pad to move forward, to learn a lesson.

"I wanted to see them," he told me, "but I think it was really important for them to see me, to see me happy and healthy. They needed to reconcile the space between that night a year ago and that moment that I was standing in front of them. I think I put them at ease."

· · ·

Back from Kansas, he felt more settled, having squared away his soldiers. Still, he was not done settling things with the U.S. Army. Next would be his peers, his buddies who wanted to be in touch. The West Point football brotherhood was pervasive. Chuck, of course, was his go-to confidant. And Pasquina had stayed on his medical case despite his own massive obligations at the hospital. Will Huff, who had flown with him from Landstuhl, was working his way toward a position directing athletics at nearby Towson University in Maryland. Coach Young and Coach Kish were both in touch. And the Giants still invited him back to talk with players and even help with team practices. His schedule was filling.

One day in August another former coach, Johnny Burnett, came to visit. Burnett coached the defensive backs at West Point, so he spent a lot of time with Greg and Chuck on the field in the 1980s. Kurt Gutierrez, who passed the number 98 to Greg at West Point, came along. They had lunch in downtown Alexandria. Greg was wearing his Power Knees, which gave him more flexibility when he was out and about. But as the three men walked toward their vehicle, Greg fell behind. It did not bother him. In fact, he had a bit of a spring in his step, even if it was a mechanical one. The lyrics to his new "theme song" seeped into the back of his brain.

"Who's the cat that won't cop out, when there's danger all about? Shaft." He chuckled to himself. The theme song had lately become a motivational melody and that morning it had wormed its way into his head.

He started up historic King Street, moving slowly past the shops and restaurants, working the tips of his canes into the mortar along the rough, red brick walkway. Charming as the stone pattern was aesthetically, and accurate as it may have been historically, the uneven surface created by the smooth, slippery, unevenly spaced surfaces made for a field of landmines that had to be negotiated delicately. He lifted his head slightly, trying to take in the whiff of breeze dancing lightly off the Potomac, carrying the heavy smell of oily water and feeble fish.

He heard the scrape of metal on stone, as the right cane slipped off a brick's surface, then slid into a crevice. He pulled, but his own weight lodged it, while the rest of his body maintained momentum. Tipping forward on his left leg, right leg rising behind, he balanced for a fraction of a second before legs, cane and rear-end clattered to the ground. The sound of separating fabric sent a chill up the back of his neck.

Shit.

A quick inventory revealed no apparent injury, except to his pride. He looked around to see, first, who might have seen him so clumsily kiss colonial history, then, who might help him get up. While he for the most part had mastered the task of keeping his legs under him while vertical, getting them back under him while horizontal was another thing altogether.

Two elderly women approached.

"Oh, my goodness, are you all right?" one asked, setting down her shopping bag while the other dropped her pocketbook and picked up one of his canes.

"I think so, ma'am," Greg answered. *Seriously? Where the eff was Gutierrez? What happened to Coach?*

"What can we do to help you get back up?" they asked. The women were both made up and dressed for a ladies' afternoon about town.

"I'm not sure." He felt crimson creep over his cheek bones. *There is no way they are up to this task.* But what else was he going to do? "Maybe if you hold that cane steady, I could climb up it and at least get onto one of these knees."

The women positioned themselves. He looked around for someone bigger. Stronger. No one in sight. *I am a freaking colonel in the U.S. Army! I am supposed to be helping them cross the street!*

But the women were determined. He rolled onto his belly, managing to get on all fours from there.

"Oh no, it seems you've ripped the seat of your pants," pointed out the purse lady.

"I thought I heard something tear back there," Greg said. This was getting more mortifying by the minute. "I guess there's a trip to the tailor in my future."

"Yes, it seems like an even tear right at the seam. Easily repaired," said one of them. Practical advice, but he wished they would stop staring at his derriere.

"Just hold that steady," Greg directed, grabbing the cane. He hoisted himself up, sliding his right arm into the bracket. From there, he pulled his right leg onto its foot.

"I'm Greg, by the way."

"Well, it's nice to meet you Greg!"

"Okay, ladies, if you could just . . ."

One of them picked up the other cane and slid it beneath his left arm.

Sweaty, dusty, grateful, and once again vertical, he beamed at the women.

"Now that was teamwork," he laughed. "Thank you, ladies. I don't know what I would have done if you hadn't come along. Thank you, again!" The ladies picked up their bags and waved goodbye. Re-assembled, he brushed himself off and continued toward his car. He wondered if Coach and Kurt had figured out yet that he was missing.

"A sex machine to all the chicks—SHAFT—you're damn right." The song seeped back into his mind. Oh, the irony, he thought. He wondered now who might be watching the bionic man, clomping down the street, ass out, bobbing to his sex-machine theme song.

• • •

It was not just the humbling lift from the little old ladies in Alexandria that made a new addition to the Gadson family seem appropriate. The fall—but more the awkward rescue, bore the reality of his new life into his subconscious. No matter how well he was recovering, there would always be a small degree of possible peril. Welcoming an assistance dog into their sometimes chaotic mix was something Greg had been considering for a while.

Nate, the English Labrador retriever, bounded into their lives with gusto. He was stocky and jet black, galloping from room to room on his first day home, sniffing through Gabby's well-used lacrosse laundry and politely nuzzling his new mom and siblings. Trained by America's VetDogs in upstate New York, Nate was 4 years old and accustomed and well-mannered enough to gracefully navigate a noisy urban street as well as a fine (smelling) steak restaurant. On duty, he barely wandered a few inches from Greg's iron ankles or wheels. When Greg drove, Nate snuggled up behind the driver's seat, his tummy gently vibrating to the turn of the engine, content to be as close to Greg as possible. But at home, when he knew his master was safely engaged elsewhere, he was often belly up, waiting for a cuddle or rub. After just a week, Greg felt Nate had become a part of him, like his prosthetic legs or his chair. The dog could pick up Greg's canes if he dropped them, or stand steadily at attention if Greg fell, providing his master leverage to get back up.

"The two of you even look alike," Kim said, shortly after Nate's arrival. "He's black and has that same square head!" Nate both blended and he enabled. The sweet-eyed, soul-swelling baby beast gave Greg four more feet to rely on, an unconditional presence, and a constant, tangible blob of love Greg could reach down and touch any time of the day or night. He could also nobly and stealthily help his new master up off a cobblestone sidewalk should that need arise again. Falling was still inevitable. Nate made it more tolerable.

There was not much a man, his truck and his dog could not do.

CHAPTER TWENTY-THREE

"There were doubters. Some people thought it was dangerous.
Greg Gadson blew them all away."
—Mike Corcoran, Prosthetist

Near the end of 2008 Greg was ready to settle into some anonymity. He used the Joint Chiefs Internship program to begin classes at Georgetown University, studying public policy management. School would be challenging but it would also be a fitting solo gig—if he failed he would not be letting anyone down but himself. The university gave him a handicapped parking spot and Nate traveled with him, sometimes carrying his books. His studies along with his physical rehab appointments two or three times per week were keeping him quietly busy.

The serenity did not last for long. He soon learned that one does not counsel an NFL team toward an unexpected Super Bowl victory without attracting some attention. But he never imagined seeing his face on the cover of a major American magazine. And he never really thought of himself as "inspiring."

But the editors at America's then "best-selling consumer magazine" did. The cover headline on the May 2008 edition of *Reader's Digest* read, "35 People Who Inspire Us," and featured photos of various athletes, actors, and a selection of everyday folks who had accomplished extraordinary things. Greg's mug peered out at RD readers from the top of two rows of featured faces, alongside Maria Shriver, Harrison Ford, and a few lesser-known folks, such as a mom-philanthropist and an entrepreneur inventor. He found himself not only featured on the cover of the magazine, but the subject of a two-page photo spread inside. Posed seated, holding a football, Power Knees stretched out in front of him, he beamed at the camera. As much as he loved taking photos, he hated posing for them.

But there it was. *He had become a centerfold.* This ought to inspire a whole new category of "Zoolander" jokes, Greg thought.

The article told the story of his relationship with the New York Giants, and even featured a photo of him palling around with Eli Manning in the locker room. The caption referred to them as "two champions." And there was a pull-out quote, attributed to him:

"I still have a long way to go. I don't believe you ever really arrive in life. You live life."

Not *bad*, he thought, for an Army colonel just getting the hang of handling media. But he had spoken from his heart. There were other articles—one in *Sports Illustrated* and another in *People*. He only hoped these blips upon his small media platform were enlightening to the masses still incoming at Walter Reed.

A report generated by surgeons at Landstuhl, the base in Germany where nearly every medically evacuated soldier passes through, showed the number of American military personnel undergoing limb amputations was increasing. In 2009, 75 U.S. soldiers lost limbs. In 2010, 171 military personnel sacrificed an arm or a leg to the wars. Most of the casualties were due to IED explosions. Many came likely as a result of the surge in Afghanistan.

The increase was like rocket fuel to Mike Corcoran, Dr. Paul Pasquina and the therapy team at Walter Reed. The more cases crossing the threshold of the hospital, the harder the team worked. The more complicated the case, the further they probed for solutions. Seeing these young men and women losing their athleticism, their drive and their mobility, motivated them all to push the boundaries of therapeutic medicine to the cutting edge of possibility.

Mike's relationship with Össur, the prosthetics company, helped to propel technology. When they developed a product, Mike worked to refine it. If they had a question, Mike's ear went to the ground for answers. So, when Össur was ready to unveil their new Power Knee II, Mike was their hands-on operator.

It had been nearly two years since Greg had first been wheeled into the rehabilitation area of the hospital. He and Kim, along with Mike, therapists Bob and Kyla, and along with fellow soldiers like Andrew Kinard and Josh Bleill, had spent countless hours there and had grown to be a family—a family with a mission—based in the "Land of the Misfit Toys." And the elves were getting craftier.

Mike needed a test pilot for the new technology. He needed someone who was driven, intelligent and focused. He also did not want someone who would tell him what he wanted to hear—he needed honest feedback. The subject for his experiment would also have to be credible. It would not hurt if the person had a reputation at stake—some rank—someone who would be very motivated toward success.

Greg seemed the obvious candidate. The two had become close friends through the last two years of struggle, each coming to respect the other's energy and success. Greg was not going to let a little thing like missing legs keep him from performing tasks required of a lieutenant colonel. And Mike was not going to let his experiment fail. He had sockets molded to fit Gadson in early April. The custom Power Knee II arrived a week later.

Once again, a small crowd gathered in the MATC the morning Mike and Paul pulled the new knees from their cases.

"These are the very cutting edge," Mike explained. "The knees work using artificial intelligence and sensors which cue actuators to move. They can actually *sense* when a person lifts their thigh muscle, or stub, to take a step."

He helped Greg slip his stubs into the new liners and sockets. Greg felt the cool, smooth plastic form a vacuum around his thighs. The fit was decent. His hand dropped down, grazing the top of Nate's head, then, sure the feet were under him, he leaned forward to stand, sending a signal to the knee to straighten. The motor kicked in, assisting his rise. Nate stood to walk along with him.

"All right, you're up!" Mike called, staring steadily at Greg's knees.

"Yeahup," Greg said, feeling the familiar introduction of new technology. He paused. *Set the fear of falling aside. Defy the logic. Trust the science.*

Leaning on his canes, he lifted his right stump to take a step. The knee gradually kicked out, setting the foot on the floor.

"Go ahead and put weight on that now," Mike directed.

Greg let his torso move forward, supported by the right leg. His left leg drew up for another step, the knee responded and he took another step.

Mike and Paul studied the motion.

"Might need a tweak or two," the Irishman said.

"How does that seem?" Pasquina asked.

"It's a lot like the old one, but smoother. Lighter. It really does move with me, almost anticipates my step," Greg answered. He felt a little wobbly and, of course, there was the typical dampness at the base of his neck.

"They'll take some getting used to."

"Yeah, but I'll be okay." He was getting used to being an experiment.

"Camera ready by tomorrow. PR is planning a press conference to unveil these. The Össur folks will be here too."

"Yeah," Greg said, sitting down on a bench with a thud. He grabbed a towel and wiped his face. "Camera ready by tomorrow."

The next day I was part of the media scrum at Walter Reed, watching Greg step carefully around the track in the MATC, then walk outside into the spring air, demonstrating this very new technology for television and print journalists. Trees blossomed pollen into the blue Washington sky, the sun wreaking havoc on videographers' lenses. Seven or eight cameras followed Greg and Mike and Paul as they showed off their trophy patient and his bionic extremities. Paul talked about the sleeker, quieter, lighter second-generation knee, which he expected would be widely used by both unilateral and dual amputees. It was fun to feel a little on the inside, since Greg had given me a heads-up about the event. I tossed him a question about the battery life of the knees and how they might affect his day-to-day activities. "I can already see myself doing things that I would normally not do, like going shopping and actually browsing instead of just going in to get something," he answered. A few reporters slowly nodded. This next generation of prosthetic could not only help a person move more efficiently, it could assist him in some playful dawdling as well.

• • •

The bionics boom was beginning. "The Six Million Dollar Man," a 1970s television series relic, became a new reference point. But now the engineering was on the outside. Silvery metal appendages were being created and tested in several laboratories, including the Department of Defense's DARPA, or the Defense Advanced Research Products Agency. Their LUKE arm, which could be controlled through a series of skin and electronic patches, by a person's thoughts, was fascinating fodder for news stories, but not practical yet for everyday use.

National Geographic, a magazine known for its use of dramatic photographs, was working on a spread about bionics. It reached out to recipients of mechanical arms, legs and eyes. Mike and Greg were asked to pose and ponder.

Greg soon learned that all those slick, sultry, surreal looking photographs in *National Geographic* were not just snapped with a bottom shelf Kodak. Being an amateur photographer himself, the first shoot with Mark

Thiessen and a raft of assistants was fun. He checked out their equipment, watched as they meticulously set lights and lenses. But it was more than a daylong, on-location shoot. It required four days and three locations. He was impressed by how demanding the art could be, how painstaking.

One shoot required him to walk on his Power Knees around an outdoor track on Fort Belvoir. He figured the makeup folks had not brought enough sponges and paper towels to sop up the sweat he broke laboring around on the black asphalt. Mike walked along with him, carrying a laptop, pretending to be entering stats. It was not an unrealistic photo op. Mike often picked away at his keyboard while Greg clomped around. It was just that at that moment they were concentrating more on looking the part than playing it. By far the longest, and most annoying shoot was in a studio. Since producers and photographers could control the lighting there, they worked every available option.

"Smile!" called out the producer, instructively.

He drew back his cheeks.

"Try to look more natural," the photographer corrected.

"I'm not a natural smiler," Greg said, stone faced. Still, he tried. He thought happy thoughts. He remembered the *Reader's Digest* shoot, where he smiled effortlessly.

"Okay, try again, let's see those teeth," the photographer said. Greg forced a grin.

"No, like you mean it." He tried again.

The producer sighed. Greg shook his head. "I'm not sure what you want me to do." He was stiff with exhaustion. He had been sitting on a stool wearing his prosthetics, shorts and combat boots for what felt like hours in the studio. The makeup person kept dabbing at him.

Who would see the piece anyway? he wondered. *Does anybody really read* National Geographic *anymore?*

It seemed a lot of effort for one photo, when the story was not even about him. But at the end of four days, he was glad he had done it. Big picture, it would give Mike and Walter Reed some cool exposure. But he felt his modeling days were definitely numbered.

The *National Geographic* bionics article came out in January of 2010. Once again, there was a large photo of him featured among the various limb-challenged models. He was seated on a stool, wearing the shorts and combat boots, looking straight at the camera. In the photo they chose, he was *not* smiling.

CHAPTER TWENTY-FOUR

"Mick was part of me but also my interactions with other guys
who were wounded. Every one of them was part of Mick."
—Colonel Gregory D. Gadson (Ret.)

"Oh, don't worry about it," she said. "Things like this happen."

Greg looked directly into the almond-shaped, greenish-hazel, thickly lashed eyes of one of America's most famous bad-girl sweethearts.

"It's all because of me, though," he said.

"Nah, I think Pete got something he can use. We did a lot of takes." Rihanna blotted her forehead. The temperature was pushing 90 degrees. Her soft Caribbean accent was as charming as it was soothing. She was so at ease. Comfortable in her own gleaming brown skin.

I used to be like that, he thought.

He straightened in his chair. Because he was new to acting, Director Peter Berg had instructed him to stay in character at all times. Not too tough, since "Mick," in his mind, was a collage of himself along with all the wounded souls he'd accumulated in his subconscious over the last couple of years. He was pretty comfortable with "Mick." The cast and crew were directed to support his learning curve by helping him to stay focused.

For the first time in a while he was feeling self-conscious. He looked down at his broken prosthetic. He rubbed the armrests of the borrowed wheelchair. Greg knew very little of the movie-making industry. He was learning, though, that there was a lot of downtime involved. Time to just sit and watch the spectacle. Time to let your mind wander. Time to ponder the random chain of events that had led him to be sitting in a director's tent, steaming in the Hawaiian heat, being comforted by a mega-famous superstar.

It had not been long after his unsmiling face, prosthetic legs and combat boots appeared in the January 2010 issue of *National Geographic* that he'd received a call from the Navy's entertainment liaison office, asking if he could consult on a movie set. He thought it odd that the call would come from the Navy. Actually, there was nothing about that call that was *not* odd, but the Navy part seemed the strangest, since last time he checked he was still in the Army.

Staying in the Army had taken some, well, legwork. When they notified him of his imminent departure into civilian life, Greg had generated enough paperwork—medical records, letters of recommendation, all sorts of bureaucratic tree-killers, to prove he was indeed fit for duty—that he was still able to make a contribution. "The Army's not really paying me to run," he joked. Still it was a relief to receive the COAD—Continuation of Active Duty. The status not only made him eligible to remain on active duty, it enabled him to start a new job.

Greg would be the director of the Army's Wounded Warrior Program, also known as AW2. The Army created the program the year he was wounded—in 2007—mostly to fill gaps in the Veterans Administration's efforts to handle the number of soldiers transitioning out of the military after they were hurt or had become ill. The year Greg was wounded, the VA had only six or seven people handling the entire country. Veterans had many decisions to make regarding their various benefits, employment, and general survival as they transitioned back into civilian life. It was overwhelming to the soldiers, their families and the staff. When Greg took the reins in June 2010, there were around 10,000 military personnel who needed some sort of assistance through AW2. It was a huge job and his placement there demonstrated the Army's renewed confidence in his abilities. He would report to Brigadier General Gary Cheek, a fellow West Point alumnus whom he'd worked for back in Afghanistan. Cheek seemed relieved to have Greg's assistance.

The call from the Naval entertainment office was followed closely by a call from movie director Peter Berg.

"First I want to thank you for your service," Berg started out. "I saw your photo in *National Geographic*. It's pretty dramatic."

"Yeah, it took a while for them to get that" Greg said. "I think I didn't really have the look or whatever they wanted."

"Well, you had what it took to get the New York Giants to the championship," Berg said, "I'm a big Giants fan."

"All they had to do was believe in themselves. I didn't do it. They did."

"Listen, Greg, I was wondering—would you be interested in being in my next movie? It's a science fiction thriller, where the Navy winds up saving the world from an alien invasion."

"The *Navy*?" Greg laughed a little. "You know I'm in the *Army*. I thought you just wanted a military consultant. You want me to be *in* it?"

"Yeah," Berg answered, "I'd like you to play a wounded sailor, who helps fend off the attack. Can I send you a script?"

Acting? Aliens? *Sailor*?

"Uh, sure," Greg said, certain that absolutely nothing would come of this conversation.

"Send it." He was not sure he would read it.

Later, an exchange with General Cheek left him even more certain that this movie, if it was actually made, would be made without him.

"So, who's Peter Berg?" the general asked.

"Did you ever see the show on TV, 'Friday Night Lights?' He did that. He's had some other movies."

"And Peter Berg wants you to play a naval officer?"

"Actually, that's been updated. They've changed it to a Marine."

"A Marine?" Cheek leaned back in his chair.

"Well it's all set on the water—on a ship."

"Let me think about it, Greg. I have to say I've never had any experience with this."

"Thank you, General. And something else I—"

"What's that?

"I don't want people to think I went after this. Like I want to be some Hollywood darling or whatever. *Berg* called *me*."

"Roger."

And then, silence from the center ring. The Pentagon was quiet and so was Hollywood for that matter. Maybe this movie thing was just a passing whim on the part of a producer with a soft spot for wounded veterans. Greg was not an actor, anyway, and never had designs on becoming one. He had other things to worry about—about ten thousand things. Ten thousand and three, if you counted his wife and kids. And he was still managing his own recovery. Part of that included adventure trips offered by various veteran service organizations. He had developed a friendly relationship with Cheryl Jenson at Vail Veterans. After all, it was Cheryl and her organization that first showed him how much he could still do only months after he'd been wounded. Horseback riding and fishing with Jaelen that first summer were true turning points because both challenged him physically and enveloped him emotionally. He learned that he could climb onto a horse and stay there. His confidence also grew with the freedom of slipping onto the back of the huge swaying animal and moving through the woods of Colorado with no chair, no prosthetics and not much supervision. The two events Cheryl organized each year—in March there was an accessible snow skiing weekend—were on his calendar and would stay there for years to come. In addition to the Vail Veterans activities, he cranked himself through any number of bike rides organized by the

Wounded Warriors program and the Face of America organization.

If anything could distract him from all of his work and obligations, it was his lifelong passion: football. He was still a member of the New York Giants football team. His role as mentor had continued since that thrilling win in 2008, but he was more established now—less of a special guest and more of a teammate, roaming the halls at the Meadowlands, sharing casual conversations with players looking for his advice. In the four years since Super Bowl XLII, the players as well as the coaches had become almost superstitious about Greg, anointing him as something of a personal guru. Chase Blackburn, who had leaned in so intently on Greg's inaugural speech back in 2007, and Dave Diehl, who valiantly hoisted Greg onto the team bus more than once, became students and confidants. Players like running back Ahmad Bradshaw, defensive ends Justin Tuck and Osi Umenyiora, all sought his counsel from time to time, searching for physical and emotional solace.

Coach Coughlin witnessed Greg's calming influence, how his presence increased their confidence and connected them as a team. He liked having Greg around. After the Giants beat the Patriots for the championship again in 2012, Greg met the team at Tiffany's in New York to receive his second Super Bowl ring. He attended the glitzy ceremony wearing a polished suit, striding confidently on prosthetic legs. He no longer worried about his future, and in fact looked forward to whatever challenges lay ahead. And he knew the role he had played with and for this team had drawn him back into life.

"You know, life goes on," Greg said to Coughlin after the ceremony, "but I couldn't have done it without you."

"I'm glad," Coughlin answered, "because it's two-way then. We couldn't have done it without you either."

. . .

The potential movie gig was certainly not at the top of his mind, but he suddenly remembered to check in during a deep-sea fishing trip to Alaska. In between reeling in many family-meal-sized salmon and trout, he doubled back with General Cheek.

"General, has there been any decision regarding my request?"

"Not yet, Greg. Is Peter Berg set on the Marine thing? Seems folks in the center ring might be more amenable if you played an Army officer."

"Not a Marine."

"Not a Marine," Cheek repeated.

"What's the verdict?" the director asked later on the phone.

"I'm not even sure how to—" He sighed. If his part in the project was not dead already it would be in a minute. "It seems like they're stuck on the Marine thing. If I could play the part of an Army soldier, instead of, you know, Navy, they might approve it."

"I don't think that'll be a problem at all," Berg barely took a breath.

"So, that's not a change that will affect the story you're trying to tell?"

"Nah. Go Army."

"Go Army. Hooah!"

And so in that one astonishing moment it was settled. Greg would essentially play himself, a recovering wounded U.S. Army officer, in Peter Berg's next film.

When Greg called to tell me about his new role, he explained that the story would be based on the old board game called "Battleship."

"I played that game as a kid, with my brother," I told him.

"Yeah, with the plastic pegs."

"Right!" I laughed, thinking of how little technology it took to amuse us back in the '70s. The game was played with rounded red and white markers, which plugged into plastic boards.

"You had to bomb the crap out of those little plastic boats to sink them. So, there's going to be a lot of bombing? Of ships?"

"I guess *some* bombing. It's a science fiction movie."

"Based on an old board game?"

"Right." Greg laughed. "I have a pretty small role, really. But it'll be fun. We're filming in Hawaii."

"What's your character's name?"

"Mick. I think. Something like that. I play an angry wounded guy."

"So not a big stretch, then," I teased.

• • •

The movie script arrived at the Gadson home soon after. Then another, updated script arrived. Then another. Pretty soon, there was a whole box of them sitting on Greg's desk.

"Are you going to even look at those?" Kim asked.

"I might. I don't know. They keep changing it."

She picked up the latest version.

If you are one of the people reading this who has not stumbled upon the movie "Battleship" while lying on the couch, channel surfing and eating Doritos, I do not want to spoil it for you. However, I think it is probably okay to tell you that, in the end, the U.S. Navy and the one Army guy win.

The next-to-last scene of the film features an awards ceremony, in which almost everyone who helped save the world from aliens gets various medals for bravery, presented to them by Liam Neeson, who plays the part of the tough admiral who is also the father of our troubled hero's (Lieutenant Alex Hopper, played by Taylor Kitsch) love interest, Sam (Brooklyn Decker). Sam is also Army officer Mick Canales' physical therapist, which is how he, Mick, gets roped into these hairy heroics in the first place.

Berg told Greg the awards ceremony scene would be shot first, since Greg was new to acting and that scene would be the easiest. All he had to do was walk, shake Liam Neeson's hand, look proud yet humble, then take his position on the stage, standing in a row of other proud yet humble looking actors.

The scene was shot at the National Memorial Cemetery of the Pacific, also known as the "Punchbowl," because it's nestled inside a crater, formed between 75,000 and 100,000 years ago. It was first used as an altar where the early islanders would perform ritual human sacrifices to their gods. The grounds opened as a cemetery in 1949 with the interment of five war dead: one unknown service member, two Marines, legendary war correspondent Ernie Pyle—and an Army soldier.

Greg was not dressed in an Army uniform for the scene, though. He was costumed in "aloha attire"—a Hawaiian shirt and shorts, so his prosthetic legs would show. But he did feel a little like a human sacrifice.

At first, people seemed to be milling about all over the cemetery's concrete walkways and imposing steps, which rise to meet Lady Columbia, the maternal statue keeping constant watch over those sacrificed. Eventually, everyone was called to order and places. Greg's direction called for him to sit next to Decker in the audience of Navy soldiers, and when his name was called, he was to stand, walk slowly toward the stage, step up a small curb, shake hands with Neeson, then take his place on the platform. Too easy.

The director finally called "action!"

Because his was the least of the hero roles, he went first, beginning the final scene's momentum where eventually Lieutenant Hopper (Kitsch) faces his commanding officer and, he's hoping, his future father-in-law.

"Lieutenant Colonel, United States Army, retired, Mick Canales," Neeson's voice boomed. Greg stood and boldly made his way toward the vaunted actor, realizing only then that he had never met the man before. When they shook hands with cameras rolling, it would be the first time Neeson would lay eyes on the brand-new actor. Greg got his "colonel" on, and maintaining character, looked Neeson straight in the eye, quashed a habitual "nice to meet you" and instead allowed just the slimmest of smiles to curve his lips, the faintest glimmer of recognition to graze his eyes. They had, after all, just saved the world. Greg then turned, shoulders squared, chin out and chest back, and walked as crisply as he was able to his place on the stage.

It was perfection.

So, they did it again.

And they did it again. Each time they ran the scene, they would cut, there would be consultation between the director and producer. Camera shots would be changed while grips, makeup artists and other movie-making underlings would scurry from light to reflector and face to face. Again would come the "action" call, and Greg would stand, walk, step, shake, turn and once again plant himself. Every time there seemed to be a different camera angle to pursue. Every time, the air got hotter. And every time, the small curb seemed a little higher. Eventually the tropical steam took out a few crew members. Still, they continued to shoot.

Greg felt sweat soaking through his floral getup. He was not sure if anyone there realized how difficult it was for him to stand for long periods of time. Fatigue began to numb his fragile dexterity. What started as a simple task had become a test of his endurance.

"Action!"

"Lieutenant Colonel, United States Army, retired, Mick Canales."

For what felt like the millionth time, Greg walked toward the stage, keeping his gaze fixed, his Army face stern, respectful.

Stand. Step. Step. Step. Watch the curb . . .

But this time, instead of keeping his eye on the pavement, he fell into it. All he could see were the legs of white folding chairs and a sea of Navy dress shoes. And all he could hear was the huge sucking sound of 400 horrified lungs.

The next thing he saw was the metal part of his leg, curbside. It had snapped off the socket, which was still stuck on his stump. He sat on the ground—not for first time in his life—studying his mangled leg. While not as disturbing as the first time, it was still pretty traumatic, considering his immediate audience.

He sat for only a second before everyone nearby, including Berg himself, was lifting him off the ground. Problem was, he only had one leg left to stand on. Someone went in search of a wheelchair. Meantime, he leaned on Berg.

As usual, when he kissed the concrete, his pride took the heaviest beating. Now it was compounded by the fact that when the director called "cut!" this time, it was terminal. No leg meant no walking, stepping, shaking or planting. The leg was not the sort of thing that could be fixed with duct tape. His fall brought the production to a halt.

Thankfully a wheelchair materialized, then a few folks helped him to the director's tent, where he could recover.

Rihanna's acting coach joined them in the shade.

"Ya know, you have to really *believe* in what you're doing," the coach encouraged. "It'll get easier."

Greg heard her. He figured he could pretend. But he was not sure he could pull off the believing part. This was not football. Or a battlefield. Or the Super Bowl. It was all just so *fake*. The crew wrapped for the day. Berg supplied a spare personal duffel bag where Greg deposited his leg and leg pieces.

"I guess you were right about having a prosthetist on the set," Berg admitted to Greg. Greg had suggested the prosthetic staff a few weeks earlier, but Hollywood had not wanted to pick up the tab.

"Proper preparation . . ."

Berg laughed. "We have a few weeks before our next scene with you. Find someone. We'll get them on the payroll."

Greg headed back to Washington, one movie scene and one more humiliating fall under his belt. But Berg did not fire him. One of America's top pop stars told him it was all going to be okay. And no matter what happened next, there was little hardship duty involved in working along-side the famously beautiful Brooklyn Decker. So long as he could keep pulling it off.

His home life existed between trips to Hawaii. In all he would travel to the Pacific three times and and one time each to Texas and Baton Rouge, Louisiana. In between, and sometimes from the road, he managed AW2 soldiers, learning more and more about the specific needs of a transition-ing force. Mostly it seemed they needed psychological support. Suicides among members of the military were on the rise. The stats showed those losses were not necessarily combat-related. Part of his job was to initiate programming to keep these young veterans from self-medicating, or even-tually subduing their mental anguish permanently. He had some deeply held insights on suicidal tendencies, but was not yet ready to go public.

Once in a while Greg would send me a photo from Hawaii. One was with Rihanna. Another was of him lying on the ground in a strange pose. It reminded me of a rendering of Jesus at Gethsemane from my Catholic childhood. The lighting made it look cultish. There were grass and moun-tains behind him, but it was tough to figure out what he was doing.

"That was when we were shooting the fight scene," he explained on the phone later.

"Who were you fighting?"

"The alien. The alien is this big stunt guy. His name is Bubba."

I could not even picture it. Even with the picture, I could not picture the whole scenario. I pitched The Pentagon Channel desk a story about LTC Gadson shooting a movie with Peter Berg in Hawaii. They immediately shot me down. Too long. Too far. Too much. I would have to hear about it all later.

· · ·

Greg took Mike Corcoran with him to Honolulu for the second shoot, in which one wounded lieutenant colonel gets mouthy with his physical therapist and is warned by local police that aliens have attacked.

The scene is on a lush tropical mountainside and Sam is trying to get Mick to do his physical therapy, which involves walking on an uphill trail. Mick is crabby. Mick is frustrated. Mick does not want to cooperate with his therapist, no matter how beautiful or charming she is, or how stern she becomes. He is fairly pissed off over the loss of his limbs. Greg did not have to dig too deeply to access this emotion.

What struck Greg about the set's location was the tightness. He barely had to move to change scenes. All the crew did was change camera angles, and it made everything look different. The set also reminded him a bit of the military. Everyone—hairstylists, makeup experts, lighting professionals, photographers, wardrobe—all had their tasks to perform, their missions to execute. They were all part of the team. It made him feel a little more at home.

Greg had to learn lines for this scene, which, in keeping with the theory of shooting easiest-to-hardest, would be the second easiest. Mostly, Mick is surly, at one point telling Sam, "My grandmother could climb this mountain."

For a moment, Greg was back in the MATC at Walter Reed. *Three sit-ups? That was all he could do?* It was that sort of frustration he could draw on for this scene. He thought about those days when brushing his teeth was as awkward as hanging wallpaper. And he remembered double amputees: Andrew Kinard, Josh Bleill, Marco Robledo. Each one of the guys he had worked so hard with, back in the "Land of Misfit Toys."

"My *grandmother* could climb this mountain," he groused, looking at the dirt trail under his metal feet. The dredging up of those old emotions was working. Soon Mick and Sam are chased down by police.

"The island is under attack," the Hawaiian park police warn Mick. "I need you and your friend off of this mountain right now."

Sam turns to go, but Mick continues up the incline, defiantly delivering the first of several slightly amusing lines.

"I ain't never seen an alien. Have *you* ever seen an alien?"

. . .

Initially Greg's role in the movie was very small. But as he adapted and worked with his coach, Berg and the writers added things. Every morning he would arrive at his trailer and his coach, also named Mike, would have what screenwriters call "sides," or the portion of the script they would be working on that day. He was not sure how far ahead writers were working but almost always there was new stuff. At first, the threat of last-minute add-ins made him a little uneasy. But he got used to it. Some days it seemed they were dreaming up dialogue as they went along.

Mick may never have seen an alien before but Greg knew he was eventually going to have to fight one. And even in Hollywood, it's tough to punch an extraterrestrial when you have no legs. He knew he could get one good swing in, but that would be all. The recoil from the force of his swing would send him flying backwards, straight onto his ass, where it would be hard to get much done. Even magical movie making would not overcome the simple physics of fist fighting. Berg and his crew had to come up with a plan to keep him vertical.

The first attempt involved a harness system in which his end was hooked to a corset around his ribs, and the other end was hooked to a forklift. It literally lifted him off the ground. He wondered if this was what Peter Pan felt like when they shot that movie. And Peter Pan, by the looks of him (who was always played by a small woman), weighed about 150 pounds less than Greg. Besides, the corset was as uncomfortable as it was dysfunctional. There was no way he was going to get a clean swing at the hulking beast from this contraption. Obviously, they have never worked with a no-legged man before, Greg chuckled to himself. The crew went back to the warehouse.

The next contraption looked like something that might have been used to hold up a mannequin in a department store window. It had a square, steel base from which protruded a rod that attached to his back. It only took a moment for everyone to figure out that this device was not going to hold him up, either. He could not move naturally. Last he remembered, since he had not thrown a punch since boxing class at West Point, he would need full mobility from the waist up so he could throw the full weight of his body into his shoulder. The rod really did not allow him to move much more than his arms. The crew pondered the problem some more. In the meantime Greg's role continued to expand. The fight scene would now be an important one, in which he saved the damsel, Sam, from an attacking alien, thereby preventing the alien and his space-pals from sucking out all of earth's resources, rendering the planet uninhabitable. Or maybe just without cell service. Either way, he had to figure out how to stay upright.

The fight scene, the second most difficult, was filmed in Baton Rouge. Up until then, Mick had been belligerently defying Sam, and sending her to do the dirty work. She has to pull car keys off the belt of a dead park police officer, killed by the space alien. And she has to drive the car into a communications tower, causing it to implode and stop sending "come hither" signals to all of the alien's friends and family. But now, Mick is beginning to pivot. He is plotting. He is taking control of the situation. He is working up to his ultimate on-screen "fuck it" moment. As the crisis gathers, it becomes apparent Mick is going to have to shed his "victim" persona and get on with the hero stuff. As the camera comes in close, Mick looks sideways at Cal, the impish scientist (played by Hamish Linklater), and in perfect Batman-ese utters, "Let's see if we can buy the world another day."

And they're off.

Sam successfully crashes the vehicle, but her leg becomes somehow lodged inside. The time for talk is over because, of course, by now the alien is stomping around outside the smashed Jeep. The anger, bitterness, resentment, and struggle of 1,000 wounded soldiers seethes across Mick's face. He is literally getting out of the passenger seat, ready to fight for his life, Sam's life and even that of the impish scientist. He is mad, and he is not going to take it anymore—and this alien is going to pay.

"I got this," he says to Sam. Once more, Greg is the small but stealthy defensive end, plowing into his much larger opposition. He is a colonel, leading his unit. He is Army. He is on an extreme close-up. He is large and in charge. The camera tilts down as huge, mud-covered boots and steel rods set down in the dirt and Mick emerges from the car. He is staring straight into the bulging eyes of a very ugly non-human.

The production crew finally decided that it was best not to have to keep Greg on his feet for the fight scene. So they rigged a cushioned, fully-backed chair to a camera dolly. While he could not bob and weave he could slide back and forth on a single axis with his butt firmly planted. The chair could swivel slightly and each time Greg threw a punch, a stagehand hiding below the slider would control the chair, accordingly, ensuring a natural looking twist through Greg's chest and abdomen. The camera would be kept on a medium or tight shot, so nothing below his waist was visible. It was comfortable and effective, much to the relief of the crew, but at an unfortunate cost to Bubba.

For the fight scene, Bubba wore a smooth, gray, thick, neoprene-looking suit, shaped like the alien, but the textures and colors of the costume would all be computer generated. The suit had reference points here and there, to help the artists in post-production create and cover the suit with shiny, grooved gold and silver armor.

Greg sat in his chair on the dolly, waiting for Berg to call "Action." He strained as he threw punch after punch. Despite the exertion, he was enjoying the breeze of his swing, the physicality of the work. Sweat soaked his "Army" T-shirt. After a number of run-throughs, Berg called "Action!" Greg grimaced, picturing his menacing enemy, believing in the threat, the danger, the urgency. He found music helpful in getting himself worked up for these angry scenes. When he needed to be sad, he played The Spinner's "Mighty Love" in his mind. It was one of his mother's favorites and he played it for her in his Tundra SUV when he'd picked her up from the hospital just a few weeks before she'd died. Now, Red Rider's "Lunatic Fringe" screamed through his brain. *We can hear you coming . . . no you're not going to win this time . . . we can hear the footsteps . . . Can you feel the thunder? Oh, oh, oh, oh. . . . Uh oh!*

He felt his knuckles catch the side of the padded alien hood. Bubba "weebled" backwards.

"Cut!" Berg yelled.

"Oh shit!" Greg's lungs pushed out the curse before his brain could stop it.

A freshly clocked Bubba stared at him through tears.

"Sir," he said calmly, "Could you please not do that again?"

Greg felt horrible. He hated that he'd hurt someone. He apologized several times, finally just racking it up to, perhaps, too much "believing."

The show, naturally, went on.

As one might expect, Sam the damsel is released from her stuck position in the car, but the fight continues. The alien begins to get the upper hand. Greg is on his back, while the alien, blinded because he cannot see without the oversized helmet and protective glass that Mick punched off his pasty, whiskered head, tries to stab him with his whirring propeller-like hand. But what Greg is actually looking at is a paper towel in Bubba's hand, which will later be covered with the image of a propeller-like hand. Still, Greg is able to appear terrified, as Mick is nearly overcome. Greg is eventually able to also turn terror to rage, at least on his face, for the remainder of a pretty long battle.

As much as he enjoyed the work, the days were long. For twelve or thirteen hours he would run lines, adding things, dropping others. For something as brief as "I got this," there would be twenty takes, Berg calling out different lines for Greg to try. No one could even remember what any of them were later. "I got this," was a perfect moment. It seemed all the coaching and motivational ear bugs paid off. He was learning how to stay in character. He was learning, even here in the Louisiana bush, how to believe.

. . .

The first scene (keeping with the reversed schedule) shot at the Center for the Intrepid (CFI) in San Antonio would, of course, be the most challenging. The Center for the Intrepid is the Texan version of Walter Reed's Military Advanced Training Center (MATC) where Greg had spent so much time during his recovery. It is staffed and stuffed with the latest in rehabilitation experts and gear. And it is where we first meet Mick and Sam. Mick is walking on a CAREN—a Computer Assisted Rehabilitation Environment, like the one I saw on my initial tour of the MATC at Walter Reed. It generates a virtual reality, with video scenes of cities and other landscapes, and a moving platform to simulate different uphill or downhill grades. It's a training machine created to help wounded warriors learn to walk on prosthetics. Here we see Mick at his meanest, harnessed into the CAREN, walking, but fighting with the tech at the controls. His new physical therapist is introduced. He is unphased by her beauty or her cheer.

Greg looked at his lines, wondering how he would dig for the emotion of this scene. He remembered an afternoon in May, the sun shining on taut white sheets at the end of his bed in Ward 57. He remembered the burden on his family. The vision of the impossible path ahead—crawling, stumps dragging through the gravel. The explosion, the dust, Fredrick Johnson's sand-scraped voice.

Now, as Mick, he feels like he might grab Sam by the neck. Instead, he looks her straight in the face and says, "I lost my fight when I lost my legs." He calls himself "half a man," and into a camera shot so tight it would make even a Kardashian wince, he finishes, "And half a man ain't enough to be a soldier. That's all I've ever known."

And *that* was a wrap. Mostly.

There was one scene that needed, months later, to be reshot. The producer decided that his final scene, the one where he takes the stage with Neeson, would be more powerful if he was wearing his dress uniform. Luckily, they figured out a way to get rid of the aloha look using green screen trickery, so the entire cast and crew did not have to be re-activated. Trickery could not, however, solve the problem of the uniform, itself, which would no longer go around his now much-larger topside. Muscle mass he developed in his upper arms from pushing his chair, along with a thickening of his belly, made him look more like a Tootsie Roll than an Army officer. He never thought of his dress uniform as a costume, but in this case it was. So Hollywood got him an upgrade.

By November, the film was in the can, as they say, and Greg went back to their home near Fort Belvoir, to focus on the AW2, his soldiers and his kids who were whizzing through their teenage years and careening toward adulthood.

Post-production took a year and a half. By the time he was told to get ready for the world premiere of the movie, he had nearly forgotten about it. It debuted in Japan in early April of 2012.

Halfway around the world, he was reunited with the other cast members on the red carpet at the Yoyogi National Gymnasium in Tokyo. It was not lost on the paparazzi that Rihanna was making her acting debut. Her hair was luxurious and long, in contrast to her chopped military movie-making look and she wore a "silk pajama" number, as a nod to local fashions. She, along with Decker, Kitsch, Berg and Alexander Skarsgård (who played Kitsch's—or Hopper's—brother) all posed together in front of posters and make-believe cannons, smiling insanely, trying to appear casual before the sea of people and flashes, before finally taking their seats to watch the movie. Once again, he found himself seated next to Brooklyn Decker. Kim sat on his other side, inconspicuously, as she preferred. Greg wore a dark suit with a bright red tie, but most of the other men wore cool California sport coats.

Greg watched in awe at the special effects and amazing handiwork of editors and producers. But what really shocked him was the amount of time *he* was on the screen. In his mind, he played such a minor role that it could have been dropped altogether. But as he watched himself perform, becoming part of the plot, part of the tumult and churn that spits out the happy ending, he realized he had been a key player, woven in from beginning to end. His character had his own side story, which he had been able to deliver to an audience, who did not know him from a bowl of cereal. Somehow, far away from the reality of war, he had become an *actor*.

"Battleship" premiered in Los Angeles a month later, on May 10th, eight days before the release. This time, Mike Corcoran and Linda Anderson and her daughter Daniellecame along with Greg and Kim. Chuck was doing his time in Afghanistan. Kurt and Marcy Gutierrez were there too.

Greg gazed up at the sleek silver Nokia Theatre, a building that could seat more than 7,000. It boasted one of the largest stages in the country. Wearing a suit coat and slacks this time, he was extra careful not to rip his pant legs on the steel hinges of his Power Knees as he turned sideways and slid out of the car. He stepped out onto an ocean-blue carpet, made especially for the premiere. All of his guests went to their seats, while he and Hamish Linklater, much less the impish scientist on this evening, lingered to the click and whirr of the cameras. Greg smiled and waved, like he was supposed to, before heading inside.

Rihanna's arrival set off a scene of celebrity madness. This time she wore a backless, nearly front-less white gown, stunning the Navy personnel invited to fill bleachers rising over the walkway. She stopped briefly, hanging onto her dress, to take a flower from one of the sailors. The paparazzi screamed and cackled, aping for her attention. Again, her waved tresses flowed flawlessly along one side of her face as she stepped gracefully, as her entourage, keeping their distance, made sure onlookers kept theirs.

The Nokia lobby was all "Battleship"-ped out. In the center was a giant notched metal sphere—an homage to the burning, rotating weapons the aliens had fired upon the Earth. Giant strobe lights lined the walls. Larger-than-life movie posters hung everywhere, framed by what looked like iron rods. The high ceilings amplified the noise, bolstering the hype created by all the "coming soons" sent out by the studio.

Greg and the others made their way into smaller side rooms to do media interviews. Questions were lobbed like birdies over a badminton net. They were all pretty much the same: How had he landed the role? Did the Army mind him being in the film? What was it like to work with Liam, Brooklyn and Rihanna? Was it fun? Was he going back in the Army? Was he going to pursue acting?

When it came time for all the stars to be announced, he stood in the wings of the stage, imagining the puzzlement of the Los Angeles audience. What was he even *doing* there with the likes of Neeson and Rihanna? His name was the last to be announced and he stepped out, bobbing a bit as he did now from right to left. The lights made it impossible to see exactly what was happening in the audience, but after a few seconds he realized the whole place was on its feet. Thousands of audience members were standing for him. He smiled and waved, taking it in for a moment, knowing the adulation was not really for him, but for his scarred and weary comrades back home.

After Kim and their guests headed to their cars for the after-party, Berg walked up to Greg slightly wide-eyed.

"They gave you a standing ovation," he said.

"Yeah, that was really nice. Wasn't expecting . . ."

"No. You don't understand. That's an LA audience. They don't stand up for anyone."

CHAPTER TWENTY-FIVE

*"Tradition in our Army says that one's success is not defined by
how or what we do in our current job, but how and
what our team does when we leave."*
—Colonel James MacGregor (Ret.), on taking over for his
wounded commander, Colonel Gregory D. Gadson

Greg's visibility continued to increase. He had more speaking engagements. And people seemed to recognize him everywhere he went. He could be somewhere like the grocery store or at one of Jaelen's lacrosse games, and would notice someone staring. They would look down at their phone, then back at him, back at the phone, then at him. Sometimes they would say something.

"Hey, you know who you look like? You look like that guy in that movie with the aliens and the ships—they fight off the aliens—you look just like that guy. Has anyone ever told you that?"

Greg would wait patiently for them to finish.

"Yeah, people have told me that before—because it *is* me."

And so it would go, for years to come.

Greg's widening platform was not lost on the creators of his Power Knees. The Össur company regularly featured articles about his progress with their legs. The company had been on the verge of stopping production on the computer-assisted prosthetics until they'd met Greg and were impressed by his ability to use two at one time. Developers were so intrigued, more than once they invited him, Mike Corcoran and Greg's former teammate and physical medicine and rehabilitation doc from Walter Reed, Paul Pasquina, to come to Iceland as advisors. Greg acted as the model, or test pilot, while Mike and Paul worked on the metrics. Later, after Greg retired from the Army, Össur featured him as one of its "ambassadors," sharing his story, along with several others on its website. Of course, the company PR department needed the perfect photo to bring his story to life. So once again, Greg played "Zoolander," spending an entire day in a highly produced photo shoot, getting just the right "look."

Össur provided authentic wardrobe: khaki shorts to show off the gleaming prosthetics, along with a massive down coat and comically pristine combat boots. They assembled the legs he would model, then slipped the boots onto the toeless silver feet. Then there was makeup. Finally, he was perched on a stool in full Naomi Campbell mode, in front of the screens. Photographer Doug Sanford shot from a distance, asking Greg to stand, then move about slightly. It seemed Doug was looking for a display of badassery rather than cheer, so it came as some relief that requests for smiling poses were minimal. After a quick lunch break, the cameras, lights, crew, Doug, and Greg piled into cars and drove toward downtown in a chilly, foggy drizzle. It would require some photographic magic to make anything look even functional, let alone optimal, amid the gloom and low hanging clouds.

The Washington Monument, an obvious premiere patriotic location, was made less democratic by the lack of handicapped parking, so Greg and the crew trudged a few blocks up Madison Drive, past the Smithsonian National Museum of American History, finally schlepping their gear onto the monument grounds. A couple of grips moved lights here and there. Greg stood, looking stern, his own sort of monument to the wind. Everyone shivered against a dismal sky. Doug's hands reddened with the cold. Power and batteries were essential, necessitating a few trips back to the cars. Then the crew broke set, packed up and lumbered through traffic to a second shoot location in front of the National Archives. The location change brought no luck with the weather. It was difficult to envision the result of this whole endeavor being worth the suffering.

Out of the fog that afternoon emerged true testimony to Doug and his crew's ability not only to roll with an unfortunate circumstance but to use it to level up. The photo Össur ultimately chose was at once badass, noble, iconic and beautiful. Greg stands widely on his Össur legs, combat fatigue coat spread from shoulder to shoulder, with a single cane menacing the concrete. His expression is undaunted, immobile, fierce. Behind him on a concrete block, the aesthetic foundation of America's National Archives, are inscribed the words, "Eternal vigilance is the price of liberty." The Össur ambassador page also includes a shot from the Washington Monument, but the obelisk itself is not visible, only the wind-starched flags behind him. It is accompanied by a quote from Greg, "Össur technologies have taught me about what's possible, and reminded me to keep challenging myself. Life itself is inspiring."

. . .

Greg was not only a commercial inspiration, he used his military celebrity to bring attention to some of the policy failings of the Department of Defense and the Veterans Administration. Three times he was called upon by Congress to testify on Capitol Hill. In the spring of 2009 along with various members of veteran service organizations, he addressed members of the Senate Armed Services Committee on Personnel about compensation for caregivers of wounded service members. It had to do with an antiquated catch in the law which prevented a caregiver from receiving a stipend if he or she lived in the same location as the wounded person. The poorly written law had made their family's transition even more difficult.

"I couldn't drive, I couldn't get in and out of the vehicle, I couldn't wash without assistance," Greg testified, "So my wife became that attendant for me. She became that person who did those things for me and she had to quit her job." He went on. "That took away a third of our income." Then when she and the kids moved to D.C. fulltime so the family could be together, the law rendered her ineligible for the stipend.

"It doesn't make any sense," he said to a dais of sympathetic faces. Thanks to his testimony and that of others, the policy and the stipend known as SCAADL (Special Compensation for Assistance with Activities for Daily Living) was soon updated to eliminate the geographic policy flaw.

A little more than a year later, Greg found himself in front of the House Judiciary subcommittee on human rights, endorsing the Americans with Disabilities Act on the tenth year anniversary of its passage. He was also called to testify before the House Committee on Veterans Affairs on what the military calls "battle handover," or the transfer of combat operations from one military unit to another.

Two years after Greg became a full colonel, he received what would be his final assignment in the Army. He became the garrison commander at Fort Belvoir in Alexandria.

Fort Belvoir is a World War I-era base which by the time Greg had taken charge employed more workers than the Pentagon. It's home to a number of critical Army agencies, including the Intelligence and Security Command which, put simply, collects information from all over the world then uses it to determine where to concentrate combat resources. The Defense Logistics Agency, responsible for acquiring weapons, fuel, repair parts and other materials and providing them to military assets worldwide, is also headquartered there. The Fort Belvoir Community Hospital (formerly DeWitt Army Hospital), a 1.2-million square-foot facility that became increasingly important as a care center for wounded military, is also on the grounds.

Being the garrison commander is like being the mayor of the base. He made sure the traffic lights turn red, yellow and green as necessary, and operations were generally maintained. He also spent a lot of time working as a liaison to the local community. The job was half organizational and half political. As in his time in Iraq, he was making friends with the locals, doing the "hearts and minds" dance. It was a massive job, but he enjoyed it.

At the same time his calendar was becoming more and more crowded with speaking engagements. Sports teams, veterans' organizations and corporations were inviting him to talk to their members and employees. It was flattering, and while he did many engagements for free, he was able to make a small business from others. Problem was, every time he took the podium, he needed the blessing of the United States Army. It involved negotiation, time and lawyers. The lack of flexibility was becoming cumbersome, as the more public part of his life began to take over.

Greg knew he could stay in the Army, but after having a combatant command, being a director at AW2 and then a garrison commander, he felt as if his mission was finally accomplished. He had stayed in the Army for 26 years, on his own terms, in order to serve his country, not to gain rank or status. So in June 2014, in a ceremony at the Fort Belvoir Officer's Club, he retired from the Army. Chuck Schretzman, back from a deployment in Afghanistan and planning his own military retirement, came with Stacy from Philly. Greg's dad was there, along with Kim, Jaelen and Gabby. Dr. Paul Pasquina sat in the middle of the crowd. First Sergeant Fredrick Johnson, the man who literally had breathed life back into Greg as he lay on the side of the dusty road in Iraq, was unmistakably identifiable by his scratchy-throated fast-talk. Brigadier General Rodney Anderson, who had so pointedly mentored the first lieutenant back at Fort Bragg in 1993, officiated. Greg still had that 5x7 card he had scribbled with notes—his first waypoints.

Greg ultimately stepped away from the U.S. Army just over seven years from the day Johnson, Private Eric Brown, and the others had saved his life. And while he left one of America's largest organizations behind, he knew he would always remain in the grip of the brotherhood.

. . .

The desktop version of skiing a black diamond slope at Breckenridge was, for Greg, being an entrepreneur. So, after he retired, he called on his old football mentor Kurt Gutierrez to partner with him in a government contracting business. They called the company "Patriot Strategies," in honor of Greg's military call sign, "Patriot 6." Greg was able to secure a minority-owned business status from the Small Business Administration. And the VA certified the business as a veteran enterprise. Both qualifications gave them a slight advantage in bidding on work. Still, it was at times a tight market. He loved the challenge, but mostly the independence of it all. He and Kurt were on their own, carrying their own weight, at their own risk.

He worked mostly from his home office, near the front of the house. On the front wall were mounted dozens of religious crosses—some very simple, others more ornate—that he was collecting as he traveled. Some were copper and silver, others embedded with small gems or stones, like turquoise. On shelves or mounted on adjacent walls there was of course football memorabilia, and a number of actual autographed footballs, including one signed by several Ohio State Buckeyes and one he'd received at the White House visit, signed by President George Bush and a few of the New York Giants. His double-wide desk was covered in papers and electronics, and always seemed a little messy to visitors, but he knew where most things could be found.

Kim was a STEM education teacher at Mark Twain Middle School. She taught robotics and managed a bunch of sixth-, seventh- and eighth-graders through "shop," beginning with "how to build a mousetrap," all the way up to, for some, state robotics competitions.

Gabby had already wrapped up school at Babson College, where she was a business major, and had interned at Concur, a travel and expense software company. It seemed a pretty sure bet she would wind up working there full time, and perhaps eventually move to Washington state, where the company is based. Jaelen was a West Point cadet, struggling a little academically and playing JV lacrosse.

Greg's contracting business continued to grow along with his public speaking opportunities. He'd incorporated that aspect of his life into an LLC back in 2008. Six years after the New York Giants' pivotal Super Bowl win against the Patriots, he still occasionally visited with the team. And he often spoke at West Point. There were other schools, sports teams and churches. But he also got some impressive corporate gigs, including Coca-Cola and the financial firm Ernst & Young. It seemed he was always getting on an airplane. Mostly the speaking events went smoothly. Others didn't.

Ernst & Young was where he'd taken his first official inspirational tumble. He'd been seated on a stage, wearing his prosthetic legs, during his introduction. As usual, he pitched forward a little, leaning on his cane to get out of his chair, and executed a pretty smooth maneuver to get the few feet to the podium. And he delivered a reasonably uplifting message, he thought, worthy of the well-paid and educated group of suited-up executives. He wrapped. They clapped. And he headed back to the same chair, turning then bending the metal knees forward, steering his derriere toward the seat, then squatted, plopping his full weight down. The chair crumpled like paper. The floor did not stop him either. He kept sliding backwards, quickly closing in on the edge of the stage. He heard the audience gasp as he went over the edge, falling several feet and nearly landing in the front row. Physically, he was fine. A bunch of accountants helped him back up onto the stage, where he gave an "all-clear, I'm fine" wave, then eventually made a more proper exit. The audience was more flummoxed than he was. Over the years he'd come to take the occasional fall sort of like a football tackle—just another part of the game.

In 2015 Will Huff—the former West Point teammate who had traveled with Greg from Baghdad to Landstuhl, Germany—retired from the Army and became deputy athletic director at Towson University near Baltimore. For the next few years Greg would make an annual visit there to speak to various sports teams—usually football, men's basketball, women's lacrosse and to members of the university's athletic administration. His tour began in the Towson Tiger's Johnny Unitas Stadium after head football coach Rob Ambrose called for a pause in practice. The summer sun beat down from a cloudless sky as the college players removed their black helmets and assembled along the sideline. Huff warmed up the already steaming scrum of players.

"I've held this guy's hand more than my wife's." Huff's opening line usually brought a handful of chuckles. "I held his hand in the huddle, on the field at West Point. And I held it again as he was flown from Baghdad to Landstuhl, after he was injured," Huff explained, remembering how a decade ago he'd jumped on a chopper, arriving in Baghdad as soon as he could, when he heard Gadson had been injured; how Colonel Ricky Gibbs had handed Greg over to him for escort; how he'd babbled aloud to Greg about anything he could conjure, through that interminable flight, and how he had in fact, all the while, held Gadson's hand.

Then Greg, wearing a freshly unfolded Towson two-button golf shirt, wheeled out to face the players. He loved talking to sports teams about the selflessness required in great team making.

"First, you need to know that football is not about you but where you fit in. If you are in this for yourself then you are missing the point. You are missing opportunities. This team, the one that you are a part of, here and now, will never exist again. There will never be another Towson 2018 football team. It is unique. And it's all about what you are willing to give each other. Not take. Give."

A few players took a knee. Others strained to see Greg over their team-mates' massive shoulders.

"There are three things that will guarantee you have a successful season this year. Those three things are *pride, poise,* and *team.* First, pride starts with you and accountability. Live up to the best you can be every day—not just here but in the classroom as well.

"Next is poise. Everyone wants to be in that prescient situation, where you make the play that changes the game. You're ready. You're positioned. You're poised because in practice you've done it a million times. That's the way you become poised. You practice. But poise is not about scoring the game-changing point, it's about character. It's not about winning. It's about being the best you can be every day so in that moment, you can perform for your team."

Greg fiddled with the buttons on the shirt then pulled at the sleeves.

"That brings me to that final ingredient: The team itself. Winning is a collective, not an individual accomplishment. T-E-A-M. Together Every-one Achieves More. Everyone achieves more together. It's not about what happens here on the turf. It's showing up to class, doing the work and holding each other accountable in school and in athletics."

The sun rose higher, torching the tops of their heads. Sweat trickled down necks and noses. Still, no one moved. They stood, or knelt, locked in on the message.

"Eleven years ago, I worked to inspire pride, poise and team into my unit. And it saved my life. We got blown up by a roadside bomb in Iraq, and my team, despite the devastation, in the midst of all that adversity, reacted. They reacted well because they had trained. They were poised. They had held each other accountable in training, in doing the work, in learning the lessons *before* it became a matter of whether someone lived or died. And I lived because of their pride in their mission, their poise and their commitment to team."

Heads nodded. In a way youth made them an even tougher crowd than the New York Giants. He hoped he was getting through.

"Again, your team has the chance to live for a lifetime. This man," he said, pointing to Huff, "was my teammate. Our lockers were three feet from each other at West Point. We held hands in the huddle. This man also kept me alive on that helicopter. He encouraged me to live because that's what teammates do. Lieutenant Colonel Chuck Schretzman, also my teammate, showed up at Walter Reed Army Medical Center when I arrived there. Because that is the role of a teammate. It doesn't matter if bullets are flying or if you're sweating your ass off on a field, you are committed to someone, to something for life. My West Point team of 1988 is still my team. And ten, twenty, thirty years from now, these men standing by you will still all be your teammates. So put the most you can do into everything you do today. One day, your life could change. And it'll be your teammates who get you through." It was a speech and a theme that ran through many of his motivational talks throughout the country and would carry him personally and professionally for years to come.

. . .

In addition to all the speaking commitments and keeping his company thriving, Greg was invited to be on a number of boards. He took positions at the Gary Sinise Foundation and the Face of America bike ride. And he would occasionally do photo or video shoots for other veteran service organizations. One day in the summer of 2020, he was driving through Muscatatuck, Indiana, after spending some time with a client, when he noticed a roadside billboard with a life-size photo of himself on his hand cycle. He read aloud the Disabled American Veterans' slogan, "Support More Victories for Veterans." That's just not something a person sees every day, he thought, laughing a little. It was almost as weird as watching himself in a movie.

• • •

Greg also appeared in a public service announcement video for the American College of Financial Services in Philadelphia, which provides educational grants for veterans. I tagged along so we could get a little quality car time. We also stopped in to see Stacy and Chuck, who were now living in a beautiful high rise near Washington Square. In the months and years since Greg and Chuck both retired, Chuck had been battling ALS, also known as Lou Gehrig's disease. The progressive neurodegenerative disease usually claims its victim in three to five years from the time of diagnosis. But as of this writing, it has been about seven years and he is still spinning through the streets of his hometown in a motorized wheelchair and doing advocate work when he can. He is an extraordinary hero in his own right.

• • •

We are enveloped by a sloppy, depressing rain on I-95 and Greg is telling me about a guy named Clint Walkingstick. Walkingstick is an artist from Oklahoma who is working with the "Has Heart" organization, which has set the goal of partnering with a veteran from each state to create a commemorative patch. Greg is representing Oklahoma because that is where he was born. Gabby was born in Oklahoma too, while he and Kim were stationed at Fort Sill.

Greg's patch has three themes, he tells me.

"Be present. Be your best. Be at peace. If you're present, you're not holding on to yesterday and you're not living tomorrow. You're being your best you, and you can be at peace. You can accept and handle whatever happens." I note that Greg's philosophies are concentrating, getting tighter, more precise. He's also more adamant. "People become angry because life doesn't follow their script. But whose script does life follow?"

I see what he is saying. Living in the present is different from living for the moment. Present living allows a person to cope with what "is." Living for today feels reckless and ramshackle—a jag away from reality.

"I tell people to drive to work," Greg says. "Then walk that same route. Slow down and connect. You know when I got injured, I went from warp speed to horse and buggy. I had to slow down. But it forced me to connect with people that I might not have, otherwise."

It was late afternoon and it had finally stopped raining. Greg futzed around with the radio or Sirius, or whatever.

"It's like, sometimes I feel like, 'do I have a sign on my back that says: Tell me your story?' Because everyone always comes up and tells me something they did or want to do or—anyway, I listen." Greg paused. "I listen to them because what they're saying might seem small but it's *not* small to them, so I make myself accessible and present."

I have been trying this new thing myself, this business of "being in the moment." It is difficult. Probably more so if you are facing death but maybe less so if you already almost died. Then again, if I were facing death, I mean, if I knew it was coming maybe sooner than I might have expected, being in the moment is probably the only way I could get from one of those moments to the next. The laws of supply and demand kick in. Each moment becomes more valuable.

He looks at the GPS and we realize we are about to miss our exit. We are over in the left lane, so he guns it, crossing over four lanes of highway, barely squeezing into the exit lane before it is separated by a concrete abutment.

"Jezus!" I yelp, grabbing the dashboard, like that's going to stop me from landing on the hood.

"We're okay. I have lots of airbags in this vehicle."

This is supposed to comfort me. I settle back into my seat. The velocity reminds me of something I have been wondering.

"So, I'm re-reading Cheryl Strayed's book called "Wild," about her hike on the Pacific Crest Trail when she had absolutely no experience and was not in particularly good physical shape because she was a recovering heroin addict and had any number of other issues. Her mother's death sent her into this crazy spiral."

"Her mother's death?"

"They were really close and—anyway, in the book she's thinking about why, after all that, she wasn't scared to do this thing—this eleven-hundred-mile hike all alone and she said it was because she didn't feel like anything that bad could happen because the worst already had."

"Huh."

"Is that why you drive like that? Because the worst thing has already happened, so you figure . . ."

He laughed. "Maybe. No, not really. It's like—uh, the Special Forces. Special Forces train so that they are comfortable being uncomfortable. Not that I would compare myself to SF, but it's like that."

"You like being uncomfortable?"

"That's just it. I'm not uncomfortable taking a chance. One of the gifts I got when I was hurt was a different perspective. Risks don't feel like risks. I don't have a death wish or anything but, again, I want to be in the moment."

I check my seatbelt. I do not want to be clinging to my last moment while he is enjoying just being in his. We are quiet for a while.

I look out the window. The terrain is flat and scabbed by winter.

"We make all these plans in life," he said. "This is what we're gonna do, we're gonna make a bunch of money—then all the sudden you get hit with this curveball and you think shit, I didn't get to do all the stuff I wanted to do because I was waiting."

Again, we are quiet. I hope I am not waiting.

We pull into a gas station and I get out and grab the nozzle. We laugh about how it appears for this big, muscly black dude to pull up at the pump and I—a very white woman—get out to pump the gas. Anyone looking on would have no idea that Greg does not have legs.

"Hey, woman, clean that windshield!!" he yells at me, glancing around to see if anyone is watching our performance. Then he takes a really cool photo of us both in his rearview mirror. I'm smiling—he just has a slight smirk.

"People say I smile more now than before I was wounded." I could see this being true. He was a badass. I think badasses are not grinners. They are smirkers.

"Why do you smile more?"

"I've come out on the other side. I'm content. I'm not bitter. I have no regrets. That's the place I've ended up. It's where I fight to stay. Staying present works for me."

"It's a fight?"

"It's a conscious decision. But a lot of it comes naturally now. Like you know how sometimes you ask me my schedule and I don't even know. I know I'm probably going somewhere, but I don't worry about it."

This is incredibly true. I have asked dozens of times. He only ever has the vaguest idea.

"All of the travel. I couldn't do it," I say. But I remember a trip we took to New York together. We nearly missed the last train home, but he has a way of parting a crowd.

"It gets busy. Sometimes I'm on the road for ten days at a time but one of my primary purposes is giving back—sharing my testimony."

"In one place or another."

"It doesn't matter where I'm at physically. I'm in a place of peace."

CHAPTER TWENTY-SIX

"Who is the man who would risk his neck for his brother man?
SHAFT! Can you dig it?"
—*Theme from the 1971 film "Shaft"*

For all of everyone's concerns about Chuck's health, Greg had let his own deteriorate. Exercise, especially in inclement weather, was a chore, and all the speaking engagements and travel made it nearly impossible. Airports and hotels were not conducive to a healthy diet.

And then there was the hospitality factor. Everywhere he went people fed him. Then they fed him more and poured cocktails. His weight soared. He tired easily. He sometimes broke out into sweats after meals and even occasionally suffered blackouts. In January 2019 his primary care doctor, Edward McDaniel, diagnosed him with Type 2 diabetes, a condition most notably characterized by high blood sugar. His blood pressure was also high—something he had wrestled with for more than a decade. The third blow in the trifecta of morbidities was the one condition he had truly learned to live with: being a double amputee statistically shortened his life span. "Double jeopardy," he thought—having worked so hard to survive, but for a more limited amount of time. At McDaniel's recommendation, he attended health and nutrition classes and tried to rein himself in, but a little of that long-ago buried self-pity began to seep from its grave, creating a vicious cesspool of food and beverages.

By January 2020 the scale in McDaniel's office read 268 pounds. Greg was frustrated and defeated, ready to accept his sentence to an early grave.

"Greg, you can absolutely conquer this," McDaniel coached. McDaniel[5] was an active duty colonel who served as director of executive medicine at Belvoir Community Hospital. The doctor's clientele included members of Congress, the executive branch and members of the Supreme Court. "You've faced worse. You're here today because you're strong-willed. Think about those tough days on the gridiron."

True, Greg thought. It had not been that long ago that he had turned his body into a weapon on the football field, then defied the enemy's weapon on the battlefield. It was McDaniel's words, along with news from his son that February that drove his determination to take back control of his health. Jaelen and his new wife, Alaina, announced they would be having twins in October. He was going to be a grandfather. He thought about his own mother and how she would have loved being a great-grandmother to Jaelen's twins, but she died too young, only 63. He knew he could do better for himself.

Then, in March the COVID-19 pandemic dawned like a curse, and a backhanded blessing. One by one Greg's public appearances were canceled. He was forced to stay home and eat in. It was his time, he thought.

Drawing on that same stamina that got one foot in front of the other in the Walter Reed rehabilitation wing, he checked himself into a different sort of self-rehabilitation—one that focused on diet and exercise. A new lightweight custom handcycle arrived (he had snapped the frame of his old one) and the weather began to break. Soon he had a regular cycling route around his neighborhood and slightly beyond. He logged each meal and calories into an app on his phone. He cut carbs with accountant-like precision.

While Greg rode through Alexandria regularly, he and I committed to a monthly cycling date. We explored Virginia's Washington and Old Domin-

---

5 Tragically, Army Colonel Dr. Edward McDaniel and his wife, retired Army Colonel Brenda McDaniel, were shot and killed in front of their own Springfield, Virginia, home May 26, 2021.

ion Railroad Trail and Maryland's Baltimore and Annapolis rails to trails. One weekend in August, my husband Jon flew Greg and Kim in our small Cessna to the Eastern Shore of Maryland while some friends and I racked up all the bikes and met the plane at Easton Airport. We pedaled a beautiful 40-miler, which included a ferry ride from Oxford to St. Michael's.

Greg was becoming a regular in my weekend cycling group, which included Ross Colquhoun, the physical therapist I'd met so many years earlier in the gun gallery at Walter Reed. Rear Admiral Kristin Acquavella also rode with us. She and Greg had originally met at one of the "Face of America" rides and Ross brought her into our group along with Navy Captain Beth Regoli. Funny how our lives circle back into one another. And how they expand. Soon after that October ride, Greg sent me a photo of him holding his two grandchildren—one in the crook of each massive arm. Jaelen and Alaina brought James Thomas and Jeremiah Thomas Gadson into the world on October 17th.

"Are you excited about being a grandfather?" I asked.

"I'm more—well—just thinking of what they're getting *into*," Greg joked at first. "When your kids have kids, it's like you complete a lap in life, but you're starting the next one—you're a grandparent—it's hard to wrap my head around that."

"What will they call you? Grandpop? Poppy?"

"They'll call me *Colonel*." He grinned, then snickered.

Few things that slowed him down, but the wonder of two new lives in the world widened his eyes with sweet bewilderment. I could see he was smitten. I could also see his cheekbones. He'd lost about 50 pounds and was nearly off the meds required to keep his blood sugar balanced. He'd reclaimed his physical health and emotional well-being once again.

Greg had lost so much weight he had to get new prosthetic legs made. He did not use them very often—the chair was simply more accommodating to his fast-paced life. But the size of his thighs had shrunk and another big event loomed—one for which he needed to be present—and standing. Mike Corcoran and his crew got to work quickly—and in a matter of days Greg slipped his thinner thighs into snugly fitting sockets.

On Oct. 31st, 2021, at the Whitehall Estate in Bluemont, Virginia, just two weeks after the birth of his grandchildren, Greg proudly walked Gabby to the altar, where she married Marcus Vallar. Gabby held her father's arm as he paced himself with a cane, stepping soundly onto a gravel walkway that rambled in front of an old white farmhouse. He wore a burgundy suit and a pink rose boutonniere. I caught my breath as I glimpsed one leg seeming to swerve out from under them both, but Gabby did not blink. She was used to the rock and roll of this life.

The bride was gorgeous, laughing sweetly with her groom as her army of bridesmaids looked on. Kim sat in the front row, quietly with Ace, their new service dog—a stunning blond Labrador. Jaelen, echoing both of his parents' looks, was a model groomsman, at once tending to his sister, his wife, the guests and his two new little boys. As the sun began its slide behind the Shenandoah Mountains, Greg for an instant recalled those late days of May 2007 when it seemed sure he would live, but no one knew how or how much or how differently. This was a day—a moment—he had been afraid to envision.

"All sales final!" he said firmly to Marcus, then beamed as he watched Gabby slip off his own steady arm and on to her new husband's. This was a mighty family, Greg thought, in part for what they had been through but mostly for who they'd been from the beginning.

AFTER ACTION REPORT

By Gregory D. Gadson

This book is not the story of one man's arrival to this moment—this place of peace. In fact, I did not have that much to do with it. It was my Lord and Savior Jesus Christ who brought me the opportunity to struggle, the room to hope and the courage to keep living. It was Him along with my family and the brother and sisterhood of friends and supporters—the ultimate team, who delivered me to this freedom.

I say "freedom" because I truly am freer now than when I had my legs. It's true. I would not change a thing. Freedom—the obvious definition—is what we fought for in Iraq and Afghanistan and Bosnia and Vietnam and in two world wars and in every other conflict in which the United States has engaged. But to me freedom is also disengagement from anguish, from worry about the future or reliving the past. Freedom is presence.

When you have lost both legs and have only one functional arm, you get *present* real fast. Back in 2007, I did not know what was coming next—how I would survive, how I would take care of my family, if I could maintain a career. The only thing I *could* do was be in the present moment, and take each second, one at a time.

There are two things I keep close to remind me to stay present. One is that patch, designed by Clint Walkingstick. It reads, "Be your best, be present and be at peace." You cannot be your best if you are not present, and you cannot be at peace if you are thinking about how you were wronged in the past or how you are going to get ahead tomorrow.

The other thing, material thing, is a dog tag given to me by a chaplain at Walter Reed. It is worn down and difficult to read now but it is engraved with one of my favorite scriptures, Joshua 1:9. "Be strong and courageous; do not be afraid, do not be discouraged for the Lord Your God will be with you wherever you go." Thank goodness.

This isn't to say there have not been sorrows. I have lost my parents, friends, fellow soldiers. My mom died too young—in her early 60s. She liked to say I traveled with angels. For many years I wore a cross she gave me on a chain around my neck. But under the weight of the body armor I had to wear in Iraq, the chain broke and I lost it. I didn't tell her. I didn't tell anyone. But not long after that I received a care package from her. There was a coin—on one side was an angel and on the other side was written my name. There was also a metal clip—I guess it was a hair clip—with an angel on it. I had it soldered into my vehicle. The coin was in my wallet, hanging on a lanyard from my neck and the clip was embedded in the Humvee the night we got hit by the IED. My mom made sure I made it through.

General Raymond Odierno's illness and death Oct. 8, 2021, took me by surprise. A former West Point football player and larger-than-life officer, it was hard to imagine anything could take him out. Sometimes it is not combat, but the general stress of the job that leads a great man to an early exit.

One of the most difficult times of my life was when Chuck Schretzman, my West Point teammate who was standing over me the moment I regained consciousness at Walter Reed, who was best man at Kim's and my wedding, whose kids grew up with mine, was diagnosed with ALS. As of this writing, Chuck, Stacy and their kids are battling valiantly and pretty successfully. He has survived and thrived longer than statistics predicted. Chuck and I are still known to argue football trivia or even race wheelchairs through the streets of Philadelphia, where they live now. He claims he can still "run" faster than me.

Another travesty has been the loss of so many members of the military to suicide. In 2020 a couple of fellow amputees, retired Army First Lieutenant Andy McCaffrey, and Corporal Rory Hamill, a Marine Corps veteran, took their own lives. Both had been active athletes and veteran advocates. The COVID pandemic took away those coping mechanisms though, and as a result we lost them.

Once as a garrison commander I was invited to the Pentagon for a "Stand Up Against Suicide" event, designed to raise awareness among military and civilian staff. I was not scheduled as a speaker, but I asked to speak anyway to the crowd of a few hundred, gathered in the Pentagon courtyard.

"I want everyone here to think back for a minute," I said, pausing while they focused their attention. "Think back to a time when things maybe weren't going so well. You weren't sure of your path. Maybe you were confused or depressed." I waited another few seconds. I wanted them to be honest with themselves.

"Now raise your hand if you've ever thought about taking your own life."

A smattering of hands went up. Then I slowly raised my own. It was the first time I admitted publicly that this amazing, exhausting, puzzling yet so gratifying life I had literally been hurled into had some very dark days. I never planned my own death. I never had the pills in my hand. But I sure did wonder more than once if it would not have been easier just to call it off. I know the Lord saved me from that darkness. And again, I had an incredible wife—Kim—and my kids Gabby and Jaelen—to help pull me through. As usual I did not know and still don't, if my hand in the air meant anything to anyone in the yard that day but it was cathartic to me. I hope it helped someone know that ending your life is the only way to be sure nothing gets better.

It is critical for me to experience life one day, one moment at a time. You never know what might happen next. I do not know if it is any sort of parallel, but I never looked at the "Battleship" script Peter Berg sent me until I was on the plane to Hawaii. See, the movie was not in some plan. That *National Geographic* shoot was not either. Neither was attending West Point, becoming a colonel, being blown to pieces or getting a visit at Walter Reed from an old football teammate. There is no script for your life. That is why you have to take every opportunity. Because everything, *everything* can change in an instant.

I do believe life is about struggle. It is okay to be wrestling with things. It means you are living. Through those days when I struggled to lift one prosthetic leg in front of the other, I had to dig, physically and emotionally. But I also felt intensely alive. Maybe it was because I had come so close to death. But the sweat and determination and the love I felt during those workouts made me very aware of my surroundings, my condition and the people around me.

I am where I am in this moment because of the experiences and people who have come into my life since May 7, 2007. I do not miss my legs. Did I want to go through getting blown up, having all those surgeries and physical and emotional rehabilitation? No. Did I want to put my family through all of that? Of course not.

My glass is half full because in my mind I did not lose my legs. I gave them. I gave my legs in service to my country. That is the sacrifice I and my family made and the reason we are free. We did not *lose* anything. We *gave* something. This has been our journey.

ACKNOWLEDGMENTS

Greg Gadson literally tumbled into my life one September day in 2007 and I could not have been luckier or more blessed. Greg was at first tentative about letting me write his story for only one reason: humility. But he and his family were also brave and dedicated to the service and inspiration their story might bring to others. And so, I wrote. Because of Greg and Kim's generosity I have been there to awkwardly hand Greg a beer as he shed tears over his loss as well as watch him show off his grandchildren and give his daughter away at her wedding. It is because of their love and friendship that I have shed my own tears—writing about how Greg nearly died or the time he looked into a movie camera and said, "I'm half a man," because I know for a time that's how he felt. I'm able to tell a great story about an American hero because he and his family allowed me to become a peripheral part of theirs. And for that I will always be grateful.

One of the soldiers in the Humvee that exploded the evening of May 7th was Brad Lee Bandy. He was a great help in providing forensics and logistics about that evening. Dr. Brad Woods, Dr. Ross Witters, and Sergeant-Major Eric Brown provided the gripping details of how they had managed to save Greg's life in the field. At Walter Reed, Dr. Paul Pasquina, Dr. Donald Gajewski, physical therapist Bob Bahr, and so many others who literally lifted Greg up day after day, filled many gaps in my story. Big thanks to the incredible Mike Corcoran, whom I continue to bug. Mike, you are your own great story.

Many thanks to our publisher Tim Schaffner, who so patiently answered all my first-timer questions, and to editor Jeffery Kurz for intercepting all my bad passes at sports writing. Much gratitude to publicists Scott Manning and Abigail Welhouse, for also enduring my rookie queries—you are both such a pleasure. Thank you also to my first editor, New England Patriots fan Jim Potter, for your dogged pursuit even when the Giants won.

My writing critique group has been invaluable. Mary Bargteil first brought me in after I flopped around in her writing class, Wendy Eckel kept our table full of snacks, cats, and laughter, Denny Kleppick brought his top-down military perspective and Susan Moger enhanced my work with her grammarian ways. Group co-founder Jon Coile breezed back in after an extended absence, and thankfully, I've not been able to shake him yet!

Shortly after meeting Greg, when I asked fellow writer Sharon Donnell via email if this seemed a worthy project, her answer was so exuberantly positive, funny, and inspirational, I taped it over my kitchen sink, where it prompted and tortured me until it had absorbed too much coffee, marinara sauce, and probably Grey Goose to hold on there any longer. Sharon, you were right.

All my gratitude to the former president of Cahners publishing, Terry McDermott and to George Slowik of "Publisher's Weekly", for your sage advice.

Videographer and friend, Alan Gaffere, thank you for always having my back behind the camera and for always making everything look better.

Workshops and classes are valuable but it's the people you meet there who hold you up. This project underwent extensive rehabilitation at the Solstice MFA Program, formerly of Pine Manor College, but currently, thanks to Director Meg Kearney and Assistant Director Quintin Collins, it's thriving at Lasell University in Boston. I walked away with a much better manuscript, and a small herd of new writer friends and mentors like Anne-Marie Oomen, who worked double time to help me put a bow on it; *Battleship*'s biggest fan, David Yoo; and Sterling Watson who explained "truth" and the arc. Wild Women writer, (literally, she wrote *Wild Women*) Autumn Stephens, and classmates Jen Grant, and Ashley Johnson, you are my best takeaways. Joanne Carota, whom I first met at "Writers in Paradise," is the reason I signed up.

Back home, big thanks to Kathryn Temple for improving my neighborhood by being a beautiful writer and distinguished Georgetown English professor, and to Jenn and Craig Barnabee and Judy Zdobysz for listening to me prattle on about the manuscript. Jenn gets double thanks for being a beta reader along with Megan Roshon and Speedy Johnson (who gets the prize for the most entertaining scribbles in the margin.) My friend Mitzi Bernard, the art and energy you put into the world gives us all hope. Sara Schlachter-Best, thank you for your sanity, sincerity, and kitchen-table therapy. Mom, thank you for continuing to ask, "How's the book?" for sixteen years. And heavenly gratitude goes to my Dad who left us in 2001, before so many things.

To the real beauties of the family, Rhodesian Ridgebacks Lillian and Delilah, the ever-patient and hungry oversized foot-warmers, I'll love you forever.

Finally, to that critique group co-founder who I can't shake: Jon Coile, my now-husband—you are my heart, my inspiration and eternal cheerleader. May Jack Nicholson play you in a movie one day. Love you 'til the dogs come home. And then some.